Those Who "Can't..." Teach

True Stories of Special Needs
Families to Promote Acceptance,
Inclusion, and Empathy

Shelley Kenow

New Branch
SOLUTIONS

Those Who "Can't..." Teach
True Stories of Special Needs Families to Promote Acceptance, Inclusion, and Empathy
Shelley Kenow
New Branch Solutions

Published by New Branch Solutions, Cedar Hill, MO
Copyright ©2020 Shelley Kenow

Project Management and Book Design: DavisCreative.com

Editor: Kathryn Barnsley, krbedits.com

Library of Congress Cataloging-in-Publication Data

Library of Congress Control Number: 2020922386

Shelley Kenow

Those Who "Can't..." Teach: True Stories of Special Needs Families to Promote Acceptance, Inclusion, and Empathy

ISBN: 978-1-7360460-0-5 (paperback)
       978-1-7360460-1-2 (hardback)
       978-1-7360460-2-9 (ebook)

Library of Congress subject headings:

1. FAM012000 Family and Relationships/Children with Special Needs
2. BIO033000 Biography and Autobiography/People with Disabilities
3. EDU026000 Education/Special Education/General

2020

ATTENTION CORPORATIONS, UNIVERSITIES, COLLEGES AND PROFESSIONAL ORGANIZATIONS: Quantity discounts are available on bulk purchases of this book for educational, gift purposes, or as premiums for increasing magazine subscriptions or renewals. Special books or book excerpts can also be created to fit specific needs. For information, please contact , New Branch Solutions, Admin@newbranchsolutions.com

This book is dedicated to all those
individuals and families who have been told
in words, deeds, or body language,
"You can't..."

Acknowledgments

To the families whose lives are laid bare within the covers of this book; I cannot thank you enough for your time, honesty, trust in me, and willingness to share your stories. I hope you are as proud of your individual chapter as I am. I am a better person for knowing you and treasure all that you have taught me. You have inspired me and helped me see that, *Those Who "Can't"…Teach.*

To my four biggest cheerleaders and supporters: my husband, our daughter, my mom and my mother-in-law, thank you! The love, faith, encouragement, suggestions, and belief you all have in me is the reason this book is completed.

Thank you, Kathryn, at KRB Editorial Services, LLC for all your research, comments, suggestions, and hard work in making it all flow so beautifully and accurately.

Thank you staff at Davis Creative Publishing Partners for holding my hand during the publishing process.

I thank God for making me a special educator, giving me the idea for the book, the fortitude to stick with it, and the patience for the process.

Table of Contents

Preface

There are several reasons I wrote this book. From the time I was nine years old, I knew I wanted to be a general education teacher. However, over the years, God put it in my head to be a special education teacher. I always brushed the thought aside, thinking I could never work with "those" kids for various reasons. I am thankful God did not let me go down the path I thought was for me. He put me in situations and jobs that changed my mind.

I had the privilege of being a special educator for over twenty-five years. During that time, I got to know many families where one or more members had a special need. These individuals and their families had a very different approach to life than I did. As much as I observed and learned about their lives from the outside, it was only the tip of the iceberg of all that goes on in any given minute in any of those families. I wrote this book to bring light to the differences and similarities these families have compared to others.

One goal for this book is to enlighten readers to see that "those" kids and "those" families are kids and families first. I hope that once readers finish this book their hearts will be more open and they will have a better understanding and appreciation of the life of a family with special needs.

I look back at myself going through school, thinking I could not teach students with special needs, and I wonder how I developed my initial outlook that kids who were different were somehow "less" or that they "can't." It was not intentional on my part, and I certainly was not directly taught to think that way. It just seemed to happen. I believe that is why I did not think I could teach kids who learn differently.

However the idea started, it did not last long. I have had the privilege and honor of knowing so many families and teaching their children, my perception changed early on in my career. Different is just different. As parents, we need to teach our kids this lesson. As teachers, we need to understand and accept all our students, and we need to emphasize to our students that different is not less or unable.

A second goal for this book is to prompt us as individuals to look into ourselves to see if we hold this bias. Most importantly, if we discover we do hold the bias, we need to correct it. Unfortunately, there are educators who have the same bias I did. They let that bias diminish their expectations for their students' success in school and in life. Some teachers believe that because of the modifications and accommodations to schoolwork, homework, and testing, a student with an individualized education plan (IEP) cannot or should not be allowed to earn anything higher than an average grade. If they do earn a grade higher than average, even on grade-level material, I have heard some teachers say it should not mean the same as someone whose material was not modified or accommodated. This is a failure to meet our students where they are and encourage them to achieve their potential.

A third reason for writing this book is to help educators have a better understanding of all the students they teach. Many educators also have no idea what a family with a member with special needs goes through on a daily, monthly, or yearly basis. Some families faced death multiple times, some had to send their child hundreds of miles away to find an appropriate setting, and others faced the disbelief of their disability. Having a disability affects every minute of every day for the person's lifetime, not just the minutes they are seen in public.

Fourth, the proceeds from the sale of this book will afford me the opportunity to provide access to my services as an IEP coach and advocate at a reduced or free rate to families who are currently going through the special education system.

Every story in this book is real; the names and identifying details have been changed to protect the privacy of the individuals. Many sections are directly quoted from the family members interviewed. Some terminology used in this book was the norm at the time these stories took place. I understand that today some of those words have become offensive. It is not my intention to offend anyone, but for purposes of authenticity and to see the progress made in these areas today, I believe it necessary to leave them as they were told to me by the families.

Section I

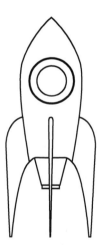

My Story

On Saturday, December 1, 1979, just days before my ninth birthday, I was sitting on the couch when my thirteen-year-old brother suddenly burst through the front door, half carrying, half dragging our father who was bleeding badly from his head. My brother told me not to look, but I could not help myself. My dad had a gash from the top of his forehead on the left, across his right eye, and over to his right ear. I had never seen anything so horrific in my life. I thought my daddy was going to die.

My brother and dad had been cutting firewood about six miles from our home. My dad cut a tree that fell upon another tree that acted like a slingshot to the first tree. The first tree came back, sliced my dad's head open, and knocked him to the ground. My brother had stepped away for a minute when he heard Daddy's chainsaw idling for too long. He went back, found Dad, dragged him to the truck five hundred yards away, and drove home. Daddy ended up needing over seventy stitches and was in the hospital for my birthday and Christmas.

On Monday, my teacher, Mrs. Nolan, could tell something was wrong. This was long before social media and instant news. She asked me to stay back at recess time, and I told her what happened. She let me cry on her shoulder that day and many more times during the three and a half weeks my dad was in the hospital recovering. She helped me make cards for him and she asked me every day how he was. She genuinely cared for me, my family, and our situation.

On Halloween, someone I did not recognize walked in wearing a baseball uniform. I thought we had a new student, so I began to introduce myself. It was my teacher, Mrs. Nolan. She was about five feet tall, always wore heels and makeup, and had very long blonde hair that was always fixed in a tall bun on her head. On this day, she managed to get all of her hair under a baseball cap and wore only eye black under her eyes as her makeup. She completely fooled every one of us. These two incidents were just a couple of reasons why I knew I wanted to be a teacher. She was always so enthusiastic and caring, loved her students, and loved teaching. My classmates and I seemed to always be engaged and happy to be there learning, and it was all due to Mrs. Nolan. I remember thinking this is how learning should always be, and I want to be a part of that. I want to bring joy as I educate someone.

When I was in eighth grade, I was going back to her class during my study hall to help when I passed by the special education room. I had never noticed the kids in that room before; had the room been there when I was in third grade? It was really more like a large broom closet, tucked away down a hall people passed through to get to the library or outdoors. I had a fleeting thought that maybe I would teach special education students instead of third-grade general education students, but I quickly dismissed the thought, thinking I would feel too sorry for "those" kids and never have high expectations for them to learn.

In high school, I passed by the special education classrooms in that building more frequently and had some classes with "those" kids in them. In tenth grade, I volunteered at a Special Olympics track-and-field day with a group of classmates from my high school. It was a great day, and I remember thinking how amazing some of the athletes were.

I thought how nice it was to have something like this for them. Again, I dismissed the thought of being a special education teacher.

When I graduated, I knew I wanted to be a teacher, but I was not sure I could handle being in a classroom every day, nor did I want to attend college full-time. My solution was to become an aide in the district where I had been a student, while I took a few college classes each semester at the local community college. I was so happy when my first assignment was working as an aide with Mrs. Nolan, the very woman who inspired my desire to be a teacher. I was also assigned part of the day to a second-grade teacher, Mrs. Dewling. In each classroom I was considered a Title 1 aide, which meant I worked with kids who struggled to read as fluently as their classmates or had trouble understanding what they read.

For two years I worked for these teachers, and I saw how they treated the students who learned differently. They had high expectations, they loved each student no matter what their learning level, they treated each student justly, and they each had great advice about strategies for me to use with the students. I really enjoyed working with the kids who learned differently and was amazed at how hard they worked compared to their peers.

The teachers trusted me and depended on me, and even though I did not yet have a college degree, they treated me with respect and as a fellow educator. It was such a great feeling. The lesson of how they treated me has stayed with me to this day, and I have worked hard to pay it forward to everyone I work with. I knew I could handle being in a general education classroom of my own. I was ready to finish college and become a second- or third-grade general education teacher.

In autumn 1990, I met an amazing man whom I married in spring 1992. He was in the United States Air Force and stationed at a base near my home. He encouraged me to finish the degree I started in 1989 at the junior college. In spring 1993, I finished my associate of arts (AA) degree from the junior college and enrolled full-time the following fall at a university, declaring my major as education. When I enrolled, the counselor asked if I wanted to double major in education and special education, and again I said no, unsure I would do well working with special-needs students.

During the fall semester, I became very ill and could not finish the term. Before it was time to enroll for spring classes, we found out my husband was being transferred to England in summer 1994. Not knowing if I would ever make it back to this same university to finish my degree, I did not enroll for the spring semester. While I was excited for the adventure of moving to England, I was heartbroken my dream might not happen.

In July 1994, we moved to Royal Air Force Alconbury, Huntingdonshire, England. We soon found a wonderful English home in a town in Cambridgeshire. We had a lovely garden in the back with a very cute fish pond attached to our patio. As an added bonus, our garden butted up to the primary school. Shortly after we moved in, the students arrived for the fall term, and the school administration accepted my offer to volunteer. I worked with a wonderful teacher, Miss Mickie, who taught Year 3 and 4 students.

At the same time, I volunteered at the Department of Defense Dependent School (DoDDS) on base while I filled out the paperwork to be a substitute or an aide. I was a substitute aide the most often in a first-grade classroom, which led me to conclude I now wanted to teach first, second, or third-grade general education students. My associate's degree qualified me to be a substitute teacher in the DoDD school, and one day I subbed in a fourth-grade classroom. I left that day thinking I never wanted to teach any class above third grade.

In spring 1996, I was called to be a substitute aide in a pre-K classroom at the DoDD school. This was an all-day pre-K with a nap in the afternoon. I was assigned to one student that day. I was told this little boy, Jordan, was "quite the handful," and his last aide had quit because they did not know how to handle him. During the morning, I was kicked, hit, scratched, screamed at, and had my hair pulled. This was one angry four-year-old.

Immediately after lunch was nap time for the students and a time for the teacher and me to look over work and talk. She told me how Jordan was dropped off at the base day care the second it opened and not picked up until the second it closed. When he got home, it was dinner, bath, and bed. He had no time with his parents, not because they both worked, but because they did not want him and did not know how to handle him. My heart broke for Jordan.

When nap time was over, I hugged him, and he hugged me back. The remainder of the afternoon was not as rough as the morning, and when it was time to send him to day care, he asked me if I would please come back the next day. For the next three weeks, until a new aide arrived, I showed up every day and loved on him. I still received punches, scratches, and the like, but the frequency diminished. I held him to high behavior expectations, taught him appropriate ways to show how he was feeling, and gave him consequences when he did not behave correctly. I praised Jordan when he was doing the right thing, I told him he was a good boy, and gave him a hug any time he asked. I was consistent in being there every day and in my high expectations for him.

In autumn 1996, I was offered a full-time aide position for five special education students in a general education kindergarten classroom. I doubted my ability to do the job, but hesitantly accepted the position. I was assigned to help four boys and one girl. One of the boys was Jordan. I had not realized he was in the special education program until I was told he was. He and I connected immediately, although it took a bit longer for me to connect with the other four. I worked in the kindergarten room and followed that teacher's guidance, and I was also guided by Miss Bellsna, the kindergarten special education teacher.

This was a terrific year. I learned so much from working with these teachers. The five students I worked with taught me they were just kids like all the other kids in the classroom. Of course there were behaviors and academic issues, but they were kids most of all. I found I had the same type of expectations for my students as the general education aide in the room had for hers. I did not feel sorry for the kids just because they had academic and behavior differences.

I found out after spending time with these kids that I loved being with them as much as I had loved being an aide for kids in the general education setting. I was really impressed with the way Miss Bellsna taught her students, and I greatly appreciated how she encouraged me. One very important lesson she taught me was that sometimes you have to reach out to another teacher or expert for help.

The lesson came because one of the students I was assigned to had severe behaviors—worse than any behavior I had ever encountered before. This five-year-old boy, Marcus, did not just kick, hit, scratch, and scream. He also spit at other students, threw desks and chairs, broke pencils and crayons, cursed, ran out of the room, knocked books and equipment off of shelves and tables, stood on tables and chairs, and seemed to have no respect for authority, especially if that authority was female. Every teacher and aide in our section of the building was female, so that set Marcus off quite a bit. When I started working in this classroom, Marcus had episodes several times a day, ranging from five to forty-five minutes each time. A few lasted a lot longer. He had one episode that lasted two hours and ten minutes.

The kindergarten room was the size of two typical classrooms, so when he had these episodes, we could move him or the other students to opposite sides of the room. Sometimes the episode was so severe (or he ran out of the room) that we took him into another room. The special education teacher, general education teacher, another special education aide, and I had all been trained on proper ways to restrain and when. When his actions could hurt himself or other students, we restrained him according to our training. It was a team effort to keep him safe during a long episode.

We did not just send this kid to an alternative school or expel him. There was no alternative school, and our principal was of the mindset that Marcus needed and deserved an education. The first half of that school year was quite intense. Every day it seemed I saw a new behavior that happened at a higher frequency or a more severe intensity.

In January, with the agreement of the team of teachers, the principal called in a behavioral specialist for guidance. The specialist trained the principal and every teacher, aide, custodian, cafeteria worker, and therapist in a new technique. Every one of us welcomed and implemented his advice. It taught me the brain could be trained to behave differently. The specialist told us to expect the number and duration of episodes to increase, and new behaviors could develop. This is how we knew the technique was working. It showed us the student was beginning to grasp certain actions no longer gave him a desired result, so he tried new behaviors or increased the intensity or duration of old behaviors.

None of us believed the boy was having these behaviors as tantrums to get what he wanted. We knew he did not have complete control of his behaviors. His brain needed to be trained to recognize triggers that upset him, to react differently, and to understand why certain things were the way they were and had to be. At first, the episodes became even more frequent and more severe, but we stuck to this new technique with great resolve. By the middle of March, the episodes were getting less frequent, less severe, and less dangerous. By the end of April, our records indicated his episodes had gone from multiple times a day to one every couple of days. In the eighteen days of school attendance in May, he had only one episode, and it was only a few minutes long and not dangerous to himself or other students.

Working with these five students and seeing how they learned academically and behaviorally was transformative. I realized at the end of this school year I could and did hold my students to high expectations. First and foremost, "those" kids were kids. Period. I wanted to be a primary special education teacher.

We returned to the States in summer 1997, and I enrolled again at a university. This time I double majored in special education and elementary education. I did not finish my degree until December 2002, because the military moved us to new assignments, and I gave birth to our child. My student teaching experience was in a classroom with students ranging from kindergarten to fourth grade. My mentor teacher, Mrs. Schidet, was fantastic and so full of life and love for her students.

To receive special education services, a student had to qualify under at least one of thirteen different categories. Nine of those categories were represented in this group of ten students. They were considered self-contained because they stayed together in the special education room most of their day. We had one student who was considered "resource" because he only needed to come in for a little extra help each day. Most of the students had some difficulty speaking, so they received speech language services; some also had physical or occupational therapy, or both.

Mrs. Schidet and I taught the same subjects and organized the same activities as in a general education classroom. We taught reading, math, English, science, and social studies as well as health and hygiene, cooking, behavior skills, and computer skills. We took a field trip to the local apple orchard and celebrated each holiday. My students came to school every day ready to work hard and learn.

My student teaching ended on a Thursday, and I started working on Monday covering a maternity leave in the same district. I was assigned to teach fifth- and sixth-grade special education students. I was hesitant after my harrowing experience working in a fourth-grade general education room, but I'm adventurous and thought I would at least give it a try. I fell in love with the students I worked with during those ten weeks. I am still in contact with several students from that class and their families today.

My students had an incredible work ethic. Every day they came to school ready to tackle the difficult tasks ahead of them, and most days they had pretty good attitudes. In reading, we read aloud Charlie and the Chocolate Factory by Roald Dahl, acted out some of it, and watched the movie. We compared and contrasted the two types of media. The math lessons varied from adding and subtracting single digit numbers, to multiplying and dividing fractions. As Valentine's Day approached, my students put great care and effort into making flower arrangements and cards to take to the local hospital's maternity ward. They were so excited to have a chance to brighten someone else's day. This was a class with about a fifty-fifty mix of self-contained and resource students.

As in my student teaching class, there were wonderful paraprofessionals to assist the students and me. These ladies helped my classroom run so smoothly and gave the students great care. Having paraprofessionals allowed me to truly address each student and their academic and behavioral needs individually as their individualized education plans (IEPs) required. I could get the resource students started on their material and then go to another student while one of the paraprofessionals continued helping the first student or group of students. Usually by the time the resource students arrived, the self-contained students were already working on an assignment and they could continue with the assistance of a paraprofessional.

Without assistance, it would have been impossible to reach each student individually. Most of the students in my student teaching and full-time teaching positions had attention and focusing issues, so trying to let them continue on their own would not have worked very well. I mention the paraprofessionals because I feel they do not get enough credit for all they do, and to illustrate why a person who is teaching only a few students needs to have one or more paraprofessionals in the room as well.

For the next fifteen years, I taught students with amazing abilities and some challenges too. I learned my kids were just kids who learned differently. But different does not mean bad, wrong, or less. My students were often told "can't" by society, their peers, and in some cases, their teachers. My students were told, "You can't earn a 'real' A or B," "You can't walk," "You can't talk," "You can't write," "You can't read," "You can't be successful in life," "You can't do math," "You can't behave that way," "You can't comprehend," "You can't sit there and do nothing," "You can't have recess," "You can't come to MY class," "You can't be in sports," "You can't be in choir," and the list goes on. I'll admit when I was young, I thought about the things they could not do, but once I took the time to get to know people who learned differently, my focus shifted to what they could do, and how I could help.

I watched my students be more compassionate, forgiving, patient, kind, accepting, and open to differences. I saw them face each day head-on with determination, ready for the challenge. They were more willing to try new experiences than many of their general education peers and complained less. I had the privilege of walking beside my kids and watching them reach milestones many said they would never reach. My students taught me about and gave me unconditional trust.

I had the privilege of walking beside my students' families as well. I taught the majority of my students for two or more years. Some I had the great privilege of teaching for eight to ten years, and I knew most of their families very well. I found that not only were my students being told "can't," their families were too. "You can't have a normal life." "You can't be happy." "You can't be proud of your child." "You can't have nice things." "You can't enjoy your life." Many of the families I have gotten to know over the years have shown me what true parenting should look like. These families have embraced their children's differences and proven all the "can't" statements wrong.

One of the first lessons I learned is my kids are often more concerned about what others think of them than they are of their academics. Many times when we see something in someone who is different than we are, we perceive it as wrong or somehow making that person less, but it's not. It is just different. Oftentimes we see a person who learns differently and needs modifications and accommodations as less intelligent than others, yet I have never met a person who feels someone with corrective lenses (an accommodation) is somehow less intelligent because of those glasses. Glasses, braces, sunglasses, pencils and pens with erasers attached, straws, and word processors are all types of accommodations and modifications many of us use daily, yet no one thinks twice about our intelligence because we benefit from their use.

I have been humbled time and again by the lessons I learned from my students and their families. My students taught me character is as important as academics—maybe more so. Their families showed me what true unconditional love looks like, and that their lives were happy and fulfilled. They proved different does not mean wrong, bad, or less. As a teacher, it is the goal to instill knowledge and build skills in our students so one day they can be productive adults, whatever that may look like for each individual.

Raymond

Sitting across the table from me was a confident, thriving, college junior. He played football for his college, was voted by his coaches and ninety-nine teammates as the football player of the year his first year, and earned average to above-average grades in all his classes. He had a summer job, lots of friends, a girlfriend, and a loving, supportive family. By all accounts, he was a successful person.

He looked like everyone else on his block at home and in his school dorm. He drove himself wherever he wanted, including through large metropolitan areas and around the country. He was the all-American, good-looking young man. By all appearances, he had it all and will continue to have it all. However, that was not always the case.

Raymond was the third of four boys. His mom, Debra, said the pregnancy with him was just like the others, but the delivery was complicated. She spiked a high fever, Raymond got stuck in the birth canal, his heart rate dropped, his oxygen was low, and he had to be taken by emergency cesarean section. Raymond and Debra recovered well with no lasting effects. Raymond met all his developmental milestones on time and was always within normal ranges on height and weight, even though he weighed ten pounds at birth.

The first time Debra realized something was not developing normally was when he attended preschool. At the first parent-teacher conference, she and Jeremy were told Raymond could not do anything. He did not know his alphabet, colors, shapes, and so on. Every time they talked to his teacher that year, it was the same words, "He can't . . . " The preschool teacher insisted Raymond do another year of preschool with the hope he would be more ready for kindergarten. During his two years of preschool, he did much better when the aide worked with him or when the long-term sub was working. They seemed to want to help him learn and were more encouraging with their wording.

When Raymond started preschool, he did not like it. He did not want to leave his mom when she dropped him off, and school was already a challenge for him, so he did not want to go. The teacher and principal told her she needed to stop dropping him off so he would behave better when he was at school. They told her he was acting that way only because he was the baby of the family at the time.

Debra tried having other people drop him off and having him ride the bus from a sitter's house, and nothing worked. The bus driver told her she was not sure what to do for him either, because getting him to come onto the bus was difficult, and then he did not want to get off the bus when he arrived at school. The principal told her if Raymond did not start behaving better, he would not be allowed to come back. At a time when most children love school the most, Raymond's and Debra's experiences were awful.

In kindergarten, it was more of the same: "He can't . . . spell, write, behave properly, etc." She asked the teacher what they could do at home and was told to read to him. Raymond's grandmother was a librarian and had been reading to him every night since he was born. Debra asked if there was more they could do, and the teacher did not have any other suggestions.

Raymond was learning in other areas, but his skills in naming and recognizing letters and making the correct letter sounds were not progressing at all. In those very early years, when Raymond was asked to spell "cat," he would say "L-R-Z, cat." They trudged through that year and hoped the next year would be better.

He recalled not wanting his teacher to call upon him in first grade because he knew he was not fast at reading or math. He had anxiety when the class played games and he was called up to the board to participate, or when everyone had to take a turn to read aloud. Raymond felt he was different from his classmates.

His teacher was not exactly negative toward him, but not really helpful either. She often commented he was not trying hard enough or at all, he needed to practice more at home, and he was making excuses for himself. He felt she was often frustrated with him, and looking back, he believed it was his inability to learn like the other students in the room. She continually marked his papers with red ink and drew big sad faces at the top.

First grade was the worst. The teacher put Raymond and another student off in a corner and had a better reader work with them. Debra knew this because the better reader was their neighbor, and he talked about it after school. While the other student's self-esteem was skyrocketing, Raymond's was falling deeper into the pits of despair.

Jeremy and Debra talked with the teacher several times at the beginning of the year trying to figure out how they could help Raymond more at home. Jeremy even offered to come to her classroom after school and have the teacher go over the day's lessons with him, so he could in turn work with Raymond at night. The teacher refused, saying she was not paid for work after school hours.

It was suggested to Raymond's parents he was rebelling because he was no longer the baby in the house and was trying to attract attention. Debra and Jeremy were told Raymond would turn out okay, but he would never go to college—or if he did, he would not graduate.

They were told the school had to do only so much and that was all they would do.

At one meeting, Debra grasped for any answer that explained what was happening to her son. She suggested that because the teacher was the same age as Raymond's grandmother, maybe he did not see her as a strict authority figure because his own grandmother was not strict. The school and teacher took the comment to mean she thought the teacher was too old to teach. Debra asked if he could be placed in another first-grade room to see if it made a difference. The school refused to even consider moving Raymond into another class, saying it was too far into the school year for such a transfer.

Debra said Raymond cried at night when he was trying to do homework. For him, it was a foreign language, and he had no translator. His parents were frustrated they could not find the answer to help him and the school did not seem to care enough to do more. Raymond told me of many times he wished he could do better or be better so his parents would not fight and vent their frustrations at each other about the best way to approach his situation at school.

With seemingly no help from the school, Debra and Jeremy hired an outside tutor. This tutor happened to be studying to be a special education teacher and was learning about new programs that were helping kids like Raymond. She began teaching Raymond a highly researched and scientifically based program, the Lindamood-Bell Phoneme Sequencing Program (LiPS). Oddly, the principal was not happy about the parents doing outside tutoring. He felt the program was making things worse for Raymond as he began spelling and saying words very phonetically.

On the surface, that sounds like a great thing for someone learning to read, but Raymond said aloud even the silent letters. Then Debra worried she had really messed things up for Raymond. However, very soon after the tutoring began, Raymond began to understand the association between letters and sounds, blended them together, and started to read on his own. By the end of first grade, he had gained two years on his reading ability. He was still behind his peers, but not nearly as far as he had been at the beginning of the year.

At the beginning of second grade, he had similar problems and came home with all of his papers and tests marked wrong in bright red ink. This year, instead of sad faces, the grades were put at the top of his papers. Raymond was seeing a lot of Ds and Fs and feeling pretty bad about himself. He felt the other kids in the class were looking at him and snickering when he was called upon to read aloud or play games where they had to answer questions aloud quicker than another person.

When they played games at recess, they excluded him. When kids picked who they worked with, they chose him last or not at all. No one ever said anything to him directly, but their behavior toward him made him think he was not as good as the kids who shunned him, and that there was something wrong with him. This type of behavior lasted most of his primary school career. Around fifth grade, he found some true friends who tried to include him in things at school from then on.

When Raymond was in second grade, Debra remembered hearing for the first time, "I'm never going to get it, so why should I even try?" Debra set up an appointment with his teacher just weeks into the school year. This teacher said the same things as his previous teacher, "He can't read, write, spell…" The teacher hinted maybe he would benefit from special education services. No one had mentioned this before, and Debra wondered why.

She and Jeremy had Raymond evaluated for special education, which revealed he had a specific learning disability. By the time they completed the evaluation, held a meeting to discuss the results, and developed his individualized education plan (IEP), half of second grade was over. While Debra and Jeremy were relieved there seemed to be an answer, they were furious no one had brought this up to them before. Debra feared Raymond's self-esteem was so far gone, it would take years to build him back up again. They finished out second grade by "going through the motions from eight to three every day."

Raymond felt some relief because he was getting help; however, when he left the room for his special education services, he believed the other kids talked about him and the others who received special education outside the classroom. Raymond did not need a lot of help; he was out of his general education classroom for about an hour a day. He received all of his instruction from his general education teachers and had a few accommodations and modifications to his work within the general education setting. He simply needed a little extra time to do the work and sometimes needed to hear the lesson differently.

It was at this time Raymond came into my life. He was very quiet and timid when he first started coming to me. I could tell he wanted to please the teachers but had zero confidence in himself and his ability to make them happy. He was a sponge for the help I provided. He absorbed everything I taught him, especially the praises. He felt success in school for the first time. His anxiety about being called upon diminished and he was able to cope better with his academics.

During the first few months of receiving help, he earned a 100 percent on a spelling test. Debra said there was a party in their house that night. He earned more perfect scores after that one, but because the spelling test had been his first, it stayed on the refrigerator for months.

I sat down with Raymond shortly after he started coming to me and explained my theory on how learning differently (my way of saying learning disability) works. I told him that in almost everyone's brains there was a direct path for their learning, but in Raymond's brain, his path had some detours. He would and could learn the same material as his peers, but his learning was going to look different, and it might take him longer. He seemed to really understand, and I believed because of the success he had with his tutor, he accepted the definition for himself.

Raymond did not recall much about third grade, except that his teacher was similar to his first-grade teacher. The teacher did not want to give the accommodations and modifications his IEP required: extra time on tests; a separate, less distracting location while taking the tests; a choice marked out of multiple choice questions; fewer vocabulary words to choose from; and a reduction in the number of extra reading points. Raymond overheard her say, "Now that those kids are going, we can really learn," on more than one occasion.

The teacher told him he was immature, lazy, and there was really nothing wrong with him. If he did not understand something the way she taught it, she became frustrated and took it out on him. She was displeased with him when he did not do as well without his accommodations and modifications and many times blamed him, saying he was doing it on purpose. I tried to explain to her that just because she could not see his disability, it was no less a disability. She still thought students should outgrow the need (or desire, in her words) for accommodations and modifications.

Debra also did not remember much about his third-grade year, other than Raymond needed glasses. She hoped the glasses would "cure" him, but felt in her gut it was more than just a vision issue. The third-grade teacher gave him a test within the first few days of school and did not apply any of his accommodations or modifications. Raymond was able to answer only two questions correctly out of twenty. She marked his errors in red and sent it home.

When Debra questioned her about it, the teacher said she needed a baseline so she would know at the end of the year how much Raymond had grown. She also recorded it as a grade. While Debra understood the reason for a baseline, she wondered why the teacher didn't keep it to herself for her records instead of crushing a child's self-esteem by letting him see his results, and why it was necessary to record as a grade. The teacher told her that students wanted to see their papers, and if she had not given them a grade, they would not have tried as hard as they did.

In fourth grade, Raymond had a near-death experience. He was playing tag football with some friends and family. During one of the plays, he and another player got tangled up and the player fell on him. Raymond was not hurting and continued to play. The next day, he felt a little "weird," and had some pain. It was Grandparents Day at school, and Debra's mom begged her to take him to the doctor, as she thought maybe he had cracked or broken a rib. Debra made the appointment for the next day.

That night, they grabbed a quick bite at a restaurant, and when Raymond took a drink, the liquid just spilled out of his mouth and ran down his chin. Debra asked him what he was doing, and he lifted up his shirt. He looked like he was eight months pregnant and told her his body felt like it was full of fluid. She rushed him to the emergency room.

Doctors determined he had a ruptured spleen and a cyst growing on the spleen that was absorbing the blood from the rupture. The cyst had absorbed as much as it could, and he was bleeding to death. The fluid he felt filling his body was blood. There was no telling how long his spleen was ruptured; the doctors told Debra and Jeremy that if it had not been for the cyst absorbing the blood, he would already have been dead.

The doctors wanted to fly him to a nearby children's hospital, but the weather conditions were not favorable, so they rushed him by ambulance. At the children's hospital, he had surgery to repair his spleen. His surgery was successful, but his life still hung in the balance. He was put into the intensive care unit (ICU) to be monitored around the clock.

Both sets of grandparents, his brothers, an aunt and her family, and his parents were there as much as they could be. They were all there when I visited on his third day in the ICU. They surrounded his bed and some were crying. Someone saw me and they made an opening so I could see him. I was not expecting what I saw. His grandmothers hugged me and thanked me for coming. I felt like I had walked into a wake.

Debra sounded very upbeat when she told Raymond I was there, but I could see in her eyes how worried she was. She held his hand and rubbed it the entire time I visited him. He had tubes sticking out of him, he was hooked up to an IV, and looked so pale, fragile, and lifeless that I almost cried. The rest of the family stepped aside so I could move close to him. I sat on his bed and picked up his hand. It was cold. She implored him to wake up to visit with me. He woke up for only a minute or two of the twenty or so minutes I was there.

Even though he was not awake, I talked to him in the most upbeat voice I could muster about the cards I brought from his classmates and told him all the well wishes the teachers and staff sent to him. I could tell my ability to hold back the tears was quickly vanishing. When I left, I cried and prayed the whole forty-five-minute drive home because I was worried I would never see him alive again. For the first few days in the ICU, no one knew for certain whether he would live.

On day four, he began to perk up and was awake more than he was asleep. On day five, he was well enough to be moved out of the ICU to a regular room for a couple of days of observation. They sent him home after the spleen was healed and the bleeding stopped. He still had to go back for another surgery to remove the cyst. He was home for one day when he started bleeding again and needed to go back to the hospital.

Debra rarely left his side. Her dad brought her leftovers from the meals people prepared for Jeremy and the other boys. He insisted she go eat in the lounge or go to the Ronald McDonald house to eat and get a shower. She did not want to leave him, though she knew she had to once in a while because the reality of the situation overwhelmed her and she cried. As long as she was near him, she saw he was alive, and she could be strong; as soon as she left his side, the strength disappeared. She never cried in front of Raymond, nor did she let on how serious his situation was.

He was in the hospital for several weeks and home another week or two before returning to school. While the situation was unfortunate, Raymond said his classmates gave him hope. They sent get-well cards, and many of his classmates visited him once he returned home. Those cards showed him that his classmates really did care about him and gave him the desire to keep fighting to get better.

On his first day back to school, the students and staff seemed to be excited he was back. "That was a pretty cool feeling," he said. When he returned to school, he was not allowed to go to recess or physical education for a while. Many of the kids stayed with him during those times to play games with him and keep him company.

Being out of school for more than a month and being unable to complete work for most of that time did not stop him; one of Raymond's most important characteristics was his work ethic. I was his homebound instructor for several weeks while he caught up. He did not complain, nor did he give up. He had to learn twice as much as the other students in half the time, and he did it well. At the end of fourth grade, I gave Raymond an achievement test called the Woodcock Johnson III. He scored closer to grade level than in any year before.

The test score that blew me away—to this day, I have not found anyone with such a discrepancy between grade level and ability level—was his oral comprehension. I had to read him a sentence and then by the end of the test read him a paragraph with one word missing. He had to tell me the correct word for the blank. There were no options to choose from, no hints given, and I could read the sentence or passage only once. Sometimes a few different words were considered correct, and sometimes there was really only one word that worked. His oral comprehension score was that of an eleventh-grader.

From fourth grade through the rest of his elementary years, he had multiple teachers per grade. This was good in Raymond's opinion because if one was not helpful, or he did not like the teacher, or thought the teacher did not like him, he was soon out of that class and into another. When I asked about his favorite teachers, he named half of the junior high staff, the junior high special education teacher, and me, but not one primary teacher.

When I asked Raymond if he had any teachers he felt were not good or helpful to him, several elementary school teachers topped the list. He felt the ones on the negative list simply did not understand a learning disability. He also believed these teachers found it easier to blame him than to change their style of teaching. He often felt as though they showed no interest in him personally; from his perspective, they pushed him off to the side and ignored him, rather than trying to help him. They always seemed like they were in a bad mood and did not really care about him, other students, or the subjects they were teaching, he said.

He felt the teachers on the good list seemed to really care about what and who they were teaching; took time with him and other students; got to know him on a more personal level; tried to help him find things that worked for him; made him feel safe, welcome and comfortable in their classes; and most importantly, believed in him.

Debra remembered the first general education teacher who told her "Raymond struggles with reading, comprehension, and other skills, but we are working with him and I believe he will figure it out." This was his fifth-grade teacher, the first teacher who said "struggles" instead of "can't." This teacher was willing to work with me to find different ways to teach the lesson, or different ways to modify or accommodate his work so he could truly show what he knew.

One of Debra's proudest moments so far came in Raymond's sixth-grade year. One student was always mean to a particular student. One day, Raymond finally had enough, and he stood up to the bully. Raymond got right in the boy's face, grabbed his shirt collar, and told him to leave the other kid alone. That moment gave Debra proof to back up her belief that Raymond was going to be okay in life. He had finally come out of his shell. He finished elementary school in all general education classes with minor help from the special education teacher.

She was happy Raymond did not remember many of the things she remembered, or he remembered them in a less negative way. Her prayer throughout his elementary years was "that he wouldn't remember the bad." Most of Raymond's categorizations of his teachers as favorites and not favorites made sense to Debra, as she saw in them the same things he did.

She was surprised he did not put one of the teachers on either list. That teacher was not helpful or understanding of his situation and yelled at Raymond two or three times for things that were out of his control; Debra was relieved he did not remember. She thought maybe it was so traumatizing to him that he did not know how to process it at the time, so he let it go. However, she said, "Mama never forgets." When Raymond was ready to move on to high school, she was so happy to be "done with that place." She remembered a few great teachers who believed in him and were his cheerleaders, but for the most part, elementary school was a constant battle.

The transition into high school was pretty nice, Debra said. The counselor and special education teachers helped get him on the proper track right away. He continued in all general education classes with minor accommodations. By his senior year, he was not going to the special education teacher for help at all. He had taken dual credit college classes, graduated with above-average grades, and was in the top third of his class.

With the help of his elementary school teachers and some of his high school teachers, he was able to find things that worked for him when it came to studying, taking tests, working on his homework, and bolstering his self-esteem. It was in high school where the confident young man in Raymond began to shine.

Raymond said his experiences with high school teachers were similar to the ones he had with elementary school teachers. Some seemed to care about him as a person, others wanted to see only his disability and the extra work it caused them. Of course, his favorite teachers in high school were the ones who formed a relationship with him and took some time with him to help him academically, emotionally, and socially. A couple of his high school teachers were people he could go to talk to about personal things. That someone outside of his family who was not one of his special education teachers would take the time with him made a huge impression on Raymond.

The placement tests Raymond took in elementary school placed him in basic math and English for his first year. He came home in the first few weeks of school and asked his mom what he had to do to get out of those classes. He knew he had to be there for the extra help, but most of the other kids were there because they did not care about school, had bad attitudes, and were just putting in their time until they could drop out; one day, Raymond saw a student fiddling with a marijuana joint.

He was in those classes for one year before he was able to pull himself out of them, but his experiences did not diminish Raymond's good attitude. Debra told me about an email from a teacher who was bragging about Raymond's kindness. He saw someone eating alone, got up from the group of friends he was sitting by, took his tray, and sat with that person for the rest of lunch.

Raymond and I talked about what he felt were the reasons he did not feel isolated when it came to making friends. His suggestion to anyone with any sort of disability was to get involved with a club, organization, or team through their school or in their community. There were no clubs or organizations in his school or community for kids in primary grades to belong to, though that changed in elementary school. He said being in sports really helped him teach other people that he was more than a kid with a learning disability, especially in elementary school. When the other kids took the time to get to know him because they spent so much time with him at practices and events, he said they accepted him more. He was not involved in any non-sports clubs, but he felt it was definitely a way to have a sense of belonging.

Debra, too, believed sports helped the other kids get to know Raymond for Raymond, but in her opinion, he still hung out mainly with his siblings, cousins, and one real friend. During baseball season especially, Raymond and his family were invited to gatherings, but Debra still often saw Raymond off by himself. In his primary years, he sat back and took things in rather than join in and possibly have drama. He was more comfortable being a loner rather than join in where he did not always feel he was welcome. He never had pity on himself, he just chose not to deal with potential problems.

Though Raymond struggled to stay motivated through a rough time in elementary school sports, he started to hit his stride in high school. He found participating in sports was a helpful way for people to see him as something other than the kid who needed special education. The summer before he started high school, the athletic department weight room and gym were open for anyone who wanted to come in and begin getting in shape for the upcoming school year. At the open gyms, Raymond began to make friends with others who were trying out for his sports. Those people saw Raymond as a potential friend and athlete, versus seeing his learning disability, and he bonded with many of them.

His freshman year, he played football, baseball, and basketball. He was a shadow player the first two years of high school sports, but in his third year, people began noticing him. His football coaches believed in him from day one, but he did not start believing in himself until his third year.

As he got older, he narrowed his participation to football and began track his junior year. His football teammates and coaches became another family to him. The group spent many hours together, on and off the field. For Raymond, bonds in high school sports ran much deeper than those from elementary school. In college, he found the same sort of camaraderie with his football teammates and coaches.

His high school athletic highlights included having an undefeated freshman football season, breaking several school records for track and football, and going to the state level competitions for track. His favorite memory was a winning football game against the crosstown rival in which he scored six touchdowns.

Even with all this success in his high school athletics career, much of Raymond's popularity in high school came strictly because of who he was. Raymond had a great personality, was kind to everyone, worked hard at everything, and was personable. Debra immediately confirmed his humbleness, and I had to agree. He was always more about the team's success than his own. I prodded him to share more accomplishments, but he shrugged it off and said, "I don't know, I really don't remember. I think we have them listed on a plaque somewhere. I can text them to you later." He never did.

Along with the highlights he mentioned, Debra shared a list of his senior year achievements: he was voted Most Valuable Offensive Player, broke the school record for the most yards carried in a season, was one of the team captains, scored the most touchdowns in a game, and led the team in carries. He earned spots on the all-conference and all-state football teams and played in the Shriners' game. One final high note was his winning the same scholarship award his older brothers had earned. This was no easy feat for Raymond because it was not de-pendent solely on his athletic skills; he had to write an essay and earn good grades.

In college, Raymond took all general education courses, and he still received accommodations of extended time and separate location on tests. He said his college was extremely supportive with providing him help and granting his accommodations, and most of his professors were willing to help him with whatever he needed. The major difference between college and lower education for Raymond was the need and ability to advocate for himself. He learned all the way through school, for better or worse, that he had to speak up for himself and stand his ground when it came to his accommodations and rights as a person with a learning disability.

In one class, he had a problem with the software the professor was using, and his assignments were not getting to her. This software was completely different than what the rest of the college used. His professor told him he needed to call the company to get it fixed. Raymond suggested to her that she should be the one to call, since it was different software than what the rest of school used, and he probably would not have access to change any settings anyway.

Unfortunately, the professor held it against him. Once all the problems with the software were finally taken care of and she could finally access all the work he had done, the maximum credit she gave him was 80 percent. It was the exact same work, he had not had to redo any of it, and she could see it had all been turned in on time, but she said because it was "late," he could earn only 80 percent. To Debra, it was yet another instance of his giving everything he had—physically, emotionally, and academically—and someone in authority telling him it was not good enough.

Another instance in which he stood up for himself was in football. His freshman year, he was not getting any playing time, even though he had a scholarship for football. With a few games left, the coach asked him if he was willing to play in a different position than what he had been practicing, and then he could play the last few games. He spoke to his former high school coaches about what to do and they encouraged him to turn down the offer. He chose not to play and waste a year of his scholarship opportunity, so he was redshirted for the first year. This decision allowed him to remain eligible to play four years and cover part of all five years of college with his scholarship.

Originally, he thought of getting a physical education degree, which made me very proud. He wanted to keep kids active and become a coach of football or track and field. He later changed his major to business administration, with a minor in psychology, which made me even more proud. With this degree and minor, he hoped to become a counselor and work with kids who had IEPs in high school and college so they were able to pursue their dreams, just like he was doing.

Looking back at his academic career, elementary school was so much more difficult for Raymond than high school and college because of homework. In elementary school, he had four to five hours of homework almost every night. In high school, it dropped to one or two hours. In college, depending on his classes, he averaged two to four hours a day. College was different in that he was not attending classes all day, every day, like in his earlier schooling. So while the amount of homework is similar to that of elementary school, it is not on top of spending seven hours in a classroom first. For a person who struggles to learn in the way the material is taught, elementary school was a nightmare.

Can you imagine if you had to go to work every day, all day, at a job where you struggled; people did not interact with you much; your bosses were constantly telling you that you were not trying hard enough, you were lazy, and you were making up your difficulties; and then you had to take your work home and do it for four or five more hours, several days a week, thirty-six weeks a year, for eight years? All to be told over and over again all your effort was still not good enough?

This was basically his experience for his first several years of schooling. Things got slightly better once he was eligible for an IEP, but some teachers still treated him as though he was making up his disability or he was lazy, and some students still treated him poorly. Even after all that, he still recommended a special education evaluation to someone who is struggling.

He said that because of his IEP, he had hope and things did get better. He found teachers who worked with him and cared enough about him and his learning to find what learning methods worked best for him. He had teachers who explained to him that his learning disability did not mean he would not or could not learn, but he learned differently, and his path to learning looked different than some of his classmates', and that was okay. He had teachers work with his strong attributes to help counterbalance his weaker ones. He learned the positives of having an IEP outweighed the negatives.

He did not believe he would be attending college if it was not for the help the IEP granted him. Something he said that really struck me was, "kids will judge each other, but after high school those people are not always going to be around. Yes, you will see them occasionally, but you have to figure out what is best for you, really." He recommended people find and improve their strengths because "even the best reader in the world, still reads." Conversely, he also suggested people should focus on finding ways to accept and cope with their weaknesses, and strengthen those skills too.

When Debra spoke of his elementary days, the pain in her eyes and quivering in her voice revealed the pain of her heart from those times. She remembered long nights of Raymond giving everything he had and feeling okay about his homework, just to have the paper returned marked up in red. She recalled nights of four and five hours of trying to get through one reading passage and answering questions, only to have to read another passage and answer questions for another subject the same night. In his desire to do well, he expended all this energy and effort, to have his teachers tell him in words or in red ink marks that it did not matter—he still failed.

In his school there was a program that was intended to encourage the kids to read more on their own, for fun. Many of the teachers turned the fun into homework and then a grade. The program determined, based on test scores and reading level material, the number of points each child was expected to earn by the end of the quarter. The students earned points by taking a test on the "fun" material. For Raymond, reading was a burden. This program was nowhere near fun for him. Almost every quarter he had to miss actual fun activities, like recess or assemblies, to earn his points—or miss out on the reward. On top of that, it almost always lowered his reading grade even more.

At the time, no one who was giving him those grades seemed worried about what it was doing to him. No one but Debra saw the defeated look in his eyes, the beaten dog look on his face, his self-esteem falling, his drive to put in all the effort diminishing, the feeling he would never be good or good enough rising up in him, the tears falling from his face as he gave every last ounce of his energy and effort into trying to decipher the words and the message of the reading passages. No one but Debra felt the pain of being unable to help her son and not having the answer to make it all go away or make it easier. Debra was oftentimes as exhausted at the end of the night as Raymond. Debra was so proud of Raymond's drive to continue in those tough times. Many times she was ready to give up, but he wanted to continue.

When Debra spoke of his high school days, there was relief and happiness in her eyes and voice. She said he was finally able to successfully apply himself and earned average to above-average grades. She was not sure if he matured, the teachers taught in a way he understood, something finally clicked in his brain, or a combination of all three. Whatever it was, she was forever grateful.

She was also extremely thankful for Raymond's football coach. The coach taught Raymond and the team more than just football; he taught them respect for themselves and others. He taught them that family was more than bloodlines, and it was important to always have one another's backs. He taught them that no matter how many years passed, he was always there for each one of them.

Debra is thankful to the coach and Raymond's high school special education teachers who made his transition to college so smooth and easy. When Raymond needed a little extra help in college, all he had to do was bring in some paperwork the high school had prepared for him.

Raymond was never bullied, but he had advice for students who might be. He said not to give up, and to seek authority; teachers and administrators were supposed to be there to protect the students. He also had recommendations for teachers and administrators. He encouraged them to protect the bullied students who came to them for help. He suggested talking to the students and helping them understand an invisible disability was something the student had no control over. He said teachers and administrators needed to accept the students in their care who had disabilities, in a way that showed other kids they were no different.

He felt it was up to the educators to talk to all of their students about each person's differences and communicate that no difference was right or wrong, or made a person less or more. He understood having twenty or more students in a classroom made it tough on teachers, but he really wanted teachers to understand "every student learns differently (whether they have an IEP or not) and they are not the same."

Raymond's message over the years was consistent: teachers needed to have a relationship with their students. "Really get to know your students, see what their strengths and weaknesses are so they can succeed as a student," he urged. Not an authoritarian relationship, but one in which the teacher knew the students' likes, dislikes, and things the student did outside of school. Teachers needed to make a connection, believe in the student, believe there was a disability if the student had an IEP, make all students feel safe and comfortable, and keep the standards high.

The only sad disability-related story Raymond had was the amount of stress it caused his parents. When he was struggling, especially in those early years, his parents talked to teachers and administrators, worked with him for hours in the evenings, and called others for help. He had other siblings who also needed his parents' attention. He knew it was difficult for all of them and he said, with his voice cracking, that it seemed to sometimes be a problem. He sometimes felt he was to blame when his parents were really aggravated with everything, though he did not fully understand what was going on at the time.

He felt his parents would go to the ends of the earth to help him. He believed his parents, grandparents, and siblings provided him with a strong foundation and they never gave up on him. Even in times when he failed, which he said was "learning in different way," his family still encouraged him and lifted him up. They taught him mistakes were okay if we learned from them, they helped him understand why he failed, and helped him find ways not to fail the next time. He advised any parents of a child with special needs to follow in his parents' footsteps.

Raymond said his mom was his biggest cheerleader. If he had a rough day at college, he could text his mom and she would send him a scripture from the Bible to help him get through whatever he is facing.

His favorite one she has sent was Philippians 4:4-7, "Rejoice in the Lord always. I will say it again: Rejoice! Let your gentleness be evident to all. The Lord is near. Do not be anxious about anything, but in every situation, by prayer and petition, with thanksgiving, present your requests to God. And the peace of God, which transcends all understanding, will guard your hearts and your minds in Christ Jesus."

I also asked Raymond if he had any funny stories related to his disability. He said his dad always joked Raymond could sing before he could read, and his singing was still better. He was not sure if his dad was complimenting his singing or saying how bad his reading abilities are. Whichever it was, Raymond was not offended; he just laughed. Debra confirmed Raymond truly could sing before he could read. He was in kindergarten, listening to a song on the car radio, when he suddenly started singing all the words. Jeremy and Debra looked at each other and laughed and cried all at the same time. Jeremy said, "He can't read, but he can sing the lyrics to Black Eyed Peas songs."

I asked Raymond if he remembered the time my daughter and I visited him in the hospital with a set of Hello Kitty Uno cards. He vaguely remembered. When I asked him if he remembered losing the game to her, his response through a smile was, "I don't lose." My daughter and I both reminded him that he did, indeed, lose that day and blamed the loss on the Hello Kitty cards at the time.

The final thing Raymond and I talked about was his future. He hoped to have a family and, while he knew it was a long shot, he had a dream to be in the National Football League. He believed he would be a great father if he had a child with a disability because he had experience to draw from, and he would support his child the same way his parents supported him. He would figure out what worked for his child as soon as possible so his child would not fall behind, and make the child's life as "normal" as possible.

Debra and Jeremy were wonderful parents who raised four amazing children. When Raymond graduated high school, his head football coach told Debra if his kids turned out half as good as hers, then he had done something right in his parenting. While Debra appreciated the compliment, there were things about raising her children, specifically Raymond, she wished she could have changed. For one, she wished she and Jeremy had found what was causing Raymond's learning issues sooner, and that she had not always been required to stay in damage control mode with regard to his heart and mind. She would change all the fights she and Jeremy had because of the situations and their frustrations with school. She would change how overwhelmed she felt at trying to find the answers and getting the school to help, and how lost she was at helping her son.

She would make the principals really listen to her as a parent and understand where she was coming from, instead of always backing their teachers. She would change all the teachers who never believed in her son or heard her when she had concerns. She would not allow the teachers to let his fellow students grade his papers and see how poorly he had done. She would change the communication problems between her and the school. She would change having to research dozens of colleges' requirements because she had to worry about where he could survive academically.

She would change the pain she saw in him when he tried to help his younger brother with schoolwork and then had to stop because the memory of his struggle was too strong. She would change all the pain he went through to get to where he is today. She would change the extra twenty to twenty-five hours a week he spent studying with a tutor on top of everything else he did. She hurt for where he had been, but not for where he was going. She knew he was going to be awesome. Debra was incredibly proud of Raymond and who he was, and she would never change him.

Her advice to other parents who may find themselves in similar situations was to never give up on their child. She said parents need to let their child know the diploma they receive at the end of their school career carries the same weight as everyone else's. She advised parents to speak to their children softly about situations regarding teachers and the school, and to find family or friends they can truly express their feelings to. As difficult and heart-wrenching as it may be at times, she urged parents to always be hopeful but realistic with their child when it comes to their academics. Finally, she advised parents to raise their child to be a good person and not to put too much worry on their grades.

Thank you, Raymond, for sharing your story with me and allowing me to be part of your life, even all these years after I was your teacher. You have thanked me for all I've done for you, but I think you've done just as much, if not more, for me. I do not know where your path will lead you, but I have no doubt you will be successful as long as you continue to have a great attitude and work ethic.

You taught me what a great work ethic looks like in a student. You taught me never to give up just because something is difficult. You taught me character is more important than grades and showed me what a humble, positive outlook can do for a person. You and your family taught me the importance of unconditional support for and from family members. I do not know how I could be prouder of you. I am excited to see what the future holds for you.

Thank you, Debra, for sharing your heart and your son with me for all these years. You and your family, immediate and extended, have taught me unconditional love and support for one another. Thank you for including me in your family's holiday joy by bringing me a plate full of yumminess at Christmas time. It has been a pleasure to know your family and become a small part of it.

Allen

When I was first introduced to Allen, he was screaming and kicking at his teacher. It was day one for me at a new school. I was working in a completely different atmosphere than at previous schools, where I had been a special education teacher to students who came to me for short periods of time throughout their day to receive the support they needed.

At this new job, I worked with the most severely academically and behaviorally challenged students in the school. This was not to say the students I had were considered severe or profound, but they were the most complex of the school's population. I had experience working with kids who were behaviorally challenged; in those cases, though, I was an aide—not the one in charge of and responsible for the outcome. To be honest, I was very nervous and wanted to do the best I possibly could for this little guy. I had already read his individualized education plan (IEP) before I met him. He was cute as a bug and had the roar of a full-grown tiger.

When Allen was born, his parents were in their early twenties. They had been married a couple of years and were ready to grow their family. At twenty-six weeks pregnant, Faith went into labor. She was taken from her home hospital to a hospital three hours away, and the labor was stopped. She stayed at the hospital for one month with the diagnosis of placenta previa, a condition in which the placenta does not rise to the top of the uterus; it covers some or all of the cervix, and can cause life-threatening bleeding. She went home and was on bed rest for the remainder of her pregnancy.

When Faith was full-term, she felt labor pains again and went to the local hospital. They told her she was dilated only a little, and sent her home to get a good night's rest. She could return the next day, they said. Brent and Faith returned around eight in the morning, and because she was dilated more than she was the night before, they let her stay. Later in the day she was ready and began pushing, but her pelvic bones did not stretch enough for the baby to move through the birth canal. The doctor had two options: do a cesarean section or use forceps. Brent and Faith requested the C-section. The doctor wanted to try the forceps first.

Brent and Faith were elated their baby boy had arrived and they instantly fell in love with him. However, they did not get the joy of holding him for more than a minute or two, as he needed to be thoroughly examined. The doctors and nurses took him away to check on his vitals. They told Faith and Brent this was normal after a baby was delivered, especially when forceps were used, so they were not worried that anything was wrong. They were told his oxygen was low but that, too, was to be expected.

Brent and Faith went to her room, had their dinner, and were settling in after all the excitement when one of the nurses came into the room. She explained the night nurse had done some testing and it appeared Allen had had a seizure. She followed up with, "We are going to airlift him to a hospital three hours away as a precautionary measure."

Faith still thought the best and believed it all would be okay with Allen, because no one seemed nervous or worried. The next morning, Faith checked herself out of the hospital, and she and Brent drove to where Allen had been transferred. On the third day of Allen's life, after multiple tests, Faith said, "That's when the bombshell hit." The neurologist told them Allen would never walk or talk.

Unaware that Allen was sideways in the birth canal, the doctor set the forceps on the front and back of Allen's head instead of the sides, as was normal. When Allen was delivered, his eye was pushed in, bruised, and swollen, and there were big indentations on the front and back of his head where the forceps had been. The doctors and nurses had assured Brent and Faith those were normal marks from the forceps, and his head would adjust to normal on its own.

The forceps crushed the frontal lobe of his brain. The frontal lobe controls conscious muscle movement; coordinates information from other regions in the brain; facilitates cognitive skills in humans, including emotional expression and problem solving; helps create long-term memories; manages attention and impulse control; and affects personality, speech, judgment, and sexual behaviors.

The right side of his body was physically affected the most. His neck would not move, and his right hand and foot were curled. Within ten days of birth, Allen was receiving physical therapy (PT). The therapists moved and flexed those parts of his body to stimulate his brain into thinking it could do that. For the next month, Allen remained in the children's hospital and underwent therapy every day—sometimes multiple times a day. The therapists also gave Brent and Faith exercises to do with him when the therapists were not around.

Faith and Brent lived at the hospital too. They experienced all the emotions from highs to lows, sad to mad, and back again. They pondered whether they should have spoken up more; whether the doctor did something wrong; whether the hospitals did anything wrong; and whether they should have insisted on the C-section (they demanded one with their second child and found a doctor who agreed). In the midst of all of the emotions and questions, one thing was certain in Faith's mind: they were going to love him and do whatever they could for him. During the time they were all at the hospital, many family and friends came to visit and offered support, prayers, and comfort.

Once Allen was released from the hospital, the therapies began at home at least three days a week and oftentimes three times a day. He began receiving occupational and speech language therapy, and physical therapy continued. Faith and Brent needed to bring Allen to the hospital three hours away twice a month for checkups. Allen's neurologist was doing a hospital-affiliated university study on children who had a brain injury at birth. Having Allen included in the study, Faith said, was wonderful, because they checked his progress often and did magnetic resonance imaging multiple times to see if his brain was reacting to the different stimuli they presented him. This was how they knew so quickly about his delays and were able to address them earlier and with the right therapies.

Brent took the first three months of Allen's life off of work, and Faith took off the first four months. Even when Faith went back to work, at lunch she picked up Allen from the sitter, took him to PT, brought him back to the sitter, and then went back to work. For the first year, they lived three hours away from the hospital. Around his first birthday, they moved to within an hour of the hospital. At the same time, Allen was just beginning to do a sliding crawl movement.

There was a small window of time after they moved when no therapist was coming to the house, but Brent and Faith had been taught to do so many exercises through the first year, they were able to keep working with Allen. They found new therapists who came to the house until Allen was three years old. During his first three years, Allen proved the neurologist wrong. He began babbling around eighteen months and said his first word at around two and a half years old. When he spoke clearly for the first time, his parents were elated, shocked, relieved, and in denial. His first truly understandable word was sunflower. The kitchen had yellow sunflowers painted on the walls, and Faith supposed they must have talked about them often for that to be his first word.

He continued slide-crawling for a few more months and began pulling himself up on things. He had every toy his parents could find to push or pull, to keep him moving and striving toward walking on his own. He took his first steps at around age two. When Allen reached those milestones, they thought maybe he would be delayed, but everything would be okay.

At three years old, many changes happened in Allen's life. He had surgery to correct his eye, he switched day care providers, and his brother, Joseph, was born. His right eye had never completely recovered from the forceps injury. Though his skull recovered, and there was no obvious evidence of the damage, his brain did not recover as well. The right side of his body showed the effects of his traumatic brain injury. The surgery on his right eye, however, was so successful that there was no permanent marking or evidence of the injury, and he never needed corrective lenses after the surgery.

Allen began exhibiting some strong behaviors. He screamed uncontrollably when he became upset, kicked and hit both of his parents, ran away when his parents wanted to talk to him, and became aggressive at the new day care.

When he was four, Faith took him out of the day care and put her work on hold so she could stay home with him. After a few months at home, Faith found a wonderful young lady who stayed with their family for several years. She was a tremendous help in getting Allen through some of his toughest times. When she was no longer able to stay with

Allen and Joseph, they found a young man who stayed with them until Allen was in seventh grade. By then, Allen was mature enough and managed his behaviors and emotions well enough to stay with Joseph for a couple of hours at a time after school with a wonderful aide from the school who came to help him.

The muscles in his arm, hand, leg, and foot on his right side did not work as well as his left side. He had surgery when he was five to attempt a repair of those muscles and nerves. He had countless hours of therapies throughout his life to try to stimulate the damaged part of his brain. Allen had been through nearly every kind of therapy: speech (privately and at school), behavioral health, music, swim, physical (privately and in school), social, and occupational therapy. He also had a private comprehensive therapy that included sensory motor work, eye tracking, core exercises, academic engagement, healthy nutrition, and confidence building that worked to overcome his developmental deficits. Nothing gave him complete mobility of his right side or completely healed the damage, even with braces and continued therapy. His problems with learning, memory, behavior, and other executive functioning skills continued unseen.

Allen attended preschool for two years and did well there academically and behaviorally. His teacher was structured, firm but loving, and attentive to Allen's needs and his behaviors. His progress was slower, but it was not as noticeable in those early years.

When I first met Allen, he was in kindergarten. He spent many hours in my classroom in both years he attended kindergarten. The first year, we focused a lot on figuring out his behaviors and how to manage them; the second year, we focused less on behaviors and more on academics. Not surprisingly, of his two kindergarten teachers, he recalled the second one. His first teacher was no less compassionate or caring, but because he was in meltdown mode so much of his first year, he had no memory of it.

When Allen was calm, he was one of the sweetest, cutest, most helpful students I had. When he was in meltdown mode, Allen's behaviors included kicking, yelling, punching, pinching, pulling hair, biting, head-butting, spitting, rubbing spit on people and objects, refusing to walk, grabbing at things, breaking and chewing his pencils, and throwing objects.

Faith had only good things to say about all of Allen's teachers, and especially about a few who stood out in her mind. His second kindergarten teacher was one. Within a few weeks at the beginning of the school year, the teacher really understood Allen. Faith had a few meetings with her, and the teacher seemed to know exactly what to do. She understood Allen's love of the St. Louis Cardinals (she was a big fan of the team too) and his fixation on the weather. She knew he could be easily redirected to the task at hand. She and I worked very well together, and Faith said she could not have asked for a better team for her son.

Both of us worked with him and held him accountable for his actions while we helped him learn better ways to deal with his emotions and feelings. We also tried many different positive behavior reinforcement plans throughout the year. Allen responded to a plan very well for about four to six weeks, then the system stopped working. She used different methods to teach him, spent extra time with him, and understood his behaviors were not directed personally toward her. By the end of his second year in kindergarten, Allen was closer to grade level academically and doing much better behaviorally.

Unfortunately, he had to be restrained many times to keep from hurting himself or others around him. I was trained in crisis prevention intervention from the Crisis Prevention Institute and was able to correctly hold Allen so he was never hurt or in any danger. This school did not have a separate location to take him, so we were sometimes out in the hallway. Allen told me he did not remember these episodes.

He had very similar distress episodes at home. His family recorded his outbursts to prove to doctors and therapists they needed help, because he did not exhibit these behaviors in their presence. Allen's only awareness of those behaviors was from those videos. As we talked about them, he seemed embarrassed. I was thankful he did not remember; I was sure it was a traumatic time for him.

He was better behaviorally in first grade, though still not like a typical first-grader. His episodes of emotional and behavioral meltdowns were less severe; the frequency was still about the same for most of the year. One incident involved two other students. Every day, Allen went to the same swing at recess. Several weeks into the school year, two boys decided they wanted to swing, and one of them chose the swing Allen had been using. When Allen told them it was his swing, they called him "retard" and "retarded." Allen began kicking the boys. One of the boys went to the playground teacher and told her Allen kicked him "just for being on the swing."

Without asking Allen his side of the story, the teacher marched him right to the principal's office. Because of his behavior track record, the principal immediately believed the report from the playground teacher and called Brent to come pick him up. By the time I heard of the situation, Brent had already taken Allen home. That night, Faith emailed me the full story Allen told her.

The next day, she and I went to the principal and told her Allen's side of the story. She did not believe us at first. We convinced her to call in the other boys and question them more thoroughly. The boys acknowledged calling him those names and going to that specific swing on purpose. Allen had already been punished for his part, and those boys were punished for their part too.

Later that day, the mother of one of the boys called Faith and apologized for her son's behavior. She told Faith she had spoken to her son about how wrong he had been to use those words and to treat Allen in that manner, and requested if her son ever did anything like that again, to call her directly. After that episode, the boy and Allen were always friendly to each other and even played together sometimes.

Allen's first-grade teacher always wore beautiful, dangly jewelry. We talked after every behavioral meltdown Allen had to discuss what worked, what did not work, what behaviors were shown, what happened right before and right after, and strategies to try. I recommended to her that she not wear her beautiful, dangly jewelry, as it could be destroyed or she could get hurt if he grabbed something during one of his meltdowns. She refused to stop wearing the jewelry, saying, "I'm not going to change what I wear; he'll just have to learn not to grab my jewelry."

While I understood her sentiment, there were flaws in that statement. Her thought was Allen had control and was completely rational during these episodes. It also insinuated Allen grabbed her jewelry on purpose. The part of the statement that irritated me the most was that while she was in complete control of her actions and could change, she refused to do so—yet at the same time, fully expected him to change. Through much practice and instruction, Allen's meltdowns became less intense, less frequent, and shorter in duration, but not before this teacher had a long, dangly necklace destroyed.

It was after the teacher's necklace was destroyed that the superintendent called Faith and Brent. The superintendent had all of Allen's records in front of her and began to list the episodes Allen had been involved in. She told them if Allen had one more episode, he would have to go to the alternative behavioral school thirty miles away. This was not an option Brent and Faith wanted, or felt Allen deserved. As his special education teacher, I also did not feel he needed to go elsewhere.

To send him away at this point, when he had made the amount of progress he had made, was ludicrous to all three of us. We all firmly believed if he went to the alternative school, he would learn more bad behaviors instead of continuing to improve. Faith and Brent knew their rights and Allen's rights and helped the superintendent see the school had not been following Allen's behavior plan. They were also able to show the appropriate setting to meet his least restrictive environment was right where he was.

In second grade, things were again better for Allen. He was managing his emotions and reactions better, and he was catching up to his peers academically. His teacher saw him several times at different events over the summer prior to second grade and they began to get to know each other. She felt this was a tremendous help in getting Allen to feel welcome in her class.

Something that took all of us too long to realize was how much Allen's fixation on the weather affected him. He always wanted to know what the weather was doing. It did not matter if it was hot, cold, sunny, rainy, snowy, windy, or stormy. In his elementary building, most classroom windows were covered with blinds. Some teachers kept the blinds open, others did not. When we realized he was so affected by the weather, we thought keeping the blinds closed was for the best. We thought if he could not see the weather, especially on days when it was expected to change, he would be less affected. We were wrong. We figured out that for Allen, knowing what the weather was doing, even if it was doing nothing, had a calming effect on him.

In second grade, Allen had an individual aide who was absolutely amazing with him. She rode the bus with him in the morning and she could tell what kind of day he was going to have based on their conversation on the way to school. She was the one who noticed when he was in third grade that he seemed to have his worst behavioral days on the second day of the week. When she told me about her theory and we tracked backwards on his data charts, she was correct. There was definitely a pattern.

I spoke with a behavior therapist about this situation. She did not seem surprised by our find. She said while she had no hard research on why, she saw this in her students at the behavioral school all the time. Her theory was on the first day of the week, the kids were refreshed from their break and happy to be back into a routine. On the second day, they remembered following the routine was difficult and tiring, and they could not do it again. On the third day, she theorized, the students accepted they had to work hard to manage their behaviors and do their school work. By the fourth day, they were looking forward to the weekend and seeing light at the end of the tunnel, which gave them an extra boost to manage their behaviors. On the last day, their behaviors were out of sorts again, because the break was coming.

She said at her school, they could elicit the most from their students academically on the first and fourth days of the week, and on the other days they adjusted their schedule to include more movement and use more manipulatives. I have worked with many more students with behavioral issues since then, and the pattern seems to ring true with all of them.

Throughout his remaining elementary and middle school years, there also appeared to be a pattern of a rough year followed by a good year that seemed to coincide with teachers who welcomed him and those who did not. When he was still in elementary and I was working with him, some teachers told me he did not belong in the general education setting because of his behaviors. He was impulsive in what he did and said, and sometimes his comments to females were very inappropriate.

I agreed he was impulsive and his comments were sometimes inappropriate; reminded them his executive functioning skills were not yet fully developed due to his disability; and impressed upon the teachers how far he had come. After these discussions, they had a better understanding that the best way for him to learn was to stay in the general education setting for academic instruction and come to me for assistance in academics and social skills. As the years progressed, Allen continued to improve both academically and behaviorally, but he never completely caught up in either area.

When I asked Allen to tell me anything he wanted regarding his life, he answered, "What, this horrible life?" He immediately smiled and said he was kidding. I was certain he had horrible times in his life; that Allen always saw the good in everything made me happy. He told me he had only one real friend through elementary and high school. He had another friend in elementary school, but when they ended up at separate high schools, the friendship was affected. Faith said one of the most difficult things to see as her sons were growing up was the vast difference in the way Allen was treated compared to his brother.

When the family relocated around the time of Allen's first birthday, they moved to a town with fewer than a thousand residents. Everyone in the close-knit town seemed to know everyone else. There was not much to do other than to go to school events, which were heavily attended. When Allen was in his first years of school, it seemed everyone knew of his behaviors. He sometimes had those behaviors in public, too, and Faith remembered the whispers and the looks.

As he continued through school and he was not top of his class, a star athlete, or the best at anything, kids did not pay much attention to him and neither did adults. Her other son, who was a star athlete, seemed to always be surrounded by peers and friends, and many adults talked to Faith about how good he was in the different sports.

Both of her boys were kind, generous, loving, nice-looking, caring, helpful, and fun. Many people never took the opportunity to find out those things about Allen. Faith felt this was not just because Allen had an intellectual disability with some physical impairment, but because he was not a standout at anything. She saw other children who were not superstars also get left out, forgotten about, or rejected. In general, she felt it was just socially harder to be accepted or to find one's tribe in a smaller community. If there was anything she could have changed about Allen's elementary school years, it would have been for him to be more accepted among his peers and the community.

She said the kids did not pay much attention to him, but I believe what she really meant to say was they did not pay much positive attention to him. Oftentimes on the playground, in the general education classrooms, on teams, and in social situations, the kids paid attention to him, just not in a good way. Kids learned early on that Allen was impulsive, easily agitated, wanted to get a laugh, did not completely grasp social situations and cues, and often said inappropriate things. Several kids over the years used this knowledge to convince Allen to do or say things that often landed him in trouble. As the years went on, the things the kids did to him and got him to do grew more intensely inappropriate.

One such incident involved several teenage boys on a bus coming back from a sporting event. Faith knew instantly by the looks on the boys' faces when they were stepping off the bus that something had happened. She and Brent persuaded Allen to tell them what happened, and it was so severe they went to the superintendent. The boys in question told the truth about what happened and were remorseful. A few of the kids were removed from the team, and several students were suspended from school.

To Faith's knowledge, nothing like that ever happened again, and she hoped it never would. It was the only time she ever thought a situation was safe and innocent and then it turned out to be horrible. Years later, the mother of the boy who spearheaded the incident apologized to Faith, and they shared a good cry. It was an unfortunate way for the other woman's son to learn a valuable lesson—but at least he did learn, and he never gave Allen a difficult time from that day forward.

I was Allen's elementary special education teacher for six years. During the time I had with him, he was in all general classes with the support of an individual or classroom aide. He came to me for extra support, both academically and behaviorally. I communicated regularly with his parents and his general education teachers. I could usually keep the amount of homework he had to complete each night down to a reasonable level.

Writing was always a struggle for him. In the elementary grades, many of his teachers believed a good way to study spelling words was to write them repeatedly. The first night of the week, the homework was to write the spelling words ten times each. This was a tremendous burden on their entire family. Allen usually had fifteen or twenty words, and some nights it took several hours to write them. Allen became very frustrated if he wrote one incorrectly, or his parents told him his handwriting would not be acceptable to the teacher, and he had to do them again. He oftentimes had major behavior episodes because it was so difficult for him.

He wanted to be like the other kids, and it made him angry he was not like them and could not be, no matter how much effort he put forth. He was often harder on himself than his parents or teachers were. Because he wanted to be like all the other students, he often did not want the accommodations that had been designed for him. If he knew the other kids had to write the words ten times each, he got mad when his parents or teachers told him he only had to write them five times each. Many nights he grudgingly accepted the accommodation out of sheer exhaustion.

It was a relief when writing spelling words repeatedly ended with third grade. His parents struggled with how much to push him academically and socially. They never wanted him to reach his point of no return. At the same time, they did not want him to use his traumatic brain injury as a way to get out of doing things he could do.

Faith always had a good rapport with Allen's teachers and felt most of them were truly partnering with her and Brent for Allen's education. She felt a good relationship and frequent communication between parents and teachers was key for any student to be successful in school. Brent or Faith spoke with the teachers at the beginning of each year to give them an understanding of Allen. They spoke of the things that had been successful in years past, academically and behaviorally, and what things were overwhelming or had not worked. They discussed what accommodations could be used and how much was too much, and affirmed they were always available to the teacher.

Sometimes teachers got busy and forgot what had been discussed. When that happened, Faith reminded the teachers of their conversations at the beginning of the year, or what was in Allen's IEP, and almost every time, things were fine. There were times when big projects were due or lots of homework had been given consistently and Allen would just reach his limit. At those times, which were very few and far between, Faith let the teacher know Allen would complete the work, just not in the timeframe the teacher wanted. Every year, Faith and Brent made sure the accommodation of extra time for completion of classwork, homework, and tests was included in his IEP for just this reason.

In elementary school, he was not bombarded with hours of homework every night, because it was a smaller school and the other special education teacher and I could check with him at the end of the day. If he was scheduled for an amount that either of us knew was too much, we talked to the teachers before school was over and discussed with them some other options.

In high school, the population was three times that of the elementary school, and there was not always an opportunity for his teachers to check on him at the end of the day. Many times in high school, he came home with homework in all of his classes and each subject took approximately an hour for Allen. Several times in elementary and high school, Allen was still trying to complete his homework after one in the morning.

Faith said, "A school system, I think, can only go so far until they might be hurting other people, a classroom, or somebody else's ability to succeed." Luckily, in high school he also had a wonderful coordinator through whom Faith and Brent could communicate with the school and make adjustments. In Allen's area, he would have had to travel thirty miles to attend a behavioral school. Faith and Brent were very pleased with all that Allen's schools did for him, but she pondered if there was more they could have accomplished if they had been in a more populated area.

When he was younger and the kids played tag, he was "it" the most. When the kids played kickball or baseball, he was always picked last. He was often told he was playing only defense because of his inability to catch, throw, hit, kick, or run fast. The kids let him join, then did not really play him, because they did not think he would help their team win.

Brent and Faith were sports oriented and understood this philosophy in young children; Faith remembered being young and picking the best kids to be on her team so she could win. She was not offended, nor was Allen, by the kids' actions. "It's natural to want to win," she said, "and that's how we explained it to him. We told him if he wanted to be on the team, he had to work to be better." That was exactly what Allen did.

From then on, he had a goal of making a school sports team because of his ability, not because of his disability. In sixth and seventh grades, Allen tried out for the school's baseball team. He did not make the cut either year. This only spurred him on. He really wanted to be a pitcher. He took all the advice he received in the years he did not make the team, worked harder, practiced more, and honed his skills during seventh grade.

When it was time for eighth-grade tryouts, he gave it his all again. I still remember the day he found out he made the team. It was one of Faith's fondest memories of his elementary days. The smile on his face and the look in his eyes were bright enough to light up a stadium. He had completely earned his spot on the team just like the other nineteen boys. He was very proud of himself, as he should have been. He played only a few times that year. Faith believed it was justified based on his ability compared to the other boys.

He played for two years in high school, and in his junior year, he did not make the cut. He called Faith to tell her the news. Just as she was preparing to give him a pep talk, he said not to worry, because he had decided to join the track team. Of all the events Allen could have chosen to participate in, he chose the 3200 meter, or two-mile event. He ran in some charity five-kilometer races in grade school and his first couple of years of high school, so he knew he enjoyed running long distances. He came last in every race he ran, but he finished and kept getting better each time.

When Allen entered high school, Faith had a talk with the head football coach. Allen played soccer in town growing up and was a really good kicker, but struggled with kicking and running at the same time. She explained Allen's situation with his right arm and leg as well as his cognitive difficulties and asked the coach if he would give Allen a chance. The coach cried while listening to Allen's story and said he would absolutely give him a chance.

As a freshman, Allen did the kickoffs every game. In his sophomore and junior years, he played on the junior varsity team and was the starter for kickoffs and extra points for most of the games. Allen's senior year approached, and he knew he had to work extra hard to keep his spot, as there were some younger guys who were pretty good. He and his parents had the philosophy with competitive sports that "a player deserves a spot if they deserve it."

It was not all about being a superstar, the hero of the game, or a standout to Allen. It was about proving to himself and others around him that he deserved his place, he earned his place, and he was going to do his best for himself and for his team. At this point in his life, Allen felt competitive sports was where he wanted to be, and as long as he was eligible and able, Faith and Brent fully supported him.

His experiences with the high school football team were good overall. There were times, though, that his inability to grasp social setting cues, his desire to belong, and his willingness to do things he thought would help him fit in combined to cause some instances that were not so good. To fit in, Allen often mimicked others. During his first three years on the team, Allen tried to adjust his behavior to that of his teammates by paying attention to what they did and said. He tried to smack talk with the players, and most of the time the other players just laughed at him or walked away. Faith heard about these things from other boys on the team and sometimes Allen relayed the story. He did not understand the underlying meaning of what the other person did or said.

It broke her heart. It kept her up at night to see her son give everything he had in everything he did, and others still made fun of him and did not accept him. Parents told her at social events how proud they were of their own children for how well their children treated Allen. Faith knew in almost all cases the child had not treated him well. In some cases, what the parent told her was the exact opposite of what she witnessed or was told of by someone else.

She and Brent had conversations with people in the community who praised their parenting to their faces, only to question that same parenting to other parents or family members, who relayed it to her. Community members commented how nice it was that Faith and Brent were having Allen try out for the baseball team . . . again, or that they were letting him play football. People complimented the school systems for allowing her son a chance at these activities. She never heard anyone make those same comments about her other son. His participation seemed expected and normal.

Faith described an incident between Allen and his friend's much older brother. Allen needed to be home at a certain time. The older brother lied to him. He told Allen it was the time he was supposed to be home and urged him to hurry, when in reality it was two hours early. Allen went home and was hurt when he realized what had happened. The child's parent shared this story with Faith at a ballgame and laughed about the joke her older son had pulled on Allen.

Faith was appalled and hurt that a parent thought it was funny for her son to be cruel to someone younger, especially someone with an intellectual and physical disability. She felt isolated because so few people in the community actually took the time to get to know her or Allen. No adult was ever rude or mean to Allen directly, yet their attitude, body language, and manner of speaking told her the words out of their mouths were not really how they felt.

Allen had difficulty making friends amongst his peers. He often invited the guys over, and still no one showed up. Faith consistently told Allen at some point his peers would understand and forget about how he acted in the past, and this lonely time shall pass. He had his family and God always watching over him. Faith acknowledged how hard it was for parents when their children did not fit in. She encouraged parents to believe in their children, remind them often of this support, and reassure them it will all turn out just fine.

For one year, Allen and Joseph were in high school together. Brent and Faith spoke to Joseph about being Allen's protector that year—their ears and eyes to things. They encouraged him to be an awesome brother for the year, and then he could make a name for himself his other three years. It did not take long before Joseph had to step up and protect his brother.

Both boys were on the school football team and attended summer training camp. Joseph came home on the first day of camp and told his parents things were as bad as they thought. Joseph and Brent had a heart-to-heart about what Joseph had witnessed. When camp was finished the next day, Joseph was ready to leave before Allen and had to wait, since Allen was his ride home. While Joseph waited, he asked a football player if Allen was almost ready. The player responded Allen was not ready because "he was checking out all the football players in the showers and locker room."

Faith said Joseph had a boldness she wishes she had, because of how he responded to this guy who was at least three times his size. Joseph said, "You do understand Allen was not checking out the guys in the shower. He's just trying to be like everybody else and be part of this team and that's it." Joseph did not hear anyone say anything more about Allen for the remainder of the camp.

Allen and his family made a few major accommodations over the years, including relocating, and a whole host of consistent minor accommodations too. Faith still cut his fingernails each week. He needed physical therapy three times a week, and learned to drive himself to his appointments. He received shots in his wrist yearly to try stimulating the nerves to work. He saw a neurologist once a year. They've tried multiple therapies, strategies, and behavior plans over the years.

They also figured out his oral sensory issues. Faith said it was as though he needed to taste the food on all parts of his mouth. He always took two bites before he began to chew, his chewing was very exaggerated, and he chewed for a long time before swallowing. When he was in the early primary grades, we knew he had need for oral sensory stimulation. He chewed anything he could put in his mouth. He chewed pencils like a little beaver. We massaged the outside of his jaw. We tried jerky, granola bars, gum, taffy, carrots, caramel, a chewable rubber T, rubber pencil wraps, a chewable necklace, and anything else we could think of that might help give him what he needed.

Until he was about eight or nine years old, his clothing did not have buttons, zippers, snaps, or ties, because his right hand could not operate any of those fasteners. The items he could manage on his own incorporated elastic or hook and loop fasteners, or they were pullovers or slip-ons. Allen learned to tie his shoes independently by sixth grade, but some fine motor issues lingered and made tying his football shoes difficult. Another football player tied Allen's shoes for three years without one comment.

It was obvious to people when they saw Allen that his right hand and arm were not fully functioning. People were very helpful, accommodating, and understanding when it came to his right hand. The problems arose when it came to his cognitive issues—his invisible issues. It was rare to come across a person who was negative toward someone with an obvious disability. It was all too common to deal with the person who was negative toward someone with an invisible disability, even when the negative person knew about the disability. There have been lots of misconceptions, biases, and downright wrong assumptions about Allen's invisible disabilities over the years.

One such incident took place the summer before I interviewed Faith. They were attending a baseball tournament for Joseph's team. When Joseph's game was over, they gathered their things to leave. Allen picked up his lawn chair and used his right side to hold the chair up against his chest while they waited for Joseph. A kid from another team walked by him and said in a snarky voice, "You must really be in love with that chair."

While Faith is not proud of it, she walked over to the boy, got down to his eye level, and told him "You do not understand, but the kid you just made fun of for holding the chair that way only has one good arm that can do anything." The kid was quite stunned and said he was only joking. She responded with "It does not matter, you should not have said anything at all, good luck at your game," and walked away.

During the same summer they had another experience; happily, this was a positive one. Allen was scheduled to play on a charity golf team with three other boys his age. On the day of the event, one of the boys brought an extra person along. Faith said the other boys did not allow the fifth person to take Allen's spot in the foursome. They understood he had paid to be part of the team; it was for charity; and having fun, not winning, was the ultimate outcome. Allen's family followed a competitive philosophy with competitive sports, but they had a different philosophy with a fun family game, fundraiser, or charity event.

Every year since Allen was born, his family donated gifts to the children at the hospital that took such good care of him. They invited his friends and family to his birthday parties and asked them to bring items to give to the hospital. At Christmas, they donated from their own money. As Allen grew and began to gain a true appreciation for all the hospital did for him, he wanted to help even more. One year, in addition to the gifts given specifically for the hospital, he donated every one of his birthday gifts.

When he reached an age when he did not have birthday parties, he began helping at his church. He chose a ministry that helped women who were abused by their spouses get back on their feet. The ministry met with the mother and found out what she needed and wanted, then the volunteers found donations to fit those needs. Once they had the donations, they set up the house for the family. Allen lit up when he was able to help these families. He especially enjoyed finding items for the kids' rooms. When he was in middle school, he often came to my room and helped my students. He always held the door for people, was polite, and did whatever he could to help anyone he knew.

Allen was a very handsome eighteen-year-old man as he began his senior year of high school. He had his driver's license and hoped to attend college in a southern state to study weather. Faith was confident it would be a great year for Allen. His high school special education case worker had been amazing, according to Faith. He had half special education classes and half general education during his junior year. His case worker kept Faith informed if there were issues; Faith said it was rarely necessary. As a junior, Allen showed a great deal of maturity when it came to attending classes, completing homework, studying for tests, and being prepared for his school day, and she expected it to continue his final year.

Looking back at Allen's school career, there were a few positive instances that really stood out to Faith. One such event was when he was in eighth grade, and I organized a Special Education Week. Each day of the week, I had a different student share about themselves, their disability, and what they wanted people to know about them, on the morning announcements. I gave Allen some talking points ahead of time, and he wrote his answers out beforehand so he could relax a little. Allen told his story to the entire student body, his teachers, and the administration.

I remember being in the room where we produced the announcements, with all the broadcast teachers and students. The three teachers in the room—Allen's current and former teachers—were changed that day. I watched the expressions on their faces as the interview went on and they learned about him. Many students were affected that day too.

Several came up to Allen afterward and told him how impressed they were that he had done the interview; some were amazed at all he had gone through, and others told me they had a new appreciation for him.

Another occasion that stands out in Faith's mind happened in spring 2019. Allen's high school football coach and I nominated him to be honored at A Night of Superstars. This was a night dedicated to extraordinary children with life-threatening or serious health challenges. The evening included a limo ride, red-carpet experience, and a country concert. Allen was chosen as a recipient. He dressed up in a tuxedo, had his hair done (the girls had hair and makeup done), and arrived to a group of adoring fans and paparazzi lined up alongside a roped-off red carpet. Everyone along the red carpet asked for his autograph next to his biography in the program. He also won tickets to sit behind home plate at a home game of his favorite professional baseball team. I know his parents will not forget the evening, and I hope Allen never does either.

One of Faith's favorite football memories was the senior speech Allen wrote. It brought tears to his mother's eyes when he thanked everyone for letting him be part of the team. He did not mention the bad days. Allen saw the happiness in everyone. The title of his speech was "What the Titan Football family means to me—is that anyone with all abilities has a place on this team—because we are always there for each other."

Allen took a year of training through a Goodwill program on how to interview for a job, write a resume, and determine what jobs would be good for him. Faith felt programs like this one were definitely beneficial. After several visits and an interview, he landed a part-time job at a local retail store. People in the community who had not seen Allen since grade school approached Faith often to compliment Allen's hard work, kindness and helpfulness in the store.

Faith's advice to all parents was to make their children feel special, push them to be all they can be, pray for them, and support them through the tough times of life. The support and prayers from family and close family friends throughout Allen's life were major reasons Faith believed Allen had been as successful as he was. She encouraged parents to do something special for their child each year, something they knew was just for them, something parents had to put some effort and thought into doing, so the children knew just how special they were. She advised parents to be close to the school, understand their child's rights, and work along with them, not against them.

I had no doubt he would be successful in finding a college and a program that would accept him. I also had every confidence that someday he would be working in a weather- or sports-related field.

Brent, Faith, Allen, and Joseph, I thank you for allowing me to share your story. Allen, you have taught me that with the right attitude, obstacles are just small hiccups in life. You and your family have taught me tenacity. You have taught me to set goals and never give up on them. You have taught me that no matter what, I can always continue to improve myself.

I have learned to accept what God has given me and to love myself for who I am, because that is exactly what you do every single day. You have shown a willingness to work when others have given up. You have shown me what generosity in the face of adversity looks like. You have taught me to be proud of every accomplishment I make in comparison to myself and not others. I look forward to seeing what you will do with the rest of your life.

Mike

In mid-1999, Cindy and Bob found out they were expecting their third child. Cindy was thirty-seven and Bob was twenty-nine. They were quite happy, and the pregnancy was just like Cindy's others; she had no morning sickness and gained very little weight. In March 2000, Cindy gave birth to a healthy baby boy. The delivery, the Apgar score, and his weight and height were normal. They excitedly brought Mike home to his three-year-old brother, Harry, and six-year-old sister, Wendy.

The beginning of Mike's life was almost exactly as his siblings' had been. The difference was that by six months, he was still not able to hold himself up in a sitting position, and his hands always formed fists. Cindy expressed her concern to the doctor at his well-baby checkup, but the doctor said to give it a little more time, as all children develop at different rates.

A month later, Cindy and Mike were at a local restaurant. An acquaintance of Cindy's walked over, asked if Mike had cerebral palsy, and said Mike was behaving the same way her son had at that age—and he had cerebral palsy. Cindy was shocked. Later, she told Bob what the woman had said, and they decided to look into it more. Their doctor referred them to a pediatric hospital about an hour away. Test results showed Mike did, indeed, have cerebral palsy (CP).

Cerebral palsy results from brain damage that occurs in utero, during delivery, or shortly after birth, and it affects muscle control and motor functioning. Scientists have identified several issues that may contribute to causing the damage, including gene mutations, illnesses or injury during pregnancy, and oxygen deprivation.

The list of CP symptoms is wide-ranging, as is the list of related conditions, and the combinations and severity of symptoms are different for each person. It causes developmental delays; sometimes it is not diagnosed until after a child has missed early childhood milestones. CP is incurable, but therapies and medications can help improve motor functions and relieve symptoms. In Mike, CP caused difficulties walking, holding his head up, swallowing, and moving his muscles voluntarily and deliberately, among other challenges.

The head neurosurgeon delivered the news to Cindy and Bob that Mike had CP. She told them Mike would not have a fulfilling life or amount to anything worthwhile, and his family would not have a good life either. She gave them no glimmer of anything good that would become of their beautiful son, and made no offer of therapies, counseling, or help of any kind.

Cindy said she wanted to slap the doctor at the news. Mike was an otherwise healthy and happy baby; why would someone say such a thing about him? In Cindy's mind, the only things the doctor gave her were gloom and despair.

They brought their beautiful baby home. Other than having low muscle tone, Mike was a typical infant. He was happy-go-lucky and seemed to always be in a good mood. He was able to swallow, so they could feed him baby food and formula.

Cindy had been around other children with cerebral palsy, but none as young as Mike. She believed that was one reason she did not recognize the symptoms and treated him as if he was just a little developmentally delayed. Bob said, "We dealt with the hand we were given, we loved him, and parented him the best we could."

Cindy and Bob never took Mike back to the pediatric hospital; the doctor there upset them badly. Their general practitioner became Mike's main doctor instead. Dr. Josh diagnosed Mike with developmental delay with hypertonia. This meant Mike was eligible for birth-to-three-year-old services, which provided occupational, physical, and speech therapies in their home several times a week. Mike was receptive to the therapists.

The doctor said Mike was also eligible for Supplemental Security Income (SSI) and Medicaid. SSI is a federally funded program that provides extra income to disabled children from birth to age eighteen. Medicaid is a federal and state-funded program that provides health coverage to millions of Americans, including eligible low-income people and people with disabilities. Medicaid is administered by states, according to federal requirements. Both of these programs have strict guidelines and criteria for eligibility.

The family had good insurance through Bob's work, so Cindy was hesitant to put Mike on Medicaid. After discussions with their doctor and Medicaid office staff, they enrolled him, because Mike would benefit from it after he turned eighteen. Cindy and Bob were adamant that Mike not abuse the system, and Cindy always ran everything through their family's medical coverage first.

With the help of the in-home therapy, Mike was soon able to hold his head up on his own and sit for a few seconds at a time. Cindy did some research and found a therapy in Europe that was very successful. This therapy was intense and required Mike to stay there for weeks at a time. It was also very expensive. The family's medical coverage would not help pay, as it was in another country and had not been approved in the United States. The cost for each trip was $15,000.

With the help of many fundraisers and donors, they raised enough money for Mike to go. His first therapy was in December 2002. He and Cindy stayed in Europe for three and a half weeks, and Mike participated in therapy six days a week, for six hours a day. One successful therapy they used was called suit therapy.

In intensive suit therapy, Mike wore a special suit with a customizable set of compression elements, weights, and resistance bands while he performed exercises to improve his strength, coordination, posture, and muscle tone. The suit aligned his limbs, contained his body's natural reflexes, and provided support throughout the exercises so he could build new muscle memory.

He practiced using a stander to help build his leg muscles and had sessions of stretching, gym, massage, and cage therapy. Cage therapy involved a room-sized cage that served as the frame for a system of resistance bands, straps, and pulleys. Therapists put harnesses on Mike in different configurations to isolate muscle groups they wanted him to strengthen and to focus on limb movement during exercises to improve his coordination.

Cindy knew the in-home therapy was not going to be enough, and the therapy overseas was not going to last forever. She found help in a nearby big-city children's hospital. Three days a week, she drove the two-hour round trip, and waited and watched as he went through three hours of therapy. When they arrived home, she fixed Mike his lunch—typically pureed pot pie or soup—and fed him. Then they both took a nap.

On the other two days of the week, the in-home therapists worked with him in the morning, and lunch and nap in the afternoon were about the same. While many of Mike's muscles were getting stronger, his ability to make words was not. He communicated his needs through grunts, smiles, eye movements, and head nods. He also rolled to what he wanted, or attempted to point at it.

Cindy was unable to work outside the home during the day because of all the therapy appointments. She worked at night as a care provider at a local nursing home. Cindy's schedule was quite hectic while Mike was between two and four years old. Most days, she slept little more than the few hours when she and Mike took their nap. Bob worked during the day, the older siblings were at school, and Cindy alone provided for all of Mike's needs.

Cindy recalled her days being something like this: she was up at six o'clock in the morning, got herself ready, then made Mike's breakfast of oatmeal before she got him up and dressed him; he still did not have enough muscle tone and coordination to dress himself. To feed Mike his breakfast, she propped him up with a pillow on the floor facing her and wrapped his legs around her waist, because he could not sit in a chair and keep his head up long enough to eat. Next, she brushed his teeth and combed his hair, and was ready by eight o'clock to either leave for a therapy appointment at the hospital or have a therapist arrive at their home. During this time, she also woke up her two older children and fixed their breakfast while they got themselves ready. If they had homework to finish, she helped them with that. Bob usually had to leave for work between six and six thirty, so he was not able to help with the morning routine.

On the days the therapists were in the home, she did laundry, cleaned the house, or prepped meals to freeze. However, she was never out of Mike's sight for more than a minute. Once therapy was completed, she fixed his lunch, propped him up, fed him, and cleaned him up. Then they took their nap. She also changed his diaper as necessary. When she awoke from her nap, the older siblings were home from school. She helped them with homework, started their dinner, and worked on something for Mike to eat. When Mike woke up, she carried him out to the living room and lay him on the floor to interact with his siblings or watch television.

After feeding Mike, she put dinner on the table for her other children and Bob. After dinner, Mike and Bob took a shower while Cindy cleaned up the kitchen and had her own dinner. After Mike's shower, Cindy got Mike ready for bed and herself ready for work while Bob tended to the family's small farm. She left for work around nine forty-five in the evening and usually arrived home about five fifteen in the morning. Mike slept in the same bed as his older brother so he could not roll out of bed, and if there was a problem, Harry was either able to help him or get Bob.

At three years old, Mike began early childhood education within the public school system, attending the afternoon class. He still qualified for speech, occupational therapy, and physical therapy, but now they happened during his school day. Cindy continued to take Mike to his therapy at the children's hospital three mornings a week. Cindy still worked at night, but was getting more sleep since therapists were not coming to the house. She decided to go back to college and become a nurse.

While Mike was in school, she worked at the nursing home or attended classes. Once a week, a respite provider came to the house and gave Cindy a few hours for herself. She and Bob used the time to grocery shop, discuss the week's activities, and eat a meal Cindy had not prepared. Near the kids' birthdays and Christmas, they also used the time to shop for presents.

Respite care is provided to give caregivers a break and is often funded by the state or federal government. It is difficult to get and keep a respite provider, because the pay is not great, the funding is not always available, and providers and families do not always mix well together. Cindy and Bob's provider only lasted about six months before she found a better-paying job. She and Mike had gotten along really well, and he really liked her; however, the family understood her need for better pay and more hours.

When Mike turned five, he began attending school all day. Cindy continued to work and attend college. Her schedule altered to getting up at four o'clock in the morning, getting herself ready, selecting clothing and preparing breakfast and lunch for Mike, and leaving the house at four forty-five. She then either worked all day or split the day between work and classes. Her evening schedule was still pretty much the same.

Since Cindy was gone at work, Mike's dad and siblings got him out of bed, dressed and fed him, and made sure he was ready for school, and got themselves ready for school and work. Much of this fell on his siblings' shoulders. Bob's work let him alter his schedule a little so he could help out at home a bit more, but he still needed to leave between six thirty and seven each morning. The bus usually did not arrive until about seven fifteen.

Mike and Cindy attended the therapy overseas a total of six times before Mike turned six. In his last two therapy sessions, he was actually holding onto a walker and walking with assistance on a treadmill. The therapy was successful, but cost more than money. The stress of traveling, raising trip funds, raising two other children, working, and the intensity of caring for Mike ended up being too much for Bob and Cindy's marriage.

When Mike was five, his parents divorced. They remained friends and were very good at keeping their problems away from Mike. He always felt supported and loved by both parents. Mike lived with his mother, but saw his dad almost daily. More responsibility fell on Wendy, Harry, and Cindy when Bob moved out. Bob often came over and took a shower with Mike to help Cindy, but most days the daily shower fell on Harry or Cindy's shoulders.

By this time, Wendy was eleven and she started helping her mom with laundry, cleaning, and watching her two younger siblings. Wendy and Harry learned how to feed Mike, which was also a huge help. As they grew older, stronger, and more responsible, Wendy and Harry still played with Mike and interacted with him as siblings, but became more like caregivers. They began to get him dressed and ready for school most mornings. They helped get him on and off the bus at school and at home. They changed his diapers, cleaned up after him, brushed his teeth, combed his hair, and fed him. They also got on his nerves, teased him, argued with him, loved him more than they ever thought possible, and ganged up on him sometimes, like most siblings.

By age six, Mike was still unable to completely control his muscles and communicated through sounds, eye gazing, and rolling to something he wanted. He and Cindy learned to communicate with each other in an almost telepathic way. During our interview sessions, Mike just had to look a certain way, make a certain facial expression, or make a sound, and Cindy knew exactly what he was trying to communicate. She talked to him to make sure she understood correctly, and he gave her some sort of signal to confirm or deny her thoughts. Usually she was correct. He even reminded her when it was time for a treatment or time to take medicine.

While Mike was my student, some paraprofessionals, his classmates, and I learned to read him as well. His best way to communicate was through his beautiful smile and blue eyes. Most of his communication at school was superficial; we could tell if he wanted or did not want something, or was happy, sad, or was not feeling well. Cindy's and his communication, on the other hand, went much deeper than that. They could carry on entire conversations.

Another mom told me about seeing Cindy and Mike at a spring-time outdoor event. This instance stuck with her, because her child is also nonverbal. Several times during the event, Cindy talked to Mike about what was happening and listened to his responses; each exchange was several minutes long. She asked him if he wanted anything to eat or drink, and he responded with a look, a smile, or a sound.

The onlooker said for a split second she considered that Cindy was just guessing at what Mike wanted, and there was really no true communication happening. Then she realized that she and her child probably looked the same way when they carried on a conversation, and she quickly cast her doubt aside. She wondered how often people saw her communicating with her child and thought the same thing, but did not change their mind like she did.

Sometimes, I admit, I wondered if what I thought Mike was trying to say matched his true intention. However, I believed Cindy really did understand everything he was trying to communicate.

We often have a bias based on a mistaken notion that because our nonverbal population does not speak, they also do not understand what is happening or have the ability to learn. There is nothing further from the truth. Mike was a great example of this. When he was in first grade, his general education teacher read a story from the Junie B. Jones collection, a children's series written by Barbara Park from the perspective of a precocious little girl who often found herself in very silly situations.

While the teacher read these stories, Mike was the only one in his class to understand and laugh at all the shenanigans Junie B. found herself getting into. Over the years, when his class watched increasingly sophisticated movies, his attention often lasted longer than his class-mates', and he was consistently one of the first in the class who understood the humor. He loved to hear his individual care aide, Miss Marla, read him the Harry Potter series.

Mike's memory and comprehension skills were strong. One day, Cindy and Mike were in a restaurant when he kept trying to turn around. She could not figure out what he wanted until she turned him around. When he could see the originator of the voice he heard at a table a few feet away, his eyes lit up, he smiled widely, and he started making noises and moving excitedly. As Cindy followed his gaze, the person at the table looked at Mike, and the adults realized he recognized the voice of a beloved therapist who had worked with him as part of his birth-to-three services. They had not been in touch in fifteen years.

We tried many ways over the years to enable Mike to communicate all he really knew and understood, but we never found the right key. We were on the cusp of getting there when our time together ended. We programmed an assistive communication device with pictures he could choose to answer questions. When he was proficient using the pictures, we programmed the device with words, and by his final year with me, he was choosing correct sentences.

The next step was to figure out a way for him to type what he wanted to say, rather than choose from pre-typed options. The device we had did not have that technology. We began looking into others, but were not successful before he left our building to go to high school. For Mike to use his device, he had to concentrate intently on directing his muscles to go where he wanted them to. It was difficult at first to achieve consistent control of his arm and finger to touch the answers he wanted on the board, but once he got used to the device, he progressed quickly.

His speech teacher often programmed two-part jokes for him to tell the class. It was a perfect way for him to showcase his great sense of humor. The look of anticipation on his face when he told the first part of the joke was priceless. The students and staff were always patient and kind with him, even if he accidentally hit the wrong button. Sometimes he got a kick out of intentionally pushing the wrong button, because the joke was even funnier when the answer made no sense.

Mike thought it was hilarious when we programmed a fart noise into his device. We also found a burp and a crying baby. He enjoyed being in the hallway and pressing one of those noises to surprise people. He learned when it was okay to use those noises and when we had to be serious, and for the most part, he used them appropriately.

By the time he moved to high school, he was able to add and subtract single digits, name the days of the week in order, tell what number came next up to twenty-five, read a story about his family to us, and ask simple questions.

When Mike entered early childhood education, he did not have a personal wheelchair; his family had always carried him or pushed him in a stroller. Since it was not safe for teachers or aides to carry him everywhere in his classroom or the building, the local special education cooperative provided a wheelchair for his use during school hours.

When he began all-day school in kindergarten, he received his first personal wheelchair, with his name printed in bright yellow on the headrest. The chair cost more than $8,000. Cindy sent forms, doctors' notes, therapists' notes, and other justification paperwork to Bob's insurance company to purchase the chair Mike needed. The paperwork took several weeks, and then he had to be fitted for the chair. The special-order chair took several months to arrive.

Mike used the chair until he was almost fourteen years old. Though it seemed obvious to anyone who knew Mike that he had outgrown his chair in nine years, Cindy had to go through the same arduous task of justifying why Mike needed a new chair.

When he was little, and the family carried him, some people stared or asked if he was tired or lazy. Cindy just politely replied that he could not walk, and that usually ended the line of questioning. Another major difficulty she encountered in public with Mike was restroom facilities. The cerebral palsy prevented Mike from exercising bladder and bowel control.

Cindy and Mike's six trips to Europe for therapy when he was a preschooler were very long plane rides. The logistics of using the tiny airplane lavatories were tricky enough for one person; they were impossible to use when Cindy needed to change Mike. He was five years old the last time he and Cindy traveled to Europe. She had to go to the flight attendants' area to change him. The flight attendants did not appreciate her doing that, but she felt it was better than laying him in the aisle in the middle of fellow travelers.

Airport restrooms were not any better, especially as he got older. They may have had a changing location for an infant or small toddler, but once a child was too long or heavy to fit on one of those, or became an adult who needed assistance, there was no good option.

Public bathrooms, in general, were difficult. In the early 2000s, family restrooms were exceedingly rare. When Cindy needed to go to the bathroom, she often used the larger accessible stall to safely fit Mike in the stall with her. It turned into a distressing situation when an able-bodied person monopolized the sole accessible bathroom in a well-known retail store, and Mike needed to be changed quickly. It was no comfort when a manager flippantly told her there were no private stalls in the men's room, so sometimes the employees used the accessible bathroom. Though public restroom options are better today, they still do not have changing places for bigger kids or adults who need to be changed.

Mike's health was relatively unchanged since birth, so he and his family were very settled in their routines until 2008, when he began throwing up regularly. It did not seem to matter what he had eaten, there seemed to be no pattern, and he had no other symptoms. He could go days—sometimes weeks—without throwing up, then suddenly vomit several times within a day or two. Doctors ran tests and did blood work, and nothing showed up that made Cindy or the family doctor lean toward any illness or medicinal requirements. After about a year, a doctor at the children's hospital diagnosed him with cyclic vomiting syndrome (CVS).

People with CVS experience repeated episodes of vomiting and severe nausea with no apparent cause. The episodes occur in cycles that can last hours or days. Potential triggers can be difficult to identify and manage.

Mike had several episodes at home and at school. He would be fine and doing his work, then suddenly he would stop, get a strange look on his face, and throw up, usually two or three times. When Mike vomited, it was not like a typically developed child. He could not aim the vomit toward a receptacle or give advance warning. It just came out and went down the front of him or the object nearest to him, if he was sitting up. It usually required changing his clothing and cleaning up his chair and any soiled objects, and waiting to see if it happened again.

If he was lying down or reclining, there was a danger of vomit not making it out of his throat unless someone was there to roll him over or elevate him quickly. Because of this danger, Cindy moved Mike into her room to sleep in case he had an episode. Cindy had to be on an unimaginably high alert mode for catching this; her sleep was not very sound during the months they tried to figure it out. Eventually, Mike was given medication that seemed to control the CVS, although it still did not take it away completely. Cindy never put Mike back in a room with anyone else.

A few months after the CVS started, Cindy took Mike to the local emergency room. He was dehydrated and throwing up. In the emergency room, they gave him a quickly flowing bag of fluids intravenously to help offset the dehydration. They admitted him, put him in a regular room, and gave him another bag of fluids. This second bag of fluid so overfilled his body that he projectile vomited almost eight feet.

If Cindy had not been right there, this could have been the end of Mike's story. Even so, she still could not get to him before he gasped for breath and inhaled, or aspirated, some of the fluid into his lungs. Cindy repositioned him so the rest of the fluid could move out of his throat.

Mike was very limited in how much he could communicate and move on his own. He likely would not have been able to either call for help or move to avoid choking if he had been in the room by himself. If he had aspirated any phlegm, it might have become stuck in his throat and caused him to choke to death. In either of these situations, by the time a nurse made their next round to check on him, it might have been too late.

While he did not die, he aspirated enough to develop pneumonia. A doctor prescribed gentamicin, an antibiotic, to fight the infection. Mike was very small for an eight-year-old; he was sleeping in his mother's lap. Suddenly, Cindy heard this very strange gurgling sound coming from him. His tongue and face were swollen. She immediately called for the nurse, and they gave him medicine to counteract the reaction.

He was experiencing anaphylaxis, a severe, potentially lethal allergic reaction that required immediate emergency health care. If Mike had been alone, he would not have been able to activate the call switch for the nurse to get the attention he needed. For the second time that week, if Cindy had not been there, Mike's story could have ended.

By this time, Cindy was almost finished with her nursing degree, and she fully understood what the possible consequences were. She was also still employed at the nursing home, which posed a challenge, because she knew someone had to stay with Mike around the clock, even in the hospital. Cindy was uncomfortable even using the bathroom in Mike's hospital room, because that would leave Mike unattended for a few minutes.

Even though the medical staff could tell Mike was experiencing an allergic reaction to something, they did not know exactly what at first. The doctor did not ask any questions; he flat-out accused Cindy of putting something in Mike's pureed food to poison him. On top of realizing she almost lost her son twice in a matter of days, she now had to defend how she cared for her son.

Cindy wondered why the doctor said that to her. Did the doctor think Mike's life was not good? Did he think Cindy and Bob thought their lives would be better off without Mike? They removed Mike from that hospital and took him to a major medical center an hour away, where the staff determined he was allergic to the medicine he had been given to help fight his pneumonia. Under their care, he recovered from anaphylaxis and pneumonia.

In addition to the CVS, in Mike's last two years of elementary school, he began having strange movements with his mouth and head. The movements did not happen all the time, did not seem to follow a pattern, and usually lasted a few seconds to a minute. Cindy and we figured out that if we stroked his head, arms, and neck, the movements seemed to stop.

Since CP is about muscles, Cindy just figured one of his muscles was tightening and our gentle touch was relaxing it. She did not seem too worried, and when she had his yearly checkup with his neurologist, he did not seem worried either. He gave her some other options to do with his arms if the caressing did not work; when we implemented the doctor's suggestions, the movements usually subsided. Life went back to normal for the family—that is, until November 2014.

Mike was a high school freshman. Things were going well for him, and he enjoyed the new school, new people, and new environment. One person was not new to him, however. His beloved paraprofessional from his elementary school had landed a job at the high school and continued to care for him. This was a tremendous help to the family and to the new school and staff.

Miss Marla had worked with Mike for three years already, and knew his distress signs and when he was faking something. She knew how to operate his communication device, and could feed and change him. In a very small way, she had become a second mom to him. She helped make the transition as smooth as possible for all involved.

In mid-November of his freshman year, his movements increased quite a bit and his medicine that had been controlling his CVS was not working as well anymore. He had a couple of episodes where mouth movements started and the vomiting started right after. Miss Marla thought he was going to choke or aspirate a couple of times. The school insisted that Cindy take him to the doctor, and he was not allowed back until she had a note saying he could be in school without posing a danger. He was out for several days before she could get him in to see a doctor.

For some parents, having their fourteen-year-old child at home, sick or not, does not pose a problem with work. However, someone had to be with Mike around the clock. When Cindy's schedule did not allow her to be at home, she had to depend on Wendy and Harry to be home with Mike. Bob helped when he could, but he was working ten hours a day with his job, and then trying to take care of the family farm too.

Finding a sitter for a child with special needs can be nearly impossible, even with extended family nearby. People are intimidated by the level of care required, and do not even try. In way too many instances, the parent or sibling of the person with special needs is the only competent, confident, capable caregiver. Cindy ended up missing several days of work. The doctor could find nothing wrong with Mike, so he wrote a note releasing him to school and a detailed procedure to follow if it happened again.

On December 9, Mike was running a low temperature, and he was not acting like his normal self. Cindy took him to the emergency room at the local hospital; they diagnosed him with a urinary tract infection and gave him antibiotics. A couple of days later at his follow-up appointment with his primary care doctor, Mike looked very pale, and Dr. Josh asked if the hospital had done any blood work. When he heard the answer was no, he immediately sent her back to the hospital to have Mike's blood drawn. His hemoglobin had become dangerously low.

Hemoglobin is the protein that carries oxygen via red blood cells throughout the body. There are many reasons low hemoglobin might occur, and sometimes doctors cannot find the cause. When a person has low hemoglobin, it results in anemia; in Mike's case, he had aplastic anemia, a disorder where the bone marrow does not make enough blood cells (red and white) and not enough platelets.

Mike needed a blood transfusion. The local hospital did not feel equipped to do the transfusion, so he went to the hospital an hour away. He had a severe episode of body movement while the staff tried to get the tube into his arm. The doctor decided Mike was having seizures, but the medicine they put him on did not work. They sedated him to get the blood transfusion line in place. He was in the hospital for three days before he was well enough to go home.

Cindy knew Mike was not the only patient on the floor, and she understood the hospital did not have enough nursing staff to keep someone with Mike around the clock. Still, she was worried he would choke and be unable to call for help. She missed work again to feel confident that Mike was being looked after closely enough. Cindy's employer told her she had to find her own replacements for her missing shifts. It was not a terribly uncommon practice in nursing, but it added to the stress of Mike's serious health issues. Bob wished he could be with his son during these times, but Bob's employer was providing the insurance, so he needed to stay at work.

In late December, Mike was in the hospital again. The CVS had calmed down again, but his movements continued; the doctors tried clonazepam to settle the movements. The three days he stayed in the hospital this time included Christmas day. Cindy and Mike missed Christmas with Cindy's relatives, but still celebrated with Wendy and Harry.

In late January 2015, Mike had more seizures and such bad episodes of CVS that he ended up in the hospital again. He was losing weight, and they could not seem to find anything to help with the almost constant seizures. His entire body jerked and twitched, his legs and arms were in constant motion, his hands clenched and unclenched, and his mouth constantly opened and closed. He looked like a puppet on a string, bouncing up and down. He appeared so very uncomfortable.

One of the many doctors he saw prescribed a scan of his brain. These test results showed a dark mass. Further testing helped doctors determine the mass was iron buildup. The mass was located in gray matter tissue and it blocked the part of the brain that controls motor function. Mike was not having seizures—his body was unable to regulate muscle movement. Because of its location and what it was, surgery to remove it was not an option. The doctors had to figure out therapy or medicine to shrink the buildup. The genetics team was called in, as this was extremely rare. Bob, Cindy, and Mike went through genetic testing so extensive that it took months to receive the results.

I visited Mike in the hospital and was able to stay for only twenty-five minutes or so, because I was having such a difficult time keeping the tears from flowing. I had not seen him for eight months, and expected to see my former student with the most beautiful blue eyes and nearly constant smile. I was greeted with nothing close to that.

His eyes were dark with dark circles around them from lack of sleep. He was unable to control any of his muscles, including his facial muscles that would have produced that big smile. He tried to smile once while I was there, but it was not his normal smile. He knocked his knees together frequently, and Cindy put blankets or small pillows between them so he did not hurt himself. These often moved out of place, and sometimes he still knocked his knees or ankles. She eventually used things that looked like boxing gloves with elastic straps that wrapped around his ankles and knees to keep them from hitting each other.

I was so heartbroken and shocked, having been his teacher for eight years, but as much as I hurt for him and wanted to take all this away from him, I could not. I also could not imagine the pain Cindy must have been feeling. I marveled at the strength she had to stay by her son's side and continue to be chipper, crack jokes, and pretend all was okay.

Mike's movements worsened until they were constant. He had a difficult time swallowing. He had to have the saliva secretion suctioned from his mouth and throat occasionally. He could no longer eat the foods he once enjoyed. He lived on milkshakes, protein shakes, pudding, and anything else that basically slid down on its own. What control he had gained over his muscles throughout the years of therapy was quickly fading. When I visited him at the hospital, I wished with everything I had that I could stop his involuntary movements.

Cindy did not leave the hospital the entire time Mike was there. However, this time, she invoked the Family and Medical Leave Act (FMLA) which allowed her to be with Mike, but did not require her to find her own replacement, and guaranteed a job was waiting for her when she returned.

Mike was losing weight because he was in constant motion. He had lost almost ten pounds and weighed around seventy pounds. When doctors discovered he was not having seizures but uncontrollable movements, or chorea, they gave him tetrabenazine, a medication used primarily for patients with Huntington's disease.

Mike was in the hospital for several weeks before the doctors were able to get his movements calmed down enough that he could go home. Cindy had stayed with him and had barely slept the entire time he was there. The hospital had provided a sleeper sofa, and sometimes Bob, Wendy, or Harry stayed with Mike so she could sleep. Regardless, she never felt comfortable sleeping more than a few hours at a time. They all did their best to close off the area of Mike's room where Cindy slept, but there were still lights and noises. She lost weight, because unless someone brought her food, she did not eat.

With Cindy's medical background and all the time she spent with Mike, she knew him and his needs better than anyone else. She could tell the next shift of nurses and doctors when medications had been administered and at what doses, what out-of-the-ordinary events occurred, how often he had voided and how much, what other doctors had said, and more. She was, and always will be, Mike's voice and biggest advocate.

When Mike came home, he slept in Cindy's room, and she still did not have much peaceful sleep. A few weeks later, Mike's movements were still pretty severe, he was still losing weight, and he was having increasing difficulty eating. The doctors suggested a feeding tube to get nutrients into his body. Normally, these are only done when a child is young, because older children can have height and weight issues. However, since Mike was so thin, the doctors believed it could be done; it would help him maintain and eventually add weight.

Two major factors kept Cindy from immediately going ahead with the feeding tube. The biggest one was that it required surgery. No one was 100 percent certain anesthesia would not make the movements worse or cause other problems. The second concern was that he would completely lose his ability to be fed through his mouth. After much consideration, debate, research, and discussion of the pros and cons, the doctors, Cindy, and Bob chose to have a feeding tube put into Mike's body. The surgery was a success, and Mike only had to spend two nights in the hospital.

Once Mike was released from the hospital, life began to take on a new normal. He started to look like the Mike he had been before the episodes started. After a few weeks, his weight leveled out, and it was evident the feeding tube helped. Mike also continued taking several medications. While waiting for the genetic test results, the doctors started Mike on tetrabenazine to attempt to control his muscles. He was also on glycopyrrolate to lower his secretion output, diazepam to help with his anxiety, his CVS medicine, acid reflux medicine, and a medicine he took occasionally to loosen his stool. It was at this time I began homebound instruction with him. I went to his home several days a week for a total of five hours to teach him what he was missing at school. He had been out of school for two months.

Mike was getting back to his old self and positive attitude. However, the tetrabenazine and diazepam made him very tired. He slept almost eighteen hours a day. Some days we could get a solid hour of instruction in; other times just a few minutes. Some days his fatigue forced us to stop; other days, his constant coughing ended our session for the day. Excessive saliva secretion and his inability to swallow caused his coughing; sometimes the saliva just needed to be suctioned out of his throat, and other times the coughing lead to vomiting.

He was instructed at home for two and a half months, until the end of the school year. Because he had lost so much of his muscle tone and strength, it was difficult for him to hold his head up or keep it looking forward. His mom propped up his head with pillows and neck cushions to attempt to stabilize his neck, but that worked for only a few minutes at a time. I had to create ways to get his answers from him, as pointing was not accurate anymore, touching the answer on a keypad was very inconsistent, and smiling when he wanted the answer someone else pointed to was also inconclusive.

The most accurate way I could get him to respond was with his eyes. I broke questions down into either yes or no answers, or three multiple choices. I moved the yes and no options from side to side and made sure I was not putting the correct answer on his dominant side all the time. Occasionally, he did not get his eyes to go the way he wanted, or his eyes did not move enough that I was convinced they moved at all, so he just dropped his head toward the answer he wanted. He got a kick out of that and sometimes started to giggle. In those moments, I saw the Mike who had been my student. Those are the moments I treasure.

It was decided at one of his individualized education plan (IEP) meetings with the local high school that speech and physical therapy were a waste of the therapists' time, since his sleep patterns were so irregular during the day. Each therapist had come out a few times before the meeting, but was unable to get a full therapy session accomplished because he was so tired, he was sleeping, or his muscles were not cooperating at all.

I went after school or in the evenings, so my services were allowed to continue until the end of the school year. While I worked with Mike, Cindy washed dishes, straightened the kitchen, and prepped his next meal and meds. The kitchen looked into the living room and dining room, so she was never out of Mike's sight for more than a few seconds, and she was always in earshot.

We managed to get Mike mostly caught up on his studies, but it came to a point where even my flexible schedule was not enough to meet his needs. Some weeks I was only able to get in three or four hours. His teachers were very understanding of his situation and accepted whatever work we could accomplish.

Months after the genetic test, the results finally came through. Mike was diagnosed with GNAO1. A GNAO1 mutation can cause a range of health issues; in Mike's case, it resulted in severe movements, developmental delays, and low muscle tone that affects his ability to hold his head up and to swallow. It is a recent discovery (first diagnosed in 2013), and at the time Mike was diagnosed, there were only five other people in the world diagnosed with this same genetic coding. Cindy's research indicated GNAO1 can present very similarly to cerebral palsy, and it is very possible many people who have been diagnosed as having cerebral palsy actually have GNAO1.

Naming this disorder changed the treatment plan only slightly. The Huntington's medicine had proven successful with other patients with GNAO1, so they continued him on that and added a medication that proved helpful in people with Parkinson's disease. After several months on both the Parkinson's and Huntington's medicines, Mike's movements were calmed down quite a bit.

By autumn 2015, Mike weighed about sixty-eight pounds, had GNAO1-related tremors, coughed regularly, required frequent suctioning, and was losing even more of his muscle tone. Cindy and Bob decided Mike would not go back to school. Since he was not going back to school, he was no longer eligible for homebound instruction or in-home therapy provided by the school district.

Mike sipped water by mouth with the help of gravity and used the feeding tube for nutrition. His weight was still low, though he had gained a couple of pounds. He developed dystonic movements—involuntary muscle contractions—which caused him pain. Since Mike had never been able to sit or walk on his own, his hip socket developed dysplasia, or hip dislocation. His frequent movements initiated this dislocation; his hips often popped out of place and caused great pain. It was a vicious cycle. His hip pain caused more movement, and the movements caused his hip to pop out and created more pain.

When Mike was younger, doctors told Cindy that at some point in Mike's life it was possible his hip would dislocate permanently. Surgery to repair his hip was not an option until Mike had stopped growing.

Cindy and Bob had a lot to consider: the pros and cons of another surgery, its side effects, and the cost to Mike's health. After weeks of discussion, they decided to schedule Mike for the hip surgery.

In March 2016, the day after his sixteenth birthday, he had the surgery. I took a present by his house the day before his birthday and saw how thin he looked and how his movements were still so much a part of his life, although they had gotten much calmer. Miss Marla went with me that day, and we both cried when we left. I prayed the surgery would prevent permanent hip dislocation and the pain it would cause, and that it would not cause more movements now. The surgery was successful. Doctors operated on a Tuesday, and Mike came home on Thursday.

On Sunday, his parents took Mike back to the hospital. His movements had exponentially increased to pretreatment levels, which did not seem possible. His socket replacement was infected and causing him tremendous pain. Doctors gave Mike the sedative propofol, which calmed his movements and allowed doctors to intubate him and put him on a ventilator. Mike stayed on the sedation medicine and the ventilator for several days. At the same time, he still received his medicine to decrease his secretions.

Propofol needs to be monitored carefully by specially trained doctors, and is not normally recommended for children. Since Mike was sixteen and in such distress, the doctors made an exception. Each vial contained ten milligrams, and Mike needed a vial every three hours, at a cost of about five hundred dollars per vial. All of his medicines and fluids were given intravenously (IV) or through a peripherally inserted central catheter (PICC) line.

One strange but funny side effect of propofol is that it can turn urine green. This was happening in mid-March and St. Patrick's Day was nearing, so they teased Mike about being an extreme St. Patrick's Day fan—he was the only patient who changed his urine color to celebrate the holiday. Within twenty-four hours, the medical staff believed the infection in his hip socket was healed enough that it would not cause him so much pain anymore.

Monday, Cindy took a nap by Mike in his bed. When she woke up, he was lying so still with his eyes closed, she thought he had passed away. She had not seen him like that in so long, she checked for a heart rate and whether he was breathing on his own instead of completely relying on the ventilator. When she realized he was still alive and her nerves calmed, she took a picture of him and sent it to Bob.

On Tuesday they began decreasing the propofol, and on Wednesday they extubated, or removed the tube from, Mike. Both intubation and extubation were considered minor surgeries, in the sense that the procedures were done in an operating room versus in a patient's room. In an emergency, though, intubation can happen in the patient's room, as Mike unfortunately found out.

Within twelve hours of being extubated, Mike began coughing and a mucus plug lodged in his airway. He began turning blue. Cindy immediately called for help, and Mike was intubated again. If Cindy had not been by his side, this could have been the end of his story. His left lung had collapsed. This time he was only intubated for a day and the secretion reduction medicine was decreased.

The sound of Mike coughing while intubated frightened Cindy, and she never wanted to hear it again. When they tried to extubate him again, the lung partially collapsed. The doctors decided Mike needed to be sedated again and his body paralyzed for several days to give his body the rest it needed.

Mike was paralyzed and intubated from early Friday morning until midday Monday. He was partially awake, but unable to move. On Saturday, Cindy's mom and stepdad visited Mike. Cindy's stepdad was a minister and wore a black shirt with a white collar to signify this. Cindy said the room could have looked very morbid as the three of them stood by Mike's bedside, hands on him, heads down, and praying. They all had hands on him because if Mike moved even a little bit, the paralytic medicine would need to be increased.

Cindy recalled with a trembling voice and tears on her face how Mike cried that weekend. Mike rarely cried with tears. To know what he was going through and see the tears rolling out of his eyes and down his cheeks was almost more than Cindy could bear. Mike knew enough to know what was happening and that the paralysis and intubation were not supposed to be part of his recovery. Cindy told Mike what was happening and how long things were expected to last. She has always done a wonderful job of keeping him informed.

Mike was extubated and off the propofol, but he was still on antibiotics for the lung that collapsed and for the infection lingering in his hip. His movements still occurred frequently, and sometimes his arms had to be in restraints so he did not injure himself. He needed to be suctioned quite regularly, but they did not want to increase his secretion reduction medicine for fear it would cause problems with his lung again.

For the last couple of weeks of his stay, he was moved out of the pediatric intensive care unit (PICU) to a regular floor. He still needed to be watched closely, as he was receiving a very high amount of an antibiotic called vancomycin that was hard on his veins. His original IV lasted for seven doses; they ran a different IV that lasted three doses, then another IV. He was down to one dose for one IV for a couple of days until they weaned him off. They had to use veins in both arms and wrists, both feet, and his PICC line to run enough IVs to get all the doses in. He received oxygen through a high-flow line and bilevel positive airway pressure (BiPAP) mask at a rate of thirty liters per minute. For comparison, the normal amount a patient received was somewhere between two and six liters per minute.

Once while wearing the BiPAP mask, Mike coughed so much he threw up. Cindy pulled the mask off of him quickly enough that it did not blow the vomit right back into his throat and cause him to choke. She saved him again. When he went home, he was on only one liter per minute.

All told, Mike was in the hospital for nine and a half weeks after the surgery; all but two weeks were in the PICU. This was an incredibly intense and difficult time for him and his family. Cindy had averted so many potentially deadly situations, she did not feel comfortable leaving Mike alone, even for a few minutes. She did that once. The hospital had a shower on the floor she was given special permission to use. When she returned to Mike's room just ten minutes later, he was choking and turning blue. A nurse had been assigned to Mike and another child. Just after Cindy left, the other child had an emergency and his nurse was called away to help. Cindy shuddered to think what would have happened if she had been away longer than she was. After that, she learned how to take six-minute showers, and only if a family member could stay in the room with him the entire time she was gone.

Once when I visited, around six in the evening, she had not eaten all day. Bob, Wendy, and Harry had to work or go to school, and no one else had come to visit. She needed a break, so rather than bringing food to her, I promised her I would call the nurses if Mike did something I could not handle while she went to get something to eat. She quickly taught me what to do if he began coughing again and left.

To say I was overwhelmed with the amount of trust she placed in me that day was a huge understatement. I was Mike's teacher for eight years, and I had experience caring for him, but this was literally putting his life in my hands. I was scared, but the fact she trusted me with her son and had the confidence in me to leave me alone with him gave me the courage to do what I had to do, if necessary.

I was thankful he and I just had a nice visit while she was getting her dinner and I did not have to do anything except rub his arms and legs. She was gone for maybe thirty minutes, and when she returned and saw that he was okay, I could see the relief on her face. It was very difficult for her to be away from him, and she agonized over every minute.

My own child was hospitalized once when she was very little, and I did not worry for her life when I left her side to go to the restroom or get a bite to eat. As a mother of a typically developing child who is rarely sick, I can easily take for granted that life. The life of a parent with a child with special needs is so drastically different that I marvel at and have a great deal of respect for those parents.

Working with my students over the years, I have been overwhelmed at times when I realize the enormous depth of trust my students' parents possess. Every parent who sends their child to a public school, day care, friend's or relative's house, or off with the child's friend's family trusts that person to care correctly for their child.

A parent of a child with special needs, especially a nonverbal child, does not have the luxury of not thinking twice about who is in charge of their child when they are out of sight. The depth of trust and faith these parents must have in other people is monumental. They are potentially sending their child into danger every time their child is out of their sight. Depending on the type of disability a person has, they are two to three times as likely than someone without a disability to be abused, sexually molested, used for a crime, or bullied.

For sixty-seven consecutive days, Cindy stayed by Mike's side in the hospital. She cracked jokes with him, fed him, held him, read to him, watched movies with him, took naps with him, bathed him, and the entire time had a positive attitude in front of him. When I asked her how she did it, she said she had to show him she had hope. Showing him how helpless she felt would not do him any good. She had her moments of breaking down when Mike could not see or hear her. She told me that when he was in the throes of his most severe movements and in so much pain, she felt so desperate that for a few seconds she entertained a thought of finding him a joint just so he could relax.

I truly cannot imagine what it must have been like to see him every day, practically vanishing before her eyes. He had lost weight again because of the intensity of the movements, and they were having a difficult time keeping nutrition in him. At one point, he was down to fifty-nine pounds. Several times during the hospital stay, Cindy thought she was going to lose her son. I am ashamed to admit it, but I stopped visiting him because I also thought he was going to die in the hospital.

His dad and siblings made the round trip—a more than two-hour drive—as many times in a week as they could. By this time, Wendy was twenty-two and Harry was nineteen. They were both continuing their education and working. Bob was still working on the family farm and for an outside company forty to fifty hours a week. Since Cindy was unable to work at the time, the other three needed to work to help Cindy pay the bills.

Mike received SSI until he was in the hospital more than thirty days, when it was cut off. His SSI was based on Cindy's income and the child support that Bob paid. When he needed his income the most, the government said he was not eligible after thirty days because he was living somewhere else, and his medical card was supposed to kick in to cover those expenses. The flaw in that logic was that he still needed a home to go back to, and if it was not for his siblings and father, he could have ended up homeless.

Since he did not have Huntington's disease, the doctors were not sure exactly what dosage of the tetrabenazine would work the best for him. The largest dose was a twenty-five-milligram pill; it took several attempts to figure out he needed eleven pills, three times a day. He needed 825 milligrams a day of a medicine that cost more than five dollars per milligram. The cost per month for just this one medicine was $130,000, and he was on it for several months at this level. The medicine was so expensive, and the dosage so high, the hospital did not have it readily available. Cindy procured it from an outside pharmacy, brought it to the hospital, and gave it to the nurses on the floor. One day, a nurse accidentally threw one of the pills away.

For a while, counting all the different medications he was prescribed, he took a total of sixty-six pills a day. The bill for the sixty-seven-day hospital stay, most of which was in the PICU, was several hundred thousand dollars. Thankfully, the insurance from Bob's work and Medicaid covered most of the bill.

Mike's muscles were still contracting, and Cindy did not want him to be on such heavy medication for the rest of his life, so she began researching deep brain stimulation (DBS). Deep brain stimulation has shown positive results in people whose movement disorders are not adequately controlled by medication. Doctors implant electrodes in specific spots in the brain, and attach them to a device placed under the skin on the upper chest. The device serves as a sort of pacemaker and helps regulate electrical signals in the brain that affect movement.

In mid-November 2016, Cindy and Bob decided DBS could benefit Mike. Surgeons implanted the DBS, but it could not be activated right away because the body had to decide if it was going to accept it. After a few weeks, his body accepted the device, so they went back to the hospital to have it activated. It took a few tries to get the correct amount of stimulation for his level of episodes. By Christmas 2016, Mike was having very minimal episodes, and they were not lasting all day anymore.

Cindy made the decision in February 2017 to start weaning him off some of his meds he had been on for so long. After a few months of careful observation, copious notes, and research, she reduced his pill intake to forty-five a day. He finally seemed to be at a happy medium between an unmoving, zombielike state and a wide-awake state with constant movement. Cindy kept him on that medicine regimen for several months. Several of the pills were not to control the movements, but to prevent or minimize things like acid reflux, CVS, and his saliva production, and one for his bowels, so she was able to adjust those without a doctor's permission. For several more months, she worked with his doctors and they reduced his medicine intake even more. As of January 2019, he took only three pills a day of tetrabenazine and a small dose of diazepam for his DBS.

Bob and Cindy agreed nothing was easy about getting Mike things he needed, or that greatly improved his life, or helped his caregivers. I have found that to be the case with all the families I have worked with over the years. The system is often not helpful to families who are trying to do as much as they can personally and privately to help their child. Several families I spoke with used their own personal insurance or personal savings, had both parents working, and performed many tasks on their own to avoid using the system as much as possible. However, when they really needed the system, it was not set up to truly help those who have rarely or never used it.

When Mike entered the public school system, he was also instructed to sign up for a state-run database that served as a waiting list for people with developmental disabilities who may need services from the government. The state used the information to provide services as funding became available, and to plan and budget for future needs. Individuals are selected for state services based on how long they were on the list, what their needs were, and where they lived.

Cindy was told that Mike needed to be on this list to get services. To this day, he has not been chosen, and he may never be. In my twenty-plus years of working with people who had special needs, I have never known anyone who received funding through this database. Many of the programs designed to help people with special needs used the database as their main resource for determining whether someone was eligible for their services. However, they often did not advertise that this was where they get some of their eligibility information until someone tried to apply. If the person was not on the list long enough, it became a barrier to receiving help. There was a major shortage of funding, and it seemed 99 percent of the funding went to areas that were much more populated than where Mike lived and where I've taught. As with many systems, they are set up with great intentions but delivery often falls short.

When Mike turned eighteen, his mom took him off the database list, because he had been on the list for so long and seemingly had no benefits from it. When he turned eighteen and she wanted to get adult services for him, she ran into trouble because he was not on the list. She had to put him back on the list which, like so many other things in the life of a person with special needs, was not easy.

One would think that since he had been on the list for many years, Cindy would be able to simply fill out a form and he would be reinstated. Alas, it turned into a much bigger ordeal. Cindy procured letters from doctors, filled out countless forms, verified Mike's identity by using his passport, and made a visit to the nearest administrative office, almost one hundred miles away.

As with anything else, there are people who will take advantage of a system, and therefore these steps are necessary to ensure someone had not stolen Mike's identity. It was just an extra burden on a family who already had so many more daily challenges than the average family. Had she been told that he needed to be registered to be recognized as someone with a disability in her state, she would never have taken him off in the first place; but that is not the way it was presented to her or countless parents like her.

When he was eighteen, Mike was five feet three inches, and Cindy was five feet five inches tall. The saving grace for Cindy was that he weighed less than one hundred pounds, because he was unable to help with dressing, eating, or walking. At home, Cindy had a Hoyer lift sling that helped her move him around the house. Someone was kind enough to donate this to Cindy's family. When Cindy took Mike somewhere, she had to lift him in and out of his wheelchair and in and out of a vehicle. They applied to the Variety Club for a special lift to add to their van that would allow Mike to get in and out of the vehicle while still in his wheelchair. If approved, it will be a great help to Cindy.

Mike's primary care physician, who had seen him since infancy, started making house calls to simplify Cindy's day. House calls also cut down on the germs Mike was exposed to during cold and flu season.

Several months before Mike turned eighteen, Cindy had to apply for legal guardianship of him. The process was lengthy and involved the whole family. First, a doctor declared Mike incapacitated, then Cindy hired a lawyer to petition the court for her to be his guardian. The court assigned Mike a guardian ad litem to protect his interests. The court then sent letters to Bob, Harry, and Wendy, asking them if they granted permission for Cindy to be Mike's guardian. Finally, they all went to court and a judge appointed Cindy as Mike's legal guardian. The tedious process, which the family repeated every year, was in place to prevent someone from trying to be a legal guardian to take advantage of an adult with special needs.

Mike's social security income went to Cindy to help pay his bills when he was a child. When he became a legal adult, he started receiving his money from social security every month. Cindy helped Mike set up a checking account, and he had a debit card. He paid rent and other bills as they came due, purchased camouflage chair coverings for his wheelchair, and bought new shoes for himself. Cindy kept all the receipts and bills he paid to show his money was spent on him. Mike still saw several doctors per year and paid the copays for his annual checkups with his pediatrician, movement disorder doctor, pulmonologist, neurologist, and dentist. He also saw a doctor at Shriners Hospital yearly to be checked for his wheelchair and other medical devices.

Since Mike started receiving his own money, Cindy started trying to go to work full-time. The state's Department of Rehabilitation Services (DRS) provided money for caregivers to take care of an adult with special needs. This application was, of course, long, complicated, and bureaucratic. There were hoops to jump through, red tape to cut, people to please, stacks of paperwork to submit, lists of phone calls to make, and reservoirs of patience to maintain to get services. DRS wanted to know exactly how long it took to feed, bathe, groom, and dress him. This was difficult to determine for someone without all of Mike's complexities, and more difficult to figure out for Mike. Mike's state-provided insurance was involved and had their own complex paperwork processes.

Cindy was told all through Mike's childhood that when he turned eighteen, he would get lots of help, and she and the rest of the family would be able to be the ones helping him. To that end, Cindy, Bob, Harry, and Wendy took the required classes and were certified to be personal assistants (PAs). Wendy studied to be a certified nursing assistant during high school and then earned an associate of art degree from a local community college to become one of Mike's approved personal assistants.

They all wanted to care for Mike, but contrary to what Cindy was told, the agencies in charge did not want to let them. They preferred a stranger came and provided care for Mike, when they did not know Mike or understand how he communicated. Cindy contacted a local advocacy office to help her convey to DRS and the insurance company the amount of trust she had to have in the person who stayed with her son—in part because of Mike's complex medical needs and because he was nonverbal, and in part because this person would be in her house with very expensive medical equipment, medicines, and her family's personal belongings.

Even more problematically, the stranger they hired would not be allowed to transfer Mike from place to place in the house, put him on the bus for school, give him his medicines, or lift him. He still took medicines every six hours around the clock, got on and off the bus twice a day, and had to be repositioned in his wheelchair or the recliner frequently.

Cindy wondered if she was supposed to leave work three or four times a day to come home and do those things for him. If so, what was the purpose of having someone else there? Why did she have to answer all the questions about how long certain things will take if the PA was not supposed to lift him or transfer him from place to place? She would be content staying home and taking care of her adult son if she was independently wealthy or did not need to work to pay her bills. Since that was not the case, if she stayed home with Mike, she needed to be paid as a PA.

Cindy knew of a family not far from her in which the mother was being paid to be the PA for her family member. She did not know the family's history, but felt this was just another time the system worked against those who were honestly trying their best and had done everything they could to take care of their child on their own for as long as possible. She hoped the advocacy office staff could help gain approval for them to be Mike's PAs, so Cindy could go to work and have some peace that Mike was well taken care of while she was gone.

For most of Mike's life, he was healthy, and their lives were not wrapped up in his medical problems. Cindy spoke highly of Mike's elementary school education. During his first few years there, he was completely immersed in general education classes. However, as he got older, he was slowly removed from complete immersion to a more specialized setting, so his education could be more individualized. Around second grade, he started getting his academic lessons from me, and I also became his adapted physical education teacher.

He still spent a portion of his day with his general education peers, and participated in as many activities with his same-age peers as was possible. He was included in class plays in fourth and eighth grades, he went on class field trips with his general education peers when it was appropriate, and he attended music, art, and cooking classes. Everyone in the school knew and loved Mike.

Cindy said his IEP meetings were wonderful, everyone was kind and understanding, and they wanted to do as much as possible for Mike. The only negative she could think of was that sometimes he rode in the car with her instead of riding the school bus to attend field trips. She and Mike had such great experiences in his elementary years, they had no reason to expect anything different when he arrived for high school, especially since his paraprofessional, Miss Marla, transferred with him.

Their experience in high school was vastly different. Cindy and Bob wanted Mike to attend his local high school and the school agreed they could handle his needs appropriately. Most teachers and staff at the school welcomed Mike enthusiastically. However, before his first day as a freshman, the school nurse, Mrs. Quinn, called Cindy and demanded she provide prescriptions and letters written by his doctor with explicit directions for feeding him, changing him, and what to do in an emergency situation.

While Cindy understood the staff at the new school did not know Mike, she felt as though the nurse had a phobia toward him. Mrs. Quinn never met Mike or took time to get to know him other than what she read in his IEP. In his first few weeks at school, Mrs. Quinn called Cindy several times to pick Mike up from school because he was not acting right, even though his paraprofessional said he was fine.

When Mike's CVS caused him to throw up randomly and frequently, the nurse called every time and insisted that Cindy take him home for twenty-four hours as was school policy, even though it was a syndrome, not an illness, that caused the vomiting. At one point, Mrs. Quinn called Mike's family doctor without Cindy's knowledge and implored the doctor to order an X-ray, as she was certain Mike's lungs were congested based on his cough. His X-ray came back perfectly clear.

Cindy felt Mrs. Quinn was trying to get her to take Mike out of the school so she would not have to deal with him. Mike only lasted a few months in this setting before all of his medical problems began to escalate. By the time he was ready to return full-time, Mrs. Quinn was no longer at the school.

Mike missed his entire sophomore year due to his medical issues. When he was able and ready to go back to school, an IEP meeting was called to determine his most appropriate placement and reevaluate him academically. When Cindy walked into the meeting, there were several people she did not recognize from an alternative school in a town thirty-five miles away.

Legally, she should have been notified ahead of time that these people would be there; it was not until Cindy picked up her mail later that day that she saw the notice. As the meeting went along, she realized why they were there. The local district high school had determined they probably no longer had the appropriate setting for Mike and had asked this school to send representatives to explain their program to Cindy. She felt ganged up on and betrayed by the local school district and began to cry. She had spoken to representatives from the local high school a couple of times before the meeting, and they said nothing to her about this other school. She thought going into this meeting that Mike would be welcomed back to his local school.

Cindy called me later that day, still crying. She asked me if I knew anything about the alternative school and told me what had occurred at the meeting. We talked about the pros and cons of having him placed at both settings, and she decided she would tour the other school before making her final decision. I pointed out, "Both schools will take him, but one school actively wants him and is excited at the possibility of having him."

She and Mike toured the alternative school a few days later, and Mike was accepted instantly. He enjoyed the school setting and what they had to offer him. Cindy was impressed as well. While it made her nervous to have him at a school that was a forty-minute bus ride away, she was comforted knowing they wanted him there. Mike began his sophomore year in November 2017 and thrived at his new school. He will most likely stay at this school until the day before his twenty-second birthday, when his eligibility ends.

Cindy referred to Mike as the "lemon from which they all made very sweet lemonade." Cindy said the future will be what it will be, and she will take it one day at a time. She said because of Mike, she was a better nurse and a more patient person, and she was proud to represent him to medical students and speak to groups in the medical community about him. She joked that there were perks to having a child in wheelchair: getting premium parking spaces; going to the head of the line for his favorite amusement park ride, bumper cars; always having a reserved seat at a movie theater; getting to be a pilot rider at a new therapeutic riding center in their area; and meeting lots of new people.

Her advice to other parents who have a child with special needs was to purchase life and medical insurance on the child as soon as possible, search out support groups, talk to someone about daily struggles, accept help from family and friends, and do not try to be a loner. Her advice to families who do not have a child with special needs was to appreciate the health of their child. Even when their child is running around and not listening, be thankful they can run, walk, play, be independent, and say "I love you." Just once, Cindy would love to hear Mike say, "I love you, mom."

I have learned so much from knowing Mike and his family and having the privilege of teaching Mike for eight years. He taught me there are more ways to communicate than just words or sign language; he taught me to smile even when times are difficult. I learned to appreciate my life and respect all the things I used to take for granted.

Mike taught me to push through, even when it is difficult and seemingly against all odds. He taught me patience for myself when I am struggling to learn something. He taught me unconditional love is possible. He taught me determination. He taught me to be nice to everyone by just smiling at them. He taught me to appreciate all progress, no matter how long it took or what size it was.

Thank you, Mike, Cindy, and Bob for sharing your story with us. Your family taught me about the depth of trust you bestowed on me and others who took care of your son. Your family taught me hope. Cindy, you taught me not to worry about tomorrow, but to focus on the good of today. Your family taught me to love and appreciate what I have, for tomorrow is not promised to anyone.

Section II

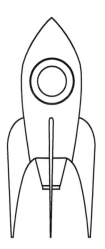

Linus

Chuck and Lucy were in their late twenties when they found out they could not have children without help. They tried in vitro fertilization without success. For her entire life Lucy had wanted to be a mother, and she was not ready to give up the dream. The next option they chose was adoption; they began the process with an agency. For months, they had to wait on background checks, interviews, reference letters, and probes into their finances. Finally, they were approved to be parents and the wait continued.

Chuck and Lucy wanted a child from Russia, but their lawyer advised them since it was an election year in Russia, they would have a better chance of adopting a child from somewhere else. He suggested Guatemala, since more than half of the children did not live past the age of five due to malnutrition. He also told them accepting a boy would make the process go faster.

A few weeks went by, and the call came in that Chuck and Lucy were assigned twin boys. They were thrilled that finally, after all these years, Lucy was going to be a mom. The process continued, and the agency did more research into the birth mother; they determined she was still legally married. This put a huge wrench into the process.

They had to track down the husband to get his permission for the adoption. Chuck and Lucy found out the husband's last known address was in Mexico. The cost, time, and potential for a "no" was too much for Chuck and Lucy, and they made the heart-wrenching decision to withdraw their names for the twins.

Many tears and a few days later, the phone call came in that there was another baby boy available. Again, the excitement returned, but within a day or two of hearing the news, they received a phone call that the birth mother changed her mind. The heartbreak was almost unbearable, and they cried many more tears.

For years they struggled and rode a wicked emotional roller coaster to do what they thought would make their dream come true. A torrent of thoughts and questions went through their minds. Would Lucy's dream of motherhood ever come true? Was this God's way of telling her she was not supposed to be a mom? Maybe it was time to give up. Maybe it just was not in the cards for them to be parents. Maybe they just needed to accept it and move on. What was wrong with them that they were not allowed to be parents? Their family, friends, and community surrounded them with love, support, and encouragement to keep trying, keep hoping, and keep trusting in God's plan.

The lawyer called again a few days later and told them if they were willing to try one more time, he had another baby boy for them. This baby had been born in early December and needed only a couple more medical clearances. Very cautiously they agreed; it was scary to get excited, but difficult to stay calm. On Christmas Eve, they received the best gift they had ever been given: a picture of their baby boy. Lucy was excited her lifelong dream was so close to becoming reality and showed the picture to everyone at church. Foreign adoption was such a big deal, the whole town was following the process.

She and Chuck celebrated the holidays—their last childless Christmas—with a spring in their steps and smiles on their faces that could not have been any brighter. Several months passed while the baby was tested and observed for any health problems. During this time, he stayed with a foster family who sent Chuck and Lucy pictures a couple more times. They had not received pictures of the other boys, so their elation grew as they realized this was their son. In September the adoption was finalized and they got to bring baby boy Linus home.

The first few weeks flew by for the family of three. Linus wanted to be held all the time, which was perfectly okay with Lucy. Sharing their new son with family, friends, and community members and getting settled into a new routine kept them busy. When Linus arrived, he was nine months old and still not showing signs of strong walking. They did not think too much about it, as his foster family had kept him in a stroller most of the time. He was not babbling or talking much either, but Lucy and Chuck were not too concerned because he was learning a whole new language.

When Linus was two and a half, his eardrum burst regularly. Chuck recalled a time in church when he noticed something oozing out of Linus's ear. His eardrum had burst. Linus had such a high pain tolerance, he was not crying or acting any differently than normal. The emergency room doctor did not believe them when they said he showed no signs of pain. Lucy said this happened so often they could tell he was having an ear problem when he started to walk funny.

The only other time Lucy mentioned as remarkable was when Linus was three; he always wanted to have her in his sight. Lucy thought maybe Linus remembered leaving his Guatemalan family and was worried it was going to happen again. Around the same time, Lucy and Chuck decided to adopt again—this time, a little girl from Guatemala. Patty and Linus became siblings and best friends. Everything seemed to be finally falling into place for Chuck, Lucy, and their family.

Lucy and Chuck agreed it was best for Lucy to be a stay-at-home mom. Lucy loved every minute of being able to stay home with Linus and Patty. They spent their days learning, coloring, making things, exploring, and bonding. Linus attended half-day preschool two years in a row, which was normal for the area where he grew up. He did well and seemed to catch on to all his teacher was teaching.

Lucy recalled discussing Linus's progress in October with his kindergarten teacher. For the first time, she learned he was struggling. To this day, seventeen years later, Lucy remembered the teacher told her, "Linus will never be at the top of his class. He will always be at the bottom." She was shocked. Why would a teacher say such a thing about a kindergartener? Why would a teacher give up on a student that early in his education? Lucy said nothing; as a first-time mom, she did not know what or even if she could say anything. Was this some sort of strange way to attempt to motivate her son?

She went home stunned and hurt. To know her child was struggling and may need some extra help, and hearing he will always be at the bottom of his class was difficult to grasp. Could this be true? What could Lucy do? Was there anything to be done? She knew sweet Linus loved school and was giving his all every day. The teacher mentioned nothing about the possibility of Linus getting any special help or being retained, just that he would always be at the bottom of his class.

Lucy chose to do extra work at home with Linus. All summer, he practiced the skills he learned in kindergarten. When first grade started, Linus hit the ground running and so did Lucy.

Each night she helped him work on his spelling words, practice his reading, and review skills from the day. Lucy had so many books in her home, it could have been considered a small library. Toward the end of first grade, Lucy and Chuck met with the first- and second-grade teachers to decide if Linus was ready to move on to second grade. He was still struggling quite a bit to read on his own fluently, so they decided to retain him. The teachers mentioned nothing about Linus receiving any extra help from the school system. Linus repeated first grade, and while he still loved to go to school, he knew it was not easy. He never stopped trying his best. Lucy worked with him nightly and throughout the summers before and after his second year in first grade.

Linus began second grade as he had each of his other years, with joy and a can-do attitude. The teachers had not communicated anything negative to Lucy, so she and Chuck thought the retention had worked and Linus was all caught up with his peers. Lucy worked with Linus every night, and read to him and with him. Even though the teachers had communicated little about Linus's progress, Lucy had seen his grades, and most of his papers were coming home with lots of mistakes.

In early December, Lucy asked Linus's teacher if there was any way the school could provide Linus some extra help from the school. The teacher told her unless he qualified for special education, there was not much the school could offer. Lucy and Chuck had Linus evaluated. The evaluation showed Linus had a specific learning disability (SLD) that qualified him for an individualized education plan (IEP).

The evaluation process did not start until after Christmas break, and by the time it wrapped up and they met to discuss the results, it was May. By the end of second grade, the IEP was written and scheduled to take effect the following year, since there was so little time left in the school year.

Linus began third grade with a positive attitude and a big smile. He rarely complained, but he did not like being pulled out of his general education classroom to receive the extra help he needed. I was his special education teacher that year. He told me he did not want to be picked on for coming out of class, because only the "dumb" kids had to leave for extra help, and he did not want to miss what was happening in his classroom. Linus had a great work ethic, and it broke my heart to hear he thought the other kids perceived him as being dumb. I explained to Linus he was not dumb; he learned differently than many other students. I told him some kids needed glasses to help their vision to learn, and some kids needed braces on their teeth to help them stay healthy, and no one ever thought those kids were dumb.

I also explained sometimes the halls were clear and we could travel from one part of the school to another quickly. At other times, the hallways were closed off or they were full of people. In those cases, we took longer or changed our route to get to where we wanted to go, but we still got there. I said our brains were the same way; sometimes the information went instantly to where we needed it to be, and other times it took a while because of things in the way. I assured him it was my pleasure to help him figure out the different path he needed to take for his brain to understand. Linus understood what I was saying, and while those words did not alleviate his worries, they helped him have a slightly different perspective of himself.

Linus came to school every day smiling and ready to tackle his academics. He knew he had to put in extra effort to understand the material, but it did not dampen his attitude in either my class or in his general education classes. I had the privilege of being his teacher for only one year. I kept an eye on him throughout junior high, and according to his teacher, Miss Love, his positive attitude toward the work did not falter, though he still struggled and was disappointed in himself when he did not do well.

He felt sometimes the teachers thought he was capable of doing the work but was choosing not to; therefore, they did not want to help him. He did not understand why a teacher thought he was faking having trouble learning. If only these teachers could see and understand how much effort he put into his studies and how much he wanted to learn and please them with good grades.

He wished he did not need the modifications and accommodations, he wished he was like everybody else, and he wished he could learn the way the teachers taught. Linus's teachers modified his tests and homework assignments by reducing the number of questions, multiple choice options, or vocabulary words per page; allowing him extra time to complete tests; adjusting reading material; and going to a different location to work on assignments so he or someone else could read the test questions aloud. He knew his tests and oftentimes his assignments were different, and the other students knew it. Linus longed to be able to learn without being different, but it was not anything he could control. He desperately wanted to be accepted for who he was. Sadly, several of his teachers and classmates along the way never did. The attitudes of some of his teachers throughout his education were very hurtful to him.

In every Christmas season, Lucy made sure the learning did not stop for Linus. She put a construction paper link on their Christmas tree for every book Linus or Patty read. She told them Santa was going to be so excited to see how many books they had read. This competition helped propel Linus to read even when he was not in school. During the summer breaks Lucy bought books from the school to work on skills. While they were camping, she gave them words to spell and define, and asked them questions about animals. Lucy felt her calling as Linus's mom was to help him be as successful as possible.

One summer, each of the kids was having a hard time saying a word. Linus said "hopsital" instead of "hospital," and Patty said "hamguber" instead of "hamburger." Lucy recalled the two of them in the car, on the way to dinner, teaching the other one how to pronounce their word. By the time they arrived at the restaurant, they were both successful. Lucy said Patty and Linus completed each other; they were always so close. When Linus was being bullied, Patty was there to make him feel better. If Patty was having a bad day or someone had not been nice to her, Linus was there to defend her or make her feel better. They had each other's backs from the first day they became brother and sister.

From the time Linus was in first grade, Lucy worked with Linus on a nearly nightly basis. Linus's fifth-grade year was his worst. The amount of work required of him, the pace of his classes, and the way subjects were taught required several hours of homework for Linus (and Lucy) every night. Linus did not play sports or join extracurricular activities at school because he wanted to do well in academics, and the amount of time he had to spend studying prevented him from doing much else.

Lucy and Chuck realized Linus learned material better by hearing or seeing it, versus just reading it, and he learned from repetition. Chuck said, "Linus could retain what you told him, but he had a harder time retaining what he read," and throughout Linus's school career a lot of his learning "depended on the teacher."

Lucy wrote vocabulary definitions on one side of an index card and the vocabulary word on the other. They studied five of these vocabulary words on the first night, usually a Monday, and added more each night until the test, usually a Friday. Lucy developed songs, made up jokes, played games, and made connections to real life people and situations. Linus excelled with this type of studying, but it was a lot of extra work on him and his mom. Oftentimes, Lucy was up prepping learning materials long after Linus and Patty had gone to bed. Without much effort, Patty learned in the way most teachers taught, which made it a little easier for Lucy to work with Linus as much as he needed.

His grades were not as important to Linus as actually learning the material. He corrected his tests and homework, studied some more, then re-did the homework and tests Lucy had rewritten. This was a student who wanted to learn, not just memorize some information and then forget it after he turned in the paper. Chuck said when Linus wanted to learn something, he figured out a way, and he would not give up until he was satisfied he had learned what he wanted.

Lucy recalled a time when Linus was in seventh grade when on top of completing his other homework, Linus studied several hours a night for a week for a science test. For whatever reason, this material was really clicking with him. He was confident and felt good after taking the test Friday; he thought he had done better on this test than most. On Monday, he was excited to see his test grade. He had earned a B and would have been super pumped, except for the teacher's reaction.

Instead of telling him "good job," or "I can tell you really understood this material," she accused him of cheating. She called him up to the front of the room and, in front of all the students, told him she thought the only way he could earn such a good grade was if he had cheated. She had no proof and his good grade was her only reason to accuse him. Heartbroken and feeling more humiliated than he'd ever been, he just stood there in disbelief. Of course, he told her he had not cheated, but that did not change her mind. He was devastated his teacher thought so little of him. Linus took everything to heart, and this weighed heavily on him for a long time.

His special education teacher, Miss Love, saw him after he received his test grade. When she saw the grade, she was ecstatic for him and was troubled that he was not also excited. Because she knew him so well, she was able to coax it out of him. Miss Love was appalled and angered, and shared some words with the teacher. The teacher never apologized to Linus privately or in front of the class. Regardless, Linus continued to work hard to learn. He was no quitter and rarely complained about his inability to learn the way most teachers taught.

Since he was not fully accepted by all of his teachers, most of the students did not accept him either. However, Linus was never picked on because of his learning disability. Most of the boys in his class just ignored him. When they did pick on him, it was because of his good nature, his size, and the fact he was not athletic.

Once, in fourth grade, he attended Miss Love's class soon after recess and she could tell something was bothering him. She took him into the hall, and he shared that several boys had picked on him because he could not run fast. They repeatedly called him fat. Miss Love collected the boys' names from Linus, and those boys were disciplined, but it did not make the hurt any less or go away any faster. Lucy said Linus had a heart of gold; he took all comments to heart and was not able to let them just slide off of him.

One night in fifth grade, Lucy and Chuck consoled Linus while he cried for hours at the kitchen table before he told them what upset him. One of the boys who had bullied him in fourth grade had never stopped. That day, this boy had prevented Linus from playing on the playground by blocking him from getting to the equipment, called him several names, and convinced other kids to call him names and prevent him from playing. Linus had reached his breaking point. He just could not understand why this one boy was always so mean to him. Linus always tried to be nice to everyone, and although he had learned not to reply to this boy's comments, that did not stop the comments from penetrating and hurting Linus.

A bright spot in Linus's academic career was his favorite teacher in eighth grade. Mr. Rakish made social studies come to life with his teaching style, incorporating visuals and stories. The students rarely had to read a textbook and answer the questions at the end of the chapters. One day when Lucy picked Linus up from school, he bounded through the school doors to the car. He was beaming. This was such a memorable moment for Lucy, because Linus rarely beamed coming out of school.

Linus said, "Mom, Mom, guess what? Today Mr. Rakish asked, 'Who in this class loves social studies?' and I raised my hand. Then he asked, 'Who in this class loves social studies and is getting a good grade in here?' and I raised my hand again. Then, guess what, Mom, he called on me, and said I could do the announcements tomorrow." It was a huge moment for Linus that Lucy will never forget. She said she had to hold back tears of joy. Linus felt normal, he felt special, and she could see by the look on his face he was truly proud of himself.

Linus had forgotten something at school, so Lucy went back to pick it up for him. She saw Mr. Rakish sitting at his desk, and she told him what a wonderful teacher he was and the story of Linus's excitement. Mr. Rakish was very touched and thanked her for making his day. He said, "That is what teaching is about—the kids in the classroom."

He told her a team he coached had recently won a state championship. The team was welcomed back to town with a parade, a school celebration, a huge write-up in the local paper, and a sign at the entrance of the town stating this team were state champions, but the parents wanted more to honor their kids. Not one of those parents or players had thanked him or told him they appreciated his work. Yet, here was a mom and son so excited about learning and being on the morning announcements they were both almost in tears of joy and very grateful.

Chuck and Lucy had thoughts and advice for teachers or parents of students with special needs. They said they would like to see teachers be more compassionate toward and patient with the students, with or without an IEP, and communicate better with parents. They advised parents to communicate with their child. Parents should ask how their day was, if they got into trouble, or what fun thing happened, and check their backpack for notes and homework, no matter how old they are.

If parents are concerned or worried their child is struggling or something is wrong, they should not be afraid to use the email address teachers give at the beginning of the year to talk to their teachers. Teachers really do care about their students, and sometimes they want to know the parents care too. When parents check in, teachers know they care. Lucy said, "Put your child first." If contact with the teacher does not change anything, keep working up the administration until someone listens. Never give up.

I wish I could continue Linus's story; however, he graduated from our school after eighth grade, and that summer he was diagnosed with leukemia. He never stopped fighting the disease, and even in his final days he had that brilliant smile on his face. He passed away when he was sixteen.

His memory and smile live on through his mother's efforts to comfort children at the hospital where he spent so much of his last fifteen months of life. Linus will never be forgotten, and his desire to learn through the most difficult challenges will forever be etched into my mind. Thank you, Lucy, Chuck, and Linus, for sharing your lives and your story.

James

With tears sneaking out of her eyes, Claire gave James a final hug and said goodbye. She and her boyfriend got into her car and drove away from James's new home. She held herself together until she was out of James's sight. When she could not contain her emotions any longer, they pulled the car to a safe stopping place before she burst into tears full of anger, sorrow, hurt, remorse, failure, and devastation.

How and why had it come to this? Why had his father treated him the way he had? Whose fault was it? Why was his father off the hook when it came to making this decision? Was she making the right decision? How could she leave her twelve-year-old son in a residential facility eight hours away from home? Was this truly the best placement for him? Did he understand she was doing this for his own good? Why didn't he get to lead a normal life like everyone else? Did he feel the only person he had left was abandoning him? Why was this the only place that would work? Why hadn't she realized he needed this kind of help sooner? Would it have mattered if she had? Why wasn't the last placement near home able to help him anymore? Why wasn't there a facility closer to home? Why, God? Why?

Claire was the youngest girl in a large family. She saw several of her siblings get married and have children and knew she wanted the same for her life as well. She was nineteen when she met Jeff, twenty when they married, twenty-one when they found out she was pregnant, and twenty-two when James was born in 1984. She was enrolled in college to become a nurse. When she was a little girl and dreamt of her future, this was it. Everything was going perfectly. Her pregnancy had gone well with just a little nausea and some early spotting. The labor and delivery only lasted a few hours, and she had a perfectly healthy baby boy.

At four months, James cut his first tooth and had his first ear infection; from then on, he seemed to always have ear infections. At thirteen months, he had his first set of ear tubes; in all, he had four sets. The ear tubes allowed fluid to drain from behind the eardrums, where buildup could cause ear infections. The tubes required surgery to insert, and usually they fell out on their own after several months to a few years. During this time, Claire worked part-time, went to school full-time, and took care of him and their home. Nothing was going smoothly. She failed one of her nursing classes, and something had to give. She had to give up school.

At his nine-month and one-year checkups, Claire told the doctor she was concerned he was delayed in reaching his milestones. The doctor said his ear infections may have caused slight delays, and boys tended to develop a little later, so she should not worry—he would catch up. He reached his milestones of rolling over, sitting up, crawling, walking, holding items, and babbling, but each one was always delayed. Claire and Jeff trusted the doctors, especially since James reached the milestones eventually. He was always a quiet, calm, laid-back, well-behaved baby who rarely cried, even when he was sick. Claire remembered thinking how lucky she had gotten with him.

Claire was already concerned about her marriage and knew she needed to complete her degree to assure her ability to take care of herself and her son in the future, so she went back to school just before James turned one. Jeff worked the evening shift and did not arrive at home until between twelve thirty and one o'clock in the morning. Most nights he could not fall asleep until two or three o'clock in the morning. James needed to sleep later in the morning to allow Jeff to sleep more than a couple of hours a night, so Claire kept James up in the evenings as late as possible. She enjoyed this opportunity to spend more time with him, but it was not just a courtesy to Jeff. It was a way to protect James.

Claire had not realized while dating Jeff that he was an alcoholic. He was happy, loving, funny, charming, and sensible when he was drinking, but not when he was sober—and he was basically completely sober only when he first woke up. Before he had his first beer, he was easily agitated and quick to respond with harsh words or actions. Claire later found out alcoholism ran in Jeff's family, which was rife with high-functioning alcoholics.

After just one semester, Claire entered clinicals, sometimes for ten hours a day. She changed the routine she and James followed to accommodate her longer days and Jeff's work schedule. She believed Jeff was doing harder drugs than just beer at this point, and she was worried about leaving James with Jeff alone. For a while, she woke up James at four thirty in the morning to bring him to the sitter, so Claire could get to clinicals by six o'clock.

When James was three, Claire graduated from nursing school and secured her first job. The hospital offered its employees day care, where James stayed while Claire worked the evening shift. Her shift ended at eleven o'clock. James and Claire spent the days together, and Claire noticed how active he was. He constantly moved some or all of his body from activity to activity within minutes. He also had small temper tantrums, which Claire attributed to his age and his frequently changing sleep patterns. James occasionally had nightmares which made him scream hysterically until Claire or Jeff could wake him.

When James was three and a half, Claire's shift changed to day-time, and James was eligible to start a prekindergarten program. Claire found a pre-K class in the town where they lived and a day care to watch him when he was not in school. Claire was at work when a day care staff member called her to come pick up James. He had gotten mad about the song they were learning, ran to the record player, grabbed the record and destroyed it. Unfortunately, this was not the last phone call she received about his behaviors.

Although she did not have to pick him up again, he was regularly in trouble for hitting other children and throwing items. James was still an only child and did not have to share items at home, so while Claire knew the behavior needed to be corrected, she also thought she knew the cause of his behaviors.

James missed the cutoff to start kindergarten when he was five, so he had another year of pre-K. His behaviors were better, but still not perfect. Claire also noticed his speech was delayed, and when he talked, he was difficult to understand. When he was five, he was diagnosed with attention deficit hyperactivity disorder (ADHD) and put on medicine at the age of six. He began to regularly have night terrors, which caused him to run screaming out of his room and down the hall; occasionally, he even attempted to exit the house.

When she told me the doctor and she agreed medicine was the right choice for him at age six, I was surprised and my face showed it. She said, "While I agree that medicine should not be the first choice, I do feel there is an unnecessary stigma around it. I feel that giving these kids what they need to be able to function is no different than giving insulin to a diabetic." ADHD is a medical condition that displays itself mostly with behaviors. In Claire's mind, it was not fair to withhold medication that benefited a child just because the difficulty was behavioral.

She felt her family and friends thought she was crazy for giving her six-year-old son medication. When people asked her the reason for putting a hyper child on a stimulant, she explained how it stimulated the regulatory part of the brain so it could function properly. The medication made such a world of difference in James's behavior, the decision to medicate was worth the ridicule and judgment Claire received from people outside the situation.

Just before he turned six, the family moved. Rather than attend a new school for only six weeks, he did not start kindergarten until they moved in mid-October. The day before the Thanksgiving break, the teacher met with Claire. The teacher, who was also a certified speech-language pathologist, told Claire that James could not handle the pace of the class, and it caused him to have bad behaviors that disrupted learning for him and his classmates. He could not stay after Christmas break.

Claire was not happy, but thought the behaviors were from the ADHD. At this point, an individualized education plan was written and he was placed in the special education classroom after Christmas break. He was in the special education classroom just a few weeks when the teacher said he could not be there with those behaviors. Even on the medicine, he was up and about in the room, occasionally still knocking objects off other students' desks, and being aggressive with other children.

They agreed to move him to a behavioral special education room. He was only in that setting for a few weeks when the school felt they did not have a proper program for him and wanted to bus him to a nearby town. He finished out his kindergarten year at the first school and began first grade in the nearby town.

Claire recalled telling him he needed to "straighten up with these behaviors or you'll get kicked out of this next school, too." It was hard for her to have those conversations with her six-year-old who she believed really was doing his best, but it was not good enough for people around him. He was still having his night terrors weekly, and instead of just screaming and running, he was swinging his fists as if he was fighting someone.

No one seemed to know what to do with him or for him. Each teacher tried behavior modification techniques with both positive and negative consequences, and nothing worked for long. The teachers he had in those early classes were not trained well enough to deal with the types of behaviors he was exhibiting. He was also not learning at the class's pace, even in his special education classes. All the adults who worked with him thought his learning was impeded because of the behaviors.

At the beginning of the following year, he was having more success than at other schools, and Claire thought they had finally found the "key that would unlock his brain." In addition to his negative behaviors, he was hyperactive and clumsy, so he often ran into things, and he bruised easily. Claire had to procure a letter from James's neurologist explaining this and testifying to the fact he was not being abused by his parents. It was just one more thing other parents did not have to deal with, but she needed to protect her son and avoid anything that could be misconstrued.

In November, Jeff got a phone call stating James needed to be picked up. He was unable to leave what he was doing and directed the school to call Claire without knowing the reason. This redirection was problematic for a few reasons. When the school tried to reach Claire at work, the teacher told the person who answered the phone every detail and why James needed to be picked up. This was the first problem Claire had with the situation. Any student—especially one with an IEP—had rights of privacy, and James's had just been violated by his teacher.

When Claire called back, the teacher told her James had pooped his pants and needed to be picked up. Claire told the teacher there was a change of clothes in James's backpack and to have him change, but the teacher refused to let him. She insisted Claire pick him up. Claire was working an hour from the school that day and told the teacher she would not be able to get there quickly and to have James change his clothes. The teacher refused again and said James would have to sit in his poopy pants until someone came and got him. This was the second problem Claire had, and she became furious with them at this point.

Claire could not leave her patients until a replacement arrived, so she continued to care for them until she was allowed to go. By the time she arrived at the school, James had been sitting in his poopy pants for two and a half hours. The school's office was enclosed in glass, in the middle of the busiest hallway of the school, with wooden benches just outside the office. All the students traveled this hallway as they moved from class to class. The office staff put paper towels down on the bench just outside the office and James sat there with instructions not to move.

Claire arrived just as school was letting out for the day, and the hallway was full of kids. The students were talking about the boy who had pooped his pants and was sitting outside the office stinking up the hallway. This was Claire's final problem with the situation and the school. She was livid and mortified for her son. When she arrived at the office, she saw her little seven-year-old son, sitting all alone on the bench looking very sad and remorseful. He had been sitting in poop all afternoon, all alone, with kids walking by talking about him and most likely teasing him or making fun of him. He was apologetic to Claire for his accident.

She, of course, was not mad at him and gave him a big hug while she told him sometimes accidents happen. All Claire wanted to do was cry for her son and the way he had been treated. However, she took him to retrieve his backpack and his change of clothes. They found the bathroom nearest his locker and he went in all by himself, cleaned himself up as best as he could, changed his clothes, and they went back to the office. Claire demanded to speak to the principal and would not leave until she was allowed to have the conversation.

She did not remember word for word what she said to the principal or to the teacher, but she knew they completely understood her son's rights had been violated multiple times, his IEP had not been followed, and they would never treat her son that way again. He never stepped foot back in that school. It had been more than twenty-five years since this incident, and Claire said it still made her blood boil.

The teacher he had at the time was a veteran teacher who was very well-respected in her school, her district, and the town. Claire was appalled she thought it was okay to let a seven-year-old sit in his own excrement for over two hours. The teacher's response was that she was not allowed to touch a student, specifically in that region, especially since he was the opposite gender. When Claire asked why she could not just have found another adult to monitor her while she helped, her response was the same. When Claire queried as to why she would not let James clean himself up and change his own clothes, the teacher said again, she could not be alone with him or touch him to help him.

The common sense that seemed to have been obvious for the situation was not present. The compassion for another human being's plight was also missing. I hold special education teachers—because they have more training, and I was one—to a higher standard than I do general education teachers. While I do not condone this behavior in either set of teachers, it was even more heinous to me that this was his special education teacher treating him this way. This was a person who was supposed to protect and accept him. In my opinion, she failed miserably.

Claire despaired about what to do with James. After what happened, he had to go back to the school where he started kindergarten until they could find somewhere more appropriate. The home district said they did not have a setting for him, and the district they bused him to was unacceptable after the incident. She truly believed that somewhere, someone would have a key to help him learn and manage his behaviors. Even though the law clearly states the school district must provide a free and appropriate education, there did not seem to be a public school setting in the area that was appropriate for James.

She enrolled him in a private school that told her they could help him. He did better in that school, and attended there for all of his second-grade year. Claire was quite pleased and was actually elected to be a school board member the next year. She finally thought there was a light at the end of the tunnel, but things deteriorated as he got further into third grade. His teacher was amazing, though she appeared to be in a power struggle with the principal. They could not agree on what worked best for James. He did well when the teacher left the classroom door open, but when the principal came and closed the door, James became aggressive and acted out. After the door was opened again, he calmed down.

Consistency and routine are necessary and beneficial for children like James, and this back-and-forth made it so bad for James, Claire knew she had to find a better setting for him. Claire was worried all the changes were having a negative effect on him. She felt he must be wondering why none of these placements were long term. She feared he was feeling rejected at school and home.

At the same time all of this was happening at school, their home life was also falling apart. Claire felt Jeff had spanked James too hard on several occasions, spanked him too often, and she had seen him slap James twice. He was a functioning alcoholic who had become verbally abusive to her and James, and his temper was quick to ignite. Claire filed for divorce when James was eight years old and it became final when he was nine. When Jeff brought James back home after one of his weekend visitations, it was obvious to Claire he had been drinking with James in the car. For his own safety, Claire would not let James spend any more weekends with his father. It was difficult to help James to understand why, and for Claire, it was one more time James's father was letting him down.

During this time, his night terrors started happening almost nightly and sometimes multiple times a night. Some of his terrors were so bad, and his fear was so great, Claire had to restrain him until she could wake him up. Neither she nor James had very good sleep for years because of these night terrors and his sleepwalking.

Claire and James's neurologist decided it might be time to bring in another professional. Claire began taking James to a psychiatrist when he was ten years old. The psychiatrist soon realized James had other things going on along with his ADHD. Something was internally driving him in the wrong direction. He was diagnosed with irritability associated with autism. They tried some behavioral therapy first, but again, it was not enough, and he had to be put on more medication. While James was on these medications, he needed to be monitored closely for any adverse effects. Some medicines were successful for a while, until his body built up a tolerance, and he had to change. Some medicines just did not work at all. Claire had to find another option.

She found another private school, closer to home. Since he did so well with the teacher in his last private school environment (as long as the door was open), Claire was hopeful her son would do well in a similar environment. Around this time, James's doctor felt the ADHD medicine was not working, and he took James off the medication.

Though a strong supporter of medications to help students like James, Claire said it was not necessarily easy treatment. A struggle for parents of children with ADHD has been the prescription refill process for stimulants. Because stimulant medicines had high potential for abuse, Claire needed to obtain a written prescription from the physician every month and hand-carry it to the pharmacy within seven days. A variety of drugs were available to treat ADHD, but many of them could have serious side effects, so decisions about medications were not made lightly.

This new school was very structured and consistent, and James did very well initially. He was there about three weeks when he became mad at his teacher and kicked her in the stomach. She was pregnant at the time. Claire and the school mutually agreed to remove James.

Claire and James were once again at the mercy of the local school district. Because the district had not been involved in his placements for almost two years and were not sure what his current needs were, they placed him in a special education classroom at his home school and assigned a personal aide to document his activity every ten minutes, so they could get a really good idea of what kind of help James really needed. After the individual observation, the public school realized they did not have an appropriate setting for him.

By the time he finished third grade eight weeks later, he had been in nine different classroom settings in five different schools, and they were looking for number ten. Though discouraged, Claire continued to fight to find what was best for her son; someone had to find the solution.

The public school could not provide an appropriate education for him, but they were still responsible to provide a free one. The school contacted Claire, had a meeting to discuss a new placement, and together they found a private school setting that seemed very appropriate for him. The public school district paid for the private school tuition; Claire did not have to. This school was an hour away, in a large city, across waterways.

Since James was the only child from his town going to this school, he was transported in a school car instead of a bus. At first, James sat in the passenger seat and he did great. However, after several months he was too much of a distraction for the driver. He did not fare much better in the backseat. One morning when they were passing over one of the waterways, James tried to exit the car from the backseat. The bridge they were going over was very busy with eight lanes of traffic. The driver almost had an accident getting James to stay in the car.

Claire was told they had to either find a new solution to getting him to school, or they would have to find a new setting for him. Her work schedule did not allow her to drive him in, but she could pick him up in the evening. James was still taking the medicine for his ADHD, and as his behaviors increased, the doctor put him on a medicine for those too.

Claire knew at all his previous schools, he had learned if he did not want to do work, he could misbehave. If he misbehaved enough, he was sent to a different location until he calmed down and was able to work again. By the time he returned to his classroom, whatever subject or activity he did not like was over, and he did not have to deal with it anymore.

The staff at this school had a different approach. When James acted out during a class or activity, they removed him, if necessary, until he was calm. Then he had to return to the subject or activity and finish it before he could move on to the next, no matter how long it took. James did not like this new approach. He reacted very badly several times, tried new behaviors, and tried to increase the frequency of the behavior; nothing deterred this staff from insisting he finished what he missed. They taught him he could not avoid difficulty, and helped him learn how to deal with struggles instead. Claire felt this was a turning point for James.

In the first couple of years James was at this school, he was also acting out much more at home. He was becoming more violent and destructive. Claire and Jeff had been divorced for a while by this point. Jeff had rights to see James and promised to come visit and do things with him, but only showed up a few of those times. He asked James what he wanted for Christmas and then sent only a card with no money or gift. He promised to call James, but the phone calls rarely came. Claire felt many of James's behaviors could be explained by the rejection he must have felt from his father, the disappointment in getting his hopes smashed over and over, and the anger at his father for not being around.

Claire tried all sorts of behavior modification techniques to no avail. New behavior plans were often effective for about three weeks, before James figured out how to manipulate the situation. Claire was always looking for the next plan, so she could be ready to change it up frequently. She rewarded him for his good behaviors, but he quickly grew tired of the rewards she offered or could afford. She took things away from him when he misbehaved to such an extent that at one point, all he had in his room was a mattress. Some thought his behaviors were attention seeking, so one behavior plan called for ignoring behaviors and providing positive attention as much as possible.

Grounding was a common discipline for adolescents at the time, but since James could not be left alone and did not have social activities outside family events, there was nothing to restrict. Many experts at the time stressed effective consequences needed to be immediate and associated with the undesired action. Finding appropriate consequences related to his negative behavior was extremely difficult throughout his childhood and into early adulthood. Claire felt this was one of her biggest struggles.

Claire had been divorced about a year when her friends suggested to her that she needed to go out and socialize more. She joined a bowling team. After a few weeks she met Ted. After a few more weeks, she and Ted went on a date. A week later they went on another date. Claire told Ted all about James, and Ted wanted to meet him.

This was the first person Claire had dated seriously since the divorce, and she was not sure she was ready to introduce James to him. Jeff had hurt James physically and emotionally so badly, Claire was very leery of how James would react. She also wondered if it was fair to ask James to get to know someone who might not be around for long. After a few more weeks, Claire decided to introduce James to Ted. They immediately hit it off. Ted had a very calming voice, and he was a big guy, so when he spoke, James listened.

Claire and Ted had been dating for several months when she needed to find an alternate means of transporting James to school. Ted was getting along very well with James. He had an evening job, and his mornings were free. Claire wondered if she should ask him to drive James to school in the morning. She really liked him and did not want to scare him away or jeopardize their relationship, but James was her priority. After a few days of thinking and praying, she asked him and he agreed. James attended the same private school until he was in sixth grade. The school staff understood and dealt with James's behaviors in a way that worked and made sense. The staff also realized his behaviors were the most severe and frequent during math and reading times. They suggested to Claire that she take him to an outside source for a comprehensive evaluation of his academic ability, behavior, speech skills, medical status, and psychology.

The school recommended a developmental center for this evaluation. The evaluation was extremely thorough. Each week, he met with a different expert for two or three hours, and each expert focused on a different area. He met with a classroom teacher, a behavior therapist, a psychiatrist, a speech language pathologist, an autism specialist, a medical doctor, and fine and gross motor specialists. James did well with all the evaluators and Claire felt the answers would be accurate.

The evaluators gave her great feedback about how well James had cooperated and how pleased they were that their individual assessments would show valid and reliable data. She believed they would finally find the answers to all his problems, but she was not prepared for the results.

At the meeting, the medical doctor's results were covered first. James definitely had ADHD, and his medicine was helping keep it under control. The doctor tested him for Fragile X syndrome, because James had presented characteristics. He was cleared. Claire was not surprised at these results. Next, the autism specialist diagnosed James with pervasive developmental disorder-not otherwise specified (PDD-NOS), which was a category of an autism spectrum diagnosis. This was not what Claire had expected to hear.

Little was known in the 1990s of the range of characteristics a person with autism could have, and the prevalence was less than 1 percent of the population. Autism is a developmental disorder that presents in a wide variety of ways and levels of severity. It affects a person's ability to communicate and interact with others, and often comes with difficulties in executive functioning. Although she was not prepared for this answer, she felt at least there was a direction the school could move toward when it came to educating James. The school teacher, speech pathologist, behavioral therapist, and motor experts spoke next. They confirmed what Claire already knew.

Based on the psychological and psychiatric evaluation results, the expert suggested James had oppositional defiant disorder (ODD). The disorder is typically diagnosed in childhood and is characterized by frequent anger, vindictiveness, argumentativeness, and defiance, especially directed toward authority figures. Again, Claire was not shocked by this diagnosis.

The next words out of the psychologist's mouth will forever be etched into Claire's mind. She was told, "Because of your son's behaviors, his PDD-NOS, and that he is retarded, we suggest a residential facility as the best placement."

Claire felt as though the floor had just given out underneath her, and her entire world was crumbling around her. She had a multitude of thoughts run through her head. What did they mean when they said, "...he is retarded"? No one had ever said those words before. Where was this coming from? She knew he was delayed, but never had anyone suggested he was that delayed. He was not stupid—slow, maybe, but not retarded.

Wait, did they just suggest sending her eleven-year-old son away? She could not do that to him, or to herself. She was all he had. His father was a jerk and had basically abandoned him; she could not do that to him too. All those schools had rejected him, and she always told him it was his behavior and not him personally. What would sending him away do to him? What was happening? Was this a nightmare? They could not be right. He could disconnect and hook up the video cassette recorder correctly, he could take things apart and put them back together. This was not right. His behaviors were causing him to lag behind, not his intelligence.

They just needed to find the key to manage his behaviors, and then the academics would catch up. Every time she asked James's doctors, they just said he was a boy and would catch up. When did that change? She guessed her plan to take him to Disneyland someday would never be possible. What else wasn't possible? She couldn't do this; she wouldn't do this to her little boy. God, why?

This was all his father's fault. She hated Jeff. He did this to her son, he should be feeling this pain too. It was not fair. How would she pay for this? Jeff never paid child support. He owed close to $20,000, but would it even be enough? A parent didn't do that to a kid, a baby; they didn't send them away. What kind of people thought sending an eleven-year-old away was the right thing? People sent a letter or a package away, but not a child. She was not doing that.

The attendees at the meeting could tell they had just told her something she did not know, and they were surprised. They all thought she knew, and that it was one of the main reasons she had brought him to their type of facility to be evaluated. They felt awful—especially the psychologist who had said it so bluntly. She would have approached the situation very differently if she had known. She apologized and asked, "You didn't know he was retarded?" If anything else was discussed at the meeting, Claire had no memory of it. For her, the world stopped spinning and time froze.

Claire had no memory of the next several days, but Ted said she just shut everything and everyone out of her life. She went through the motions of daily living, but was completely numb. Ted tried to comfort his girlfriend, and he felt bad for her, but he was not as attached to James, so the news did not affect him as much.

At some point, Claire met with the staff at James's school and told them the results of the evaluations. They told her that his diagnosis was what they were thinking, and while they had made great progress with James, they had reached the end of their ability to help him anymore. He was considered a fifth-grader at the time. The school was willing to keep him for a while, but she had to show she was looking at other places.

For the next eight months, he stayed at the school, where they maintained the progress he had made. Claire tried to find a residential facility close to home. Some of the places she visited felt and looked like a prison. Other places she visited wanted her to give up her parental rights. Nothing was right, and the pressure to find a good fit was weighing on her. Every place she looked at broke her heart even more, thinking of how she was going to break the news to James. How could she tell him, again, his placement was going to change, and with this next placement, he wouldn't be able to come home every night?

Her despair was almost unbearable. She was tired of struggling and fighting. No one seemed to be able to help her and James, and she felt there was no light at the end of the tunnel. Claire felt alone. She knew she could not continue for much longer with the way things were. She wondered how they would make the next adjustment work, and if there was even a place that would work. She questioned why no one could direct her to possible help, and no one knew what to do with or for James.

She fell into depression and contemplated suicide more than once. She was not able to leave James behind, so she knew if she died, he also had to die. For a split second a couple of times, she felt that was the answer. She fought the urge and continued to fight for him and for herself.

Ted remained by Claire's side throughout all of this, and somewhere along the way, they fell in love with each other. Ted proposed marriage and Claire turned him down. She felt it was not fair to him to take her on with everything she dealt with when it came to James. She told him if he was serious, he needed to really understand and be 100 percent on board that sometimes James and his needs came first. She did not want him to regret marrying her or worse, end the marriage, leaving her and James alone again. She was very skittish about marriage since her first one did not last, and her ex-husband had not been kind to James or understood his needs. To Claire's surprise, Ted accepted her reasons, began seeking guidance from a pastor friend, and they continued to date.

During the time Claire was looking at residential facilities, she received a phone call from James's school. James had pulled his pants down in front of several students. The school had taken care of his discipline and explained to him how and why it was unacceptable, but needed to make Claire aware. She found out from James later a student had promised to give him a nice watch if he did it. With that new information, she started thinking about all the other times James had gotten into trouble. She began to see James was gullible. She added that to his quick temper, impulsiveness, and the fact he was getting more violent and destructive, and concluded if she did not do something drastic, he would end up in prison or dead. She hated to think that about him, but it seemed like a logical possibility.

During those eight months of researching, visiting, and praying, Claire was not sleeping well, partly because of the stress, but mostly because James's night terrors became worse and more frequent, and he was getting more violent. He was almost the same height as she was and weighed between 120 and 130 pounds. His eyes were not their normal color during these episodes; his normally blue eyes were almost black. He came out of his room terrified, angry, screaming, arms swinging, and usually still running.

He knocked items off shelves, broke whatever he could, argued and yelled at the air, looked behind him as if something was chasing him, and tried to get out of the house. Once or twice, he managed to unlock the doors and ran onto the front porch before Claire could catch him. It was obvious he was scared and trying to escape from something.

Claire found herself many nights restraining him during these episodes until he woke up, so he did not hurt himself. Sometimes this lasted a few minutes; other times it lasted ten to twenty minutes or more. Some nights it happened multiple times, and other nights, not at all. When he woke up, he looked confused and was very calm. She usually told him to go to the bathroom and back to bed. He almost always complied, and when she asked him in the morning about the incident, he had no memory of it. He could not tell her during his terror what was happening either. She said it was "not him."

Claire asked James's doctor if these night terrors could be a side effect of the medicine he took for his ADHD and behaviors. The doctor said it was a possibility, and they decided to wean him off one medicine and try something else. To do that, he had to be admitted to a psychiatric hospital, as he needed to be monitored closely for bad reactions, major mood swings, or meltdowns, and protected if he became violent. The doctor chose to add a drug called Prozac, typically used to treat panic disorders, depression, and major mood swings.

James had always spoken with a garbled, fast-paced speech pattern. Shortly after taking his first dose of Prozac, he was speaking perfectly clearly and in a slower, more understandable speech pattern. Claire went to visit him that evening; he was still talking in that manner, and she could understand every word he said. While this may sound like a great side effect, it was not. He had literally not stopped talking since he had his medicine first thing in the morning. He could not stop talking. He told Claire he wanted to stop, but his brain seemed to have flipped a switch, and it was stuck in the on position.

Claire asked at the nurse's station what medicine he had been given, and told them he needed to be taken off of it immediately. The hospital did not give him another dose, yet it took three days to clear his system and for him to be able to stop talking. He did not sleep those two nights because of the constant talking. The doctor found a medicine that agreed with James and after monitoring him for a few more days, he was released.

One evening, weeks after changing his medicine, James had gone to bed earlier than normal. Claire was not tired, so she stayed up and did housework and laundry. She was sitting on the couch folding the laundry when she thought she heard James breathing. She turned around and he was standing behind her with a butcher knife in his hand. He was staring straight ahead and the knife was at his side. She was not sure when he got the knife, because she would have seen or heard him if he had retrieved it right before she saw him. She was able to slowly get up, remove the knife from his hand, and then wake him up.

Another night after James had gone to bed, Claire again stayed up. She heard a noise, turned around, and there was James with a butcher knife in his hand, only this time it was held high over his head as if he was ready to strike, and he had a demonic look in his eyes. Claire grabbed a nearby cushion and put it in front of her just as he brought the knife down. She screamed his name and he woke up.

He was having one of his night terrors. For some reason with these two, he did not come screaming and running out of his room like he had with all the other ones. When he woke up, he was very confused, but calm. Claire quickly regained her composure, told him to get a drink, go to the bathroom, and go back to bed. He did and did not wake up the rest of the night.

On the other hand, Claire did not sleep at all that night. She was scared for herself and James. She cried, pondered what was causing this, and worried it would happen again. She felt all alone and wondered if there were other parents who had gone or were going through similar experiences. She felt discouraged about ever finding the key to unlock his brain, but she was not ready to give up looking. She had to succeed. She was all he had.

The next day when she told Ted about the incident, he was scared for her too. He came over and hid all the knives and any other objects he thought could be used as a weapon. As they talked, Claire decided to take James back to the psychiatric hospital and see if they could help him. They had just dropped him off and were sitting in a nearby park. The weather was horrible and they chose to wait it out rather than drive in it. At about the time Claire began talking to him about getting married again, the tornado sirens went off. They both laughed when he mentioned it, because he remembered thinking, "We are about to die by a tornado and now she wants to talk marriage?" The conversation did not last long and did not result in their getting engaged either, but they did get a funny story from it.

James was not allowed to stay overnight at the hospital. He went there several days in a row for evaluation, until the hospital said he was okay and did not need to come back. Claire was not so sure. From that point on, she always made sure she could see the door to his bedroom after he had gone to bed.

After eight months of searching within a couple of hours from her home, she expanded her search. She visited a place four hours from home. It seemed nice, the staff were friendly, she was allowed to keep her parental rights (some facilities insisted parents give up their rights), and four hours was not a terrible distance to drive. She applied and was rejected because of the severity of his behaviors. She was dejected but determined to find "the one."

She found another facility about three hours away, but part of the behavior plan there included the entire group getting consequences for individual behavior. Because of James's history, Claire felt that environment would only lead to more bullying and negative actions toward James. She felt he needed to be encouraged rather than punished, so she kept looking.

She truly believed if she did not find something, he would go down a very bad path. She widened her search to places within eight hours of the home, and after many phone calls and record reviews, she chose a place. She told James, "You need help, and I've been trying to find a place that can help you not get into trouble anymore. Your current school has helped you as much as they can. I think I have found a place that I believe will help you. I would like us to visit." While it was excruciating for her to say, James seemed to have little reaction.

As she walked across the campus with Ted and James to see the classroom they envisioned for him, she felt a calm wash over her. She said it was like the Bible scripture of Philippians 4:7. She paraphrased: "The peace that transcends all understanding will guard your heart and mind." James liked it and thought it would be an okay place to live for a while. They applied, and he was accepted.

Claire and Ted had a meeting with the district personnel responsible for making the decision. She prayed every day leading up to the meeting: if this was God's will for her son, He would make it so. The meeting was short and direct. The principal and superintendent agreed this was what James needed and it was the appropriate setting for him. Claire became emotional when she told the superintendent how grateful she was. He was very supportive and in total agreement, even though his district had to pay all costs for school, room and board in his own apartment, and a paraprofessional twenty-four hours a day. Claire reported he was still in contact with them and James, and he has told them James was his greatest success story.

Claire made arrangements for James to move eight hours away from home. In January of 1997, they packed all his belongings: clothes, toys, bicycle, toiletries, books, movies, and room decorations. Every item Claire put in a box was a piece of her heart. While she had peace about what she was doing and why, it was still the most difficult experience she had ever gone through. Her son, her twelve-year-old son, was moving out and might not be coming back. Inside, she felt anguished on the extremely long, eight-hour drive to his new home, yet had to be strong on the outside. She had to keep reminding herself if she did not do this for him, he could end up suffering severe consequences. Ted was with them and supported her as best he could. They stayed in a hotel on Saturday night, and on Sunday they moved him into his new home. They arranged everything, settled him in, and went out for his favorite meal, pizza.

When they arrived back at the school, the staff told her it was time for her to leave. She put on the bravest front she could. With tears sneaking out of her eyes and James crying, they gave each other a final hug and said goodbye. She and her boyfriend got into her car and drove away from James's new home. She held herself together until she was out of James's sight. When she could not contain her emotions any longer, they pulled the car to a safe stopping place before she burst into tears full of anger, sorrow, hurt, remorse, failure, and devastation. She knew she was doing the right thing, but she hated that leaving him there was the right thing.

Claire knew upon leaving she would not see James for a month. They were allowed to call each other, but she physically was not be able to see or hug him for a month. On the drive home the next day, she was numb, constantly reminding herself this was the best place for him to keep him alive and out of prison. When she arrived home, she was lost. What was she supposed to do? There was no James to take care of, no James to worry about night terrors, no James for her to talk to, no James at all.

That night she called him. Her heart was torn into a million pieces as he begged her through tears to come and get him. He told her how much he hated it; she told him it would get better. He told her he missed her; she said she missed him too, but this was the place that would provide the help he needed, and he needed to stay. He understood, but still pleaded with her to come get him and bring him home. She cried herself to a fitful sleep.

The next day she went to work, but was really only physically there. Her mind was eight hours away. Tuesday night she called him again.

The phone conversation was almost verbatim from the night before; however, he did not beg and plead quite as much to come home. Again, she cried herself to a fitful sleep. For Claire, Wednesday was another day of going through the motions. For James, Wednesday was quite different. In their phone call that night, he told his mom he missed her terribly, but he liked the school and he would be okay. That night, Claire had her best night of sleep in years.

For at least nine years, she had not had a routine or normal day. Her days were ruled by those severe behaviors, outbursts, or night terrors. Every minute, she was on edge and prepped, emotionally and physically, to deal with whatever came up—even on the few days that turned out to have no negative behaviors.

Slowly, she got used to her new normal of not being on edge twenty-four hours a day, seven days a week. The pervasive, every-minute-of-every-day worry began to disappear. She started to relax sometimes. Her health started to improve, even though she never knew she had been sick. Her mental acuity became stronger with consistent, regular sleep pattern. She still worried about him, and for several months after he was there found herself holding her breath when the phone rang, especially if she saw the call was from the school at an unexpected time.

As the days and weeks passed after dropping James off, Claire and Ted spent more time together, and she realized he was who she was supposed to spend the rest of her life with. They had been to see James three times and had talked to him many times on the phone. Claire could see and hear he was okay and getting better.

One day in April 1997, Claire called Ted and said if he still wanted to marry her, she accepted. He did want to marry her, and they scheduled the ceremony for August. James was going to be home from school for two weeks, and she wanted him present. Together and separately, she and Ted went through thirteen weeks of premarital counseling.

When James came home for the wedding, Claire's family was amazed at the change in him. Claire felt redeemed in the eyes of most of her family members. He was still somewhat clumsy and did not interact with his same-age cousins perfectly, but his inappropriate behaviors were mostly gone. He went back to school until the following August, when he graduated out of the program. Claire said the staff at the school "learned James" and never gave up on him. She felt someone had finally found the key to unlock his brain, and she knew she had done the right thing when she sent her child eight hours from home.

James returned home and began eighth grade in a special education room in the public school in their home district. He was not in a behavioral classroom, nor was he in a specialized school. He was home. She did not get regular phone calls from the school anymore, he was learning at his level, and he graduated middle school the following May. Claire finally knew for certain having him attend the school in residence was the best thing for him. They learned a new normal. Life was still not a Rockwell portrait, but it was so much better than it had been. Ted provided extra stability for both Claire and James, and together they were a family.

When James started high school, a problem developed. Claire and Ted both had day jobs that required them to work longer hours than a typical school day three days a week. There were no day care facilities for kids over the age of twelve in Claire's area, and the high school did not have a latchkey program like the grade school. She had to find somewhere for James to go after school or figure out something else.

She had a niece who lived in the same city as she did. Her niece had a toddler at home and was studying to be a special education teacher.

Claire asked her niece if she was willing to provide respite care three days a week, and she happily agreed. He was only at his cousin's house a few hours a day on those three days, and he was always well-behaved and polite. It was the perfect situation. James loved to play with babies, and Claire's niece trusted James to play with her toddler while she studied, did housework, and prepped for dinner. It was a great help for all involved. Unfortunately for Claire, it only lasted for two school years, because her niece moved away from the area.

Through the school, Claire was made aware of a vocational program for intellectually and/or physically disabled persons. They accepted James into their program and provided after-school activities for him. He learned great skills and was doing age-appropriate activities, but there was still a problem. This agency was supposed to send representatives to pick him up from school on the days he worked. Many times the driver never showed, and Claire or Ted had to scramble to leave work and pick him up. She was afraid he would revert back to some of his old behaviors because of the feeling of disappointment and rejection, but he handled it well.

Some days, he delivered phone books or bulk magazines to businesses; other days, he worked on a janitorial crew. Most days, he worked at the local Humane Society. He fell in love with a dog, and it did not take much for him to convince Ted and Claire to adopt her. (She lived with them for the next ten years before she passed away.) During his senior year, James settled into an after-school routine of frequently visiting two of his friends who lived in group homes, and continuing his yearslong participation in Special Olympics.

James still occasionally had his night terrors and sleepwalking. Sometimes they were still severe enough that Claire or Ted had to bear-hug him until he was calm and awake, but they happened much less often than before he went to school in residence in middle school. Also, James's curiosity and lack of being able to always think through the consequences of his actions led him to do scary things once in a while.

He was about sixteen years old, and he needed to burn some energy. Claire and Ted lived in an area that was safe for James to run around a couple of blocks without anyone watching him. He went out and ran around those blocks for an hour. At some point in his run, he managed to catch and kill a squirrel for no other reason than he could. This concerned Claire at the time, but thankfully it was a onetime incident. Another day, he was curious what would happen if he lit a tissue on fire. He was not home alone, and Ted quickly put out the fire.

One of the medicines James took to help control his irritability associated with autism was Risperdal. When he was younger, he took it for a couple of years before it stopped working, and he began taking something else. When he was fifteen, he was put back on Risperdal at the same dosage he took a few years earlier. About a week after he started taking the medication again, he had a bad reaction. It was one of the scariest times Claire had ever had with him.

He woke up on Saturday, said he did not feel well, then threw up. James had always been a pretty healthy person, so this was unusual for him. He was only up for a short time before he went back to bed. He woke up three hours later, said he felt better, ate something, kept it down, and took a shower. When he finished his shower, he called Claire to the bathroom. When she opened the door, he had a glazed look in his eyes, his color was off, and his speech was slow.

He very intentionally swallowed several times in a row, as if something was stuck in his throat. He was also incredibly slow to respond. She said his name, and it took him several seconds to turn his head toward her and say, "What?" She thought he might be having a stroke.

As a nurse, she thought she could get dressed and take him to the emergency room, but within a minute or two, she came to the distressing realization that she needed to call an ambulance.

She was freaking out, because even though she was a nurse, this was her son. While she was on the phone with the dispatcher, she was watching him quickly get worse, and there was nothing she could do. His responses became even slower, and he could not swallow at all.

At the hospital, Claire had to explain how exactly opposite his behaviors were, compared to normal. Finally, one of the nurses said he might be having an allergic reaction to something. The doctor agreed and they gave him an antihistamine intravenously. Within a couple of minutes, he was pretty much back to himself. After about thirty minutes, the medicine wore off and he started showing the symptoms again. Once they gave him another dose and he was stable, he was transferred to a children's hospital. He was there for four and a half days until the medicine was completely out of his system.

The psychiatrist later apologized for his mistake of not starting the medicine at a lower dose. Parents and medical providers need an open and trusting relationship when caring for a child with disorders which require medications. Parents know their children best, and medical staff need to listen to and trust them. The psychiatrist made a mistake, but he owned it, and he provided excellent care to James for several years.

During middle school and high school, James participated in Special Olympics. Claire felt they had finally found a tribe that understood them. James found peers and made friends who understood him and accepted him where he was. His soccer coach was amazing too. He recognized his players had unique abilities, and he used those abilities to strengthen weaknesses and help his players have success, not just on the field, but in their lives. He did not see his players as disabled. He met them where they were and motivated them to do things they did not think they could do.

Not only was he the coach of the Special Olympics team, he was a coach for an elite soccer team and a police officer. He was firm but loving, and strict but kind. He taught James and all the other team members about sportsmanship, teamwork, dependability, and accountability.

She knew James was finally in a group that included him in everything he wanted to do. In Special Olympics there was no exclusion, no rejection, no blame for not meeting some standard, no comparison to anyone else, no weird stares, no whispers, and no judgement of who he was not. There was only acceptance, praise for effort, smiles, love, high fives, cheers, encouragement, and recognition for doing one's best. He loved participating. Claire's heart was overwhelmed with joy as she watched James play. The joy of seeing her son be himself, be relaxed, be part of a group, be successful, and be accepted was almost too much to handle the first time.

Special Olympics benefited Claire as well; she found parents who got "it." There was an organization for the parents where they could share stories of behaviors, academics, and life events with each other without fear of judgement or misunderstanding. They could offer advice from a "been there, done that" point of view. To finally find a group of people who understood her path and could help her navigate her future path was priceless. Special Olympics will always hold a very dear place in her heart.

As James wrapped up his senior year of high school, Claire thought about his future. In her profession, she met many elderly or very sick patients who were the parents of children with disabilities similar to

James's. These patients needed care for themselves, but refused to move to a place where they could receive the care, because there was no one to take care of their grown children. Claire had also talked to parents who had grown children with disabilities who had never really done anything or gone anywhere after they left the school setting. Claire had often advised these parents to look into a group home situation for their child. Now she thought about this for her own son.

She did not want James to face losing her and moving away from the home he had always known at the same time. She felt the turmoil he would go through would be too much, and she wanted to avoid it as much as possible. She also considered that he was an only child, and she and Ted had to work for many more years. James was not capable of staying home alone, and they were already dealing with care problems of where, how long, and who for after school.

What would care look like when he wasn't in school all day? If he continued in a job, how would he get there? Would he have time to visit his friends? Would he have any friends if he always had to depend on her or Ted to get him places to be with his friends? In considering all of these things and knowing he had been okay at the in-residence school, she put his name on the list for a group home. She thought it would take several years before something became available.

They were called two weeks later with a possible location in a city a little over an hour away and asked if they were interested. The facility was a full group home with sixteen beds. Claire asked James if he thought he was ready and he said, "Sure, let's go check it out. If I like it, I'll live there." The three of them went to visit, and they all liked the facility. The home was an intermediate care facility for developmentally disabled individuals (ICF/DD) governed by the Center for Medicaid and Medicare Services. An ICF is a rehabilitative assisted living home, available as a Medicaid benefit. ICF residents receive health care, training, services, and day programs that promote their independence.

The group home had twenty-four-hour responsibility for James, but Claire still held legal guardianship. Not all residents had legal guardians; it depended on the level of comprehension and individual choice. She was not responsible for him financially if someone took advantage of his disability, like giving him a credit card. James could not sign informed consents. If there was a change of his regular medicines, Claire had to sign permission. If he needed antibiotics or over-the-counter medicines, she was supposed to receive notification, but did not have to consent. All medicine was provided through Medicaid or private insurance.

All of his basic needs were provided for him; he shared his bedroom with one other person, and they each had their own televisions and other furniture. He and his roommate shared a bathroom with two other men. There was a community living room, commons area, and dining area. It was similar to living in a college dorm. The home had eight men and eight women, and they treated each other as family. They were not allowed to date their family members, but they could date residents from other homes.

He was not allowed to leave the premises unless there was a program happening and an authority figure from the home was with him. The group home was allowed to take him over state lines without Claire's permission, but if there was an overnight outing, Claire had to give written permission. Some of the residents where James lived were their own legal guardians and they did not have to get permission from anyone to do overnights, leave the premises on their own, or change their medications.

At James's group home, he and all the residents were required to leave during the day and go to work. Each group home was affiliated with a sheltered workshop where the residents went each day. The jobs at each workshop were different and there were different levels of responsibility and pay for each job. James was able to do the higher paying jobs many times.

Some jobs paid a flat hourly rate, while other jobs paid based on the amount of product the employee produced in an hour. Pay based on production was monitored very closely. If someone produced below what was considered an average rate, they were paid less for the job; if they produced more, they were paid more.

The residents had to use most of their earnings to pay for their room and board, known as Pay On Care. If the residents did not make enough working at the workshop, they could receive federal funding through the Social Security Act to pay the remainder. Each resident was allowed to keep thirty dollars per month of their paycheck or Social Security check. Residents used this money to pay for community outings, recreational activities and desired items outside personal hygiene and other necessary items. Claire felt he was doing all the things someone without a disability did: paying rent, going to work, taking care of himself, being a contributing member of society, not being a burden on his parents, and being who he wants to be.

She said he had a much better social life living in the group home than if he was living with her and Ted. The home planned events and outings every week, and he was hanging out with his friends in the common areas daily. His job at the workshop gave him money and a sense of purpose, which helped his sense of worth, his self-esteem, and his satisfaction with life in general. James's fellow residents became a family, and the built-in support system there was huge. When the sad day comes that she passes away, James will already have a familiar home environment, a routine he can fall back on, and friends to help him through the difficult time.

For Claire, the acceptance of her son going to a group home was a no-brainer. She made the decision to give him the best quality of life he could have. If he had stayed at home after high school, he would have had to work around her schedule, including transportation to a workshop or job; he may have had to stay home during the day, which required someone to be there; he would not see his friends nearly as much; he would have felt he was a burden on his parents; he would not be as independent; and she fully believed he would have been very unhappy, unfulfilled, and miserable with his quality of life.

While she had many great things to say about James's home and group homes in general, there were negatives also. First of all, she mourned for him and all he missed out on because of being someone who needed a place like this. The staff changed frequently; sometimes the only open facility was far away; and the distance created difficulty dealing with an emergency situation. Residents had to share a room, which was not always pleasant. There were 16 residents in the house, so there was not much individual attention. For someone who had attention-seeking behaviors, this was a challenge for her son. Opportunities for community outings were often cancelled because of issues outside his control, which occurred much more often in this setting than in a family home. James had his share of disagreements with his roommates over the years. She had to trust the people who worked with her son to have his best interests in mind, be properly trained, be honest, and to care about and for him when necessary. She had to trust those working closest with him would not abuse him in any way.

James lived in the group home for nine years, of which the first seven were great. There were some staff changes during his seventh year, and James had a difficult time with the newest staff members who did not understand his needs and disabilities. Claire was getting written reports, calls from James, and calls from the home about James's difficulties. The reports from James and the written reports showed the staff were undertrained and making situations worse for James, rather than helping him learn how to cope.

During one episode, James became violent and aggressive. He threatened harm to himself and others. He yelled at residents and staff, and told them he needed help. The staff called the police, who took him to a psychiatric hospital nearby for a few days. Claire recalled the hour-plus drive to the hospital seemed to take forever. When she arrived, James pleaded with her to find him a new home.

Finding him a new home was not an easy task. Before a group home accepted a new resident, they a) had to have space, b) had to be able to handle the needs of the new resident, and c) it had to be a good match for his intellectual level and functional status. A potential home had to see reports from the previous home to know if the new home could handle the individual's needs. Many homes Claire applied to did not accept him because of the reports of violent and aggressive behavior. Claire did not share with James how many homes she applied to, because she did not want him to feel the rejection he had felt so often as a child.

After a year of searching, a group home about thirty minutes from where Claire and Ted lived had an opening. Claire timorously applied. When she was called from the home, she was expecting another rejection. However, this home understood many of James's behaviors had been brought on or were exacerbated by the staff at his current home.

They looked beyond the last two years' worth of records and found James's reports to be disheartening.

They had actually evaluated him before he went to the group home several years earlier and felt he was too high functioning in comparison to the other residents at the time, and they did not want him to be bored. They found it hard to believe he was behaving the way the reports from the home described, and they felt bad that people who were supposed to be helping him had treated James that way for so long.

There had been some turnover in the residents since the first evaluation, and they felt James could fit in nicely. Claire was elated and could not wait to tell James the good news. The only thing left was for James to visit his potential new home again at the first opportunity and decide if he wanted to move. At the same time, the staff could decide whether they felt he was a good fit. The new home was also sixteen beds, but the facility was newer and in an area much closer to a big city. This location would not only allow more frequent visits with his parents, but also better vocational opportunities and social activities in the community.

James loved the new home and wanted to move in immediately. By the time I interviewed him, he had been at that home for seven years and counting. He was much happier and had an even better life than at his previous group home. His negative behaviors decreased dramatically. He became more mature, learned new vocational skills, and was one of the top performers at the sheltered workshop he attended five days a week. He was flourishing, and Claire could not be happier with his current home.

People's reactions to James were often times harder on Claire than on him. To add to the stress, she was frustrated by the lack of resources in her area, the hindrance of not knowing who to ask—or what to ask—regarding resources or help of any kind, and mostly her chagrin of not knowing what the key was to help him realize his potential. While there were more resources and answers available every day, Claire and James were among the vanguard of families pioneering a new path for kids with special needs. Even though the Individuals with Disabilities Education Act was passed over a decade before James was born, there were still not many teachers who were fully and properly trained to handle students like James. It was getting better, but there was still such a long way to go.

Her advice to parents was to keep fighting, keep searching for answers for their child, and have high standards and expectations for their child and their child's school environment. She recommended parents seek help for themselves, make sure they are not alone in their fight, and think long term for their child. She also suggested to parents not to spend too much time with people who do not understand or will not take the time to understand, even if those people are family.

If she and James went somewhere, she and her husband had to think through the situation and anticipate how James would handle the environment, the stimulation level, the activity around him, and how much social interaction would be involved. Would he get overstimulated and out of control? Would he be unable to process the situation and shut down? Would the people around him be too much for him to handle? Would they have to wait in line for very long? All these things needed to be considered before almost every activity, and they had to plan how to handle an event if one popped up. She was always checking the environment for items that might get broken or damaged if he were to have a meltdown. She saw the stares, heard the comments, and felt the scorn of those around her when he did not behave appropriately or had a meltdown in a public place.

Family gatherings were harder because of the innate belief that family would always be kind and be our biggest cheerleaders. Claire found out, especially in a big family, it was not the case. Her own mother questioned her parenting abilities many times over the years. When James was younger and started exhibiting some of his behaviors, her mother told her she needed to be stricter and have more structure in his life. Then later, when it was determined he had a disability and cognitive delays, her mother wondered why she was so strict and mean to him.

James's grandmother would have done anything for James to make his life better, and she always had his best interest at heart, but she did not really understand his diagnosis and what it entailed. James's grandmother contacted Ted once for his perspective. Ted explained what he saw at home, that what Claire was doing was necessary and best for James, and basically gave his mother-in-law a better understanding of James.

One of Claire's siblings did not understand, but learned as much as she could and followed Claire's lead on what he needed. Even though she did not always understand, she loved them both and learned everything she could, and became their biggest supporter. Some of Claire's siblings and in-laws were extremely supportive and tried to do what they could to help, but others did not involve themselves for various reasons.

Some questioned things she did, and many were skeptical of her reason for sending him to the in-residence school. A couple of her siblings and in-laws told others in the family they believed she was just sending James away so she could have more time with Ted, and some of the family blamed Ted for James being sent to the in-residence school. Claire did not offer many details and most of the family came to their own conclusions without asking her the real situation. None of her family knew or appreciated how difficult allowing James to go to in-residence school really was for her. Claire frequently said while it was the hardest decision she has ever had to make, she also believed it was the best decision for her son.

In the last few years, Claire did not take James to all the extended family events. Like many with autism spectrum disorder, James subconsciously self-stimulated for most of his life, including humming and gently, methodically rubbing his arms or legs. During one of the last events she took him to, he was once again questioned about why he acted the way he did, and the kids walked away from him. He was in his thirties, and these cousins were only six, but it was just one more in a string of rejections Claire decided not to expose him to.

His chronological age and his size indicated he was an adult, though he behaved more like a ten-year-old. It was difficult for him to feel like he fit in with any group. He wanted to play like the younger kids, but the younger kids did not understand or feel comfortable with him. He did not have the same experiences as the adults, so carrying on a conversation with them was limited. He could play some of the games adults played, but often they were visiting and talking rather than playing, so he was bored. Claire decided it was better for James if he came to only certain family gatherings or if he was specifically invited to something.

One of her brothers invited James to a major league baseball game. Also on the excursion was an adult cousin and another uncle, one of Claire's brothers-in-law. They all had a great time. James's cousin and uncle commented on how amazed they were that James could direct them back to where he lived, what a great time they had with him, and that they would like to do it again sometime.

Jeff's family was worse. While Claire and Jeff were married, it was only James's grandfather and one aunt who even developed a relationship with James. Neither of them kept in contact with James after the divorce.

Claire felt neither she nor her son were good enough for Jeff's mom and other siblings. When she married Jeff, his mother did not allow his sisters to be in the wedding because it was not going to be classy enough. His mother always made them sit on the floor in their formal living room when they visited her, so as not to get the furniture dirty. She never came to visit Claire and Jeff in their first home because it was a mobile home someone else had lived in before them. James and his grandfather were closer, but as James got older, his behaviors were more unpredictable, and his grandfather's health issues led to infrequent visits.

Jeff had never been a good dad to James. When Claire and Jeff divorced, Jeff had visitation rights, but he often did not use them. He repeatedly made promises to James he did not keep. He would tell James he was going to pick him up to do something fun, then not show up. James was getting these calls even after he moved to his first group home. James had his hopes dashed so many times, he was acting out and getting in trouble. He realized he had bad behaviors after a call, when Jeff raised his hopes, then destroyed them again. Eventually he told Claire he no longer could handle having Jeff call, and he wanted it to stop because he was tired of getting in trouble.

She helped him write down all he wanted to say, had him read it over, then they called Jeff. When Jeff answered the phone, Claire told him James had something he wanted to say, and instructed Jeff to listen without interrupting. James read the whole page in one breath, and then handed her the phone. Jeff was unhappy, blamed Claire and said she put James up to it, berated her, and called her names until she hung up the phone. He called James a few more times at the house, but James told the staff not to tell him when his dad called or to tell his dad he was not available to talk.

For a couple of years, rather than talk about his dad, he occasionally asked about his Papa Marc, Jeff's dad. A few years later, James told Claire he wanted to see Papa Marc. Jeff's dad had passed away the year before, and James had not been told, nor was he listed in the obituary as a grandchild. Claire had not been told of his passing until she inquired for James. Claire could see the hurt in James's eyes that he was not told and was unable to say goodbye or pay his respects to his grandfather, but she thought he handled the situation very well. Since that time, James has not queried about his father or his father's family.

By the time of our interview, James had become a well-mannered, generous, and hard-working man who loved his family and friends. He worked full time, had excellent attendance, and was one of the highest performers. His compassion towards his peers was very apparent, and he loved to help others. He liked to be busy, even if it was more work than play. Professional baseball, hockey and NASCAR were his favorite sports, and he attended more baseball games every year than his parents. He also enjoyed history and old television shows, and being able to watch them on YouTube provided hours of entertainment. Helping in the kitchen had become one of his favorite activities, and one of his goals was to learn how to grill. It appeared to Claire that James's true personality has been uncovered.

Claire often did what she had to do to give James the best life he could have, and she recommended all parents do the same. She rearranged her finances, rethought her priorities, changed jobs, figured out work schedules to match his school schedules as much as possible, found alternative day care, changed schools, and did lots of research depending on the need he faced at the time. She accepted her son was never going to be the same as her nieces and nephews and therefore he may not fit in, even in family functions. She accepted that for her son to live a healthy, productive life, he had to go to a school eight hours away from home for eighteen months.

She was vulnerable and accepted that her son's care was put into strangers' hands every day; she trusted those strangers to protect him. She prayed more than she ever thought she would. She cried many nights after he was asleep while they went through some of the stages of trying to get him the help he needed and deserved. Claire mourned James's exposure to the ridicule, rejection, isolation, and outright meanness he endured over the years. She provided the healthiest life she could for her son physically, mentally, behaviorally, and emotionally.

She and James had a conversation when he was in his early thirties in which he told her he wanted to get married and have a family of his own. She wondered how long he would be satisfied without being married? Was marriage a good step for him if he found someone? She worried about his sexual urges and whether he was safe when he acted upon them. Did he really understand all the consequences of having sex—the physical, the emotional and potentially financial? When she was younger and James was little, she thought about someday having grandchildren. However, she realized and mourned the fact that would probably not be a good thing.

She knew she had secured a home for him and taken care of him financially, but who would oversee his care, visit him, and make sure he was okay—especially if she and Ted were no longer alive? Will he ever see his extended family again? How long will he be content in this home? Five years? Ten years? Indefinitely? Will this facility ever have to close its doors, and if so, what happens then? She had concerns for funding the home and funding from Medicare/Medicaid for his medical and living expenses. My own daughter was an adult and these were not things I thought about when it came to her future. Claire and most parents in her situation had the same worries every day.

She advised any parent of a child with special needs to be proactive when it comes to new situations or environments. She encouraged parents to remember they are the experts in their child and to assert their knowledge when necessary. Parents need to let the doctors know when their child is not acting their normal, and do not get caught up in the word "normal." Claire also cautioned parents to not be concerned about specific diagnoses or any stigma related to being "labeled," frequently responding to others that James has "alphabet soup" because of the many acronyms used for his ever-changing diagnoses. Having specific diagnoses often allows the child to qualify for services that could really help, and should be considered a benefit.

She encouraged parents to be bold and brave when it comes to advocating for their child, even when it is uncomfortable or causes loss of relationships. She also stressed parents need to make themselves aware of their child's rights, and be assertive when needed to be sure they are abided by. Claire recalled a suggested bus ride of eighty minutes every morning and evening that was only changed when she reminded them the laws at the time restricted bus rides to one hour.

Parents of a child with negative behaviors should be prepared to try a million behavior plans, modifications, rewards, and consequences, and never give up. She advised parents to do their best with what they know at the time, accept new information if it comes, and then do their best with the new information. Parents should find a tribe to belong to, and not try to do everything on their own. She wished the Internet had been available to her the way it is to parents now. She was very proud of James and all he accomplished throughout the years. She was also proud of the man he became in spite of how the world treated him. She reassured parents that they, too, will get to have proud moments if they persevere with their child.

Claire, Ted, and James, thank you for sharing your story with me. Thank you for letting me be part of your lives. Claire, I appreciated your honesty and willingness to share your raw feelings. It was eye-opening. I have learned from you and James that no one is beyond hope, no one is unteachable or unreachable, and everyone deserves someone in their corner who never gives up on them.

James taught me unconditional love to extended family. He taught me patience, understanding, outside-the-box thinking, and not to judge a book by its cover or even a few pages. He taught me I do not know what the future holds for anyone, and to always look for the impossible answer.

Claire taught me what true perseverance looks like; what real unconditional love looks like in practice; that it is okay to seek advice from those around you even when they are younger; that having faith in and a relationship with God can and will get a person through extremely difficult times and situations; and that no matter how strong a person appears, they always need help and encouragement. I am very proud of you and thankful to have you, Ted, and James in my life.

David

O ne hundred eighty days, just get through this next one hundred eighty days, and this will all be behind you" was the advice Carol gave to her son as he started his eighth-grade year. His seventh-grade year had been the worst, but since fifth grade, the years had been behaviorally difficult.

David was seen as the problem child in his classes because he didn't have perfect behavior. His individualized education plan (IEP) diagnosis was specific learning disability, but the school staff had insisted many times during the previous five years that David had attention deficit disorder (ADD). Carol had taken him to several different doctors who disagreed. David was a kid who just needed a lot of movement built into his day; the school staff weren't always on board to allow it to happen. Carol knew once he left this building behind, things would be better for her son. She had seen her three other children, one of whom also had an IEP, go through high school and be much more accepted and successful there.

Carol's pregnancy, David's birth, and his record of meeting developmental milestones were similar to Carol's other three children. David was friendly, outgoing, and well behaved, and loved to play with his siblings and cousins. However, when David started school at age four, the teacher told Carol and Kevin their son's knowledge was not on par with the other kids'. He did another year of prekindergarten, and the same teacher said he had improved his skills and was ready for kindergarten.

Carol recalled a lot of papers with a lot of red marks in the next couple of years. The teachers felt immaturity and his status as the baby of the family contributed to his difficulties. After each parent conference, Carol left feeling like more should be done to help David. The majority of the meetings were about all the things David couldn't do. The teachers believed he would catch up, and effort more than ability affected his work, and they always gave Carol things to work on with David at home. He struggled with reading from the very beginning. Again, the teachers convinced Carol it was normal because he was a boy.

When David was in second grade, Carol had enough of the red marks and the negative teacher talk at every meeting. She asked for David to be evaluated for special education. By the time the evaluation process was over, it was past Christmas. David was found eligible for special education with the diagnosis of specific learning disability, just like his sister.

Finally, around the third quarter of his second-grade year, David started seeing success in school work. The school staff put accommodations and modifications into place, the special education teacher gave him direct instruction to fill in the gaps from previous years, and David had fewer and fewer red marks on his papers. He started to enjoy school and was eager to go when his mom dropped him off. Second grade ended on a high note.

The very first full day of third grade set the tone for the rest of the year, unfortunately. David's teacher gave him a test without his accommodations, to "get a baseline" of his abilities. Mrs. Hightower knew he had an IEP and was legally bound to receive accommodations and modifications, yet she chose to ignore it. She marked every answer but one wrong and gave it back to him.

All the success he had felt at the end of second grade disappeared. He was devastated, felt stupid, felt it wasn't worth trying anymore, and didn't want to go back to school. Carol told David it had to be a mistake, the teacher forgot or didn't know he was supposed to get accommodations, and she would talk to the teacher to see if he could redo the test. However, the damage had been done. David felt the teacher didn't want to help him succeed, didn't like him, and didn't accept him.

As the year progressed, those feelings only worsened for David. Mrs. Hightower often "forgot" or didn't have time to put the modifications and accommodations in place, and David saw the red marks again all over his papers. When the special education teacher asked her why she wasn't providing the accommodations, she responded, "How do you know when he doesn't need the accommodations anymore if you don't take them away sometimes and see how he does?"

The special education teacher's answer was a question. "Would you take someone's prosthetic leg away and expect them to run as fast as they could with the prosthetic leg?"

Mrs. Hightower said that was comparing apples to oranges. So the special education teacher suggested to her the next time she took a taxi and her driver had glasses, to ask her driver to remove the glasses and see how well he drove. Mrs. Hightower didn't like that answer either, and said to stop using analogies or questions and answer the question directly.

The special education teacher explained the IEP was a legal document that should be adhered to, and that it lists accommodations a team of people decided were best suited for David to show his knowledge. She told Mrs. Hightower to stop taking his accommodations and modifications away on a whim, and at the next IEP meeting, the team (which included her) would discuss whether to keep them in place. Sadly for David, Mrs. Hightower still forgot to provide accommodations occasionally or didn't provide them completely throughout the remainder of the school year.

Early in the year, she accused the special education teacher of giving David the answers to a test because he had scored so well. The special education teacher explained all assessment accommodations had actually been followed correctly, which was why David did so well. Mrs. Hightower was not convinced, and rarely let David go to the special educator to receive his assessment accommodations after that. Mrs. Hightower provided them or found someone else to provide them. She also complained to the administration that the special education teacher wasn't cooperative and often tried to tell her how to do her job. Administrators told the special education teacher to play nice with the other teachers.

In David's annual IEP review, discussions about the accommodations section became tense. While Carol wasn't thrilled with the results of David's year, she said she wanted to keep the accommodations and modifications listed on his IEP. Mrs. Hightower said nothing and the special education teacher asked, "Do you want them as they are listed currently or the ones that were actually followed through with this year?"

Carol realized David's accommodations and modifications had not been followed properly, and she finally had a better understanding of why David hadn't been very successful all year. When she questioned Mrs. Hightower, the teacher walked out of the meeting. The administrator, Mrs. Smith, glared at the special education teacher, looked at Carol, and justified the teacher's actions as forgetting or not having enough time.

In third and fourth grades, teachers often collected students' homework or tests and passed them randomly to other students to grade, or had the students pass their papers a certain direction for a whole-class grading exercise. While this was a timesaver for the teacher, many students hated this activity. Not only did a student see their classmate's score, they had to orally report the score to the teacher so the entire class heard. Imagine shouting out work evaluation results to coworkers or telling everyone about salary amounts, and hear everyone else's. What would that do to office morale or individual self-esteem? Kids who scored low grades were not the only ones affected; kids with high grades were teased, and the expectation to always have a high grade was stressful and anxiety-inducing. David's self-esteem dropped tremendously during the years his peers graded his work.

David started exhibiting some negative behaviors in third grade. He often talked, turned around in his seat, asked the teacher to repeat directions, and got out of his seat when he wasn't supposed to. Those behaviors continued into fourth grade, when again he missed assignments, didn't complete his homework or use his time wisely in class, behaved impulsively, lacked attention, and occasionally was accused of saying inappropriate things to classmates. The teachers in these two grade levels asked Carol if David had ever been tested for ADD; they said he was exhibiting many signs they saw in other students diagnosed with ADD and suggested to Carol that medicine could help with some of his behaviors.

During fourth grade, his grades continued to be average or below average in most subjects, his papers continued to have red marks all over them, and occasionally those teachers forgot to give him his accommodations and modifications. David didn't feel welcome or accepted in fourth grade any more than he had in third. The reports home, the parent conferences, and the phone calls in both of these grades still focused more on the things he couldn't do. Carol felt these teachers expected David to fail or be less successful because of his IEP, and they treated him negatively because of those expectations. She didn't necessarily think the teachers made a conscience effort to treat him poorly; rather, kids with IEPs often had incorrect stigmas attached to them that drove the teachers' thinking, whether they realized it or not.

In fifth grade, he had a teacher who accepted him from day one. She was good with structure, she was good with modifying and adjusting, and Carol felt she really wanted David to succeed. David felt that as well, because he seemed to really want to make her happy and he put forth even more effort than before. Carol could have conversations with this teacher and felt she was heard. The teacher didn't make excuses or blame David.

His fifth-grade teacher was similar to his second-grade teacher in that she knew he could be successful if he just had the right tools. She expected him to be successful, he knew that, and he wanted to be successful again. Carol said having a positive relationship with his teachers usually made a world of difference with David. While David did better and had a good ending to his year, he was still quite down on himself and his abilities. He was nervously hopeful starting sixth grade.

Sixth grade brought a whole new set of challenges. David was small for his age; he was the height of only a third- or fourth-grade student. When he went for his sports physical, they realized he was the same height as he was in third grade. The doctor sent him for testing. Those tests were inconclusive, so they did more tests. In October 2017, test results indicated David's pituitary gland was very small, and instead of being behind the bridge of the nose, it was located to the side.

The pituitary gland is responsible for how the muscles and bones grow. It also controls what hormones are sent and produced in other parts of the body. David's pituitary gland anomaly stunted all of his growth in his brain, muscles, bones, and heart. Doctors determined he needed growth hormone injections six days a week until he was at least nineteen years old. While he was on these growth hormones, he had to be closely monitored to make sure his heart, bones, or brain didn't grow too fast, and he couldn't take any other medicine unless specifically approved by his endocrinologist. He expected to see the endocrinologist at least twice a year for several years.

During sixth grade, David had three different special education teachers. The first one was the same teacher he had the year before. A few months into the school year, she had to be out for medical reasons, so he had a substitute. After a few weeks, the substitute found a full-time job and left, so he had a different substitute until his main teacher returned in the middle of the third quarter. The schedule changed each time a new person arrived.

While David kept up with his schedule, he was often in trouble because he left his general education classes at different times and those teachers weren't aware of all the changes. Sometimes the general education teachers didn't let him leave, and he got into trouble with the special education teacher because he didn't show up on time. The special education teacher's room assignment also changed during the school year, so sometimes he went to the wrong classroom and ended up being late.

Along with his special education teachers changing regularly, David's main general education teacher was out on maternity leave for several months. Carol called me in during his sixth-grade year to help David with schoolwork. David was doing his best to adjust to all the changes, but with all the inconsistencies and his hormone shots, he was still struggling quite a bit.

I had worked with David before, and his attitude now was very different. Though he still didn't really complain about the work, his work ethic was gone, and the cheery child I had worked with before was deeply buried. He wanted to get the work done without necessarily putting in much effort. I encouraged his effort, told him as many true positives as I could, loved him, and accepted him. While it helped a little, he was beaten down so far, it was going to take much more than I could offer him to get him back.

When I worked with David before, he was very open about his feelings and he talked to me when something was bothering him. This time, he didn't want to share his feelings or thoughts about why he was struggling or having a hard time. He gave me memorized answers on how to handle his behaviors in school, and he wouldn't directly open up about things happening there.

In the course of our time together, I was able to get him to reveal that for several years he had put his best effort into his work, but the teachers did not recognize his effort—just the grades on his papers. He felt from most of his teachers that he was a burden and someone they wished was not in their classes. He spent hours on his homework, only to have it mostly marked wrong. He would be innocent in a situation, but because he had been in trouble before, he was in trouble again. David felt no matter what he did at school, it was wrong. There were two occasions where he was guilty by association. He happened to be in the vicinity of some boys up to mischief and because he was nearby, he was blamed too. The other boys told the teacher and Carol both times David had not been involved, yet he was still in trouble. He felt his teachers didn't like him and it was of no use to try anymore.

His behaviors from third and fourth grade began again and he was getting into trouble frequently. The administration was not helpful, according to Carol. She talked to the administration about what was happening in the classrooms, and without hearing her all the way, the administrator defended the teachers, just as had been done when David was in third grade. Mrs. Smith, the head administrator, talked to Carol again about David having ADD or attention deficit hyperactivity disorder (ADHD) and suggested medicine would probably help him with his behaviors; staff also brought it up several times throughout sixth grade. Doctors tested David and found him negative again. The staff didn't believe she had taken him to be tested, or that the doctor tested him correctly.

After David began hormone treatments, Carol asked his endocrinologist about taking medicine if he was diagnosed with ADD or ADHD. The endocrinologist was adamant that David not take anything for those diagnoses, as they would defeat the function of the hormone pills. Carol took the information back to the administration, and they stopped suggesting it. However, they also did nothing to help him deal with any of his behaviors.

Carol asked to have a functional behavioral assessment to see if a behavior intervention plan would be helpful, and she was told because he didn't have an eligibility of emotionally disturbed, he didn't qualify for one. Carol didn't know this answer was incorrect and illegal, and therefore could not pursue the situation. For a child to have a functional behavioral analysis completed, two things have to happen: the child's behavior must impede his learning or the learning of others, and the IEP team must determine if an evaluation is necessary.

Every week, sometimes daily, Carol received notes or phone calls from the general education and special education teachers, telling her how bad her son's behavior was. Carol repeatedly met with teachers, and the teachers told her every time how awful David was in class. When she asked for ideas of how to help, she was told David needed to get his act together. When she asked for positive reinforcers like seating him near well-behaved students or having the teacher be nearer to him during lecture times, they told her it wasn't possible.

In one meeting with one of the substitutes, the sub told her all the things she successfully did with another child, yet never once talked about implementing those things with David. When she left, Carol had a great understanding of what could be done for the other student, but no game plan for David. The teachers expected something to change while they continued doing the same thing they'd always done. Any one of these teachers would say doing the same thing over and over again was not a good way to produce different results, even though they didn't see that was exactly what was happening with David.

Carol encountered only one person at the school who seemed to want to help David be successful. David's only male teacher was young, out of college a couple of years, and willing to try new things and work with Carol. In this class, David was successful behaviorally and academically. When Carol brought up the success to the administration or other teachers, she was told it was because the teacher was also the baseball coach, and David liked him because he was male and he wanted to play baseball.

In reality, David had a positive relationship with this teacher even before he became a teacher at his school. The teacher had been roommates with one of David's older siblings during their college years. He accepted David exactly as he was, trusted Carol wanted them both to succeed, knew Carol and Kevin worked with David at home to help him, and had an open mind about suggestions Carol brought to him.

Unfortunately for David, the teacher was let go at the end of the year. David clearly put forth the most effort for those who believed in him, accepted him, had a relationship with him, and expected positive interactions with him.

Carol tried every day before school to build David up again, made a game plan for his day, and encouraged him to keep a positive attitude and expectation for the day. She believed the only choice she had was to work on his self-esteem, because talking to the school staff or administration was like hitting her head against a brick wall. She felt most of sixth grade was a waste, devoid of anything positive for David. He exited sixth grade feeling dejected, beaten down, and worthless, and disliking school more than he ever had. He was excited for summer, but not to begin another school year.

Carol wanted things to change for David's attitude and the way the teachers saw him. Before seventh grade started, she asked to meet with all seven of his teachers. Three teachers agreed to meet; only two showed. Carol forged ahead, hoping at least these two teachers were willing to listen and work cooperatively.

She explained the hormone injections were working, and at the same time, there were potential side effects. He had four times the normal amount of hormones pumping through his body, so he could quickly become agitated, impulsive, and prone to outbursts. She explained David didn't realize he had reacted a certain way until it was over.

She wasn't asking them to accept his behaviors; she wanted them to understand disciplining him wasn't going to change the behaviors, because they were out of his control. She wanted them to understand certain situations might exacerbate the reactions.

One of the teachers was his English language arts (ELA) teacher and the other was his special education teacher. Throughout the year,

David had positive interactions with his ELA teacher. She was worried about him at the beginning of the year, because his scores showed his reading level was that of a fourth-grader. She worked with him and gave him help, accommodations, and modifications whether or not they were written in his IEP. She found out while his silent reading was below grade level, his oral comprehension was on or above grade level. She shared with Carol that David was more capable than she first believed, and maybe he was scoring low on his assessments because previous teachers had expected it of him.

This teacher invested in David and all of her students to help them succeed in their way. This teacher understood not everyone could complete work in the same amount of time. She allowed all her students to put a mark by their name on their assessments when they turned them in, to discreetly alert her they needed more time. No one else knew which classmates marked their papers.

She shared this method at David's annual review of his IEP at the end of seventh grade. Carol was extremely grateful, but the administrator seemed to be very upset the teacher allowed kids to use this option without an IEP, or with an IEP without that specific accommodation. The teacher explained how different students used the option throughout the year, and in her mind, it seemed a just way to show what they knew. The teacher left when the year was over. David's ELA teacher was his only bright spot during seventh grade. Carol said with a trembling voice that the ELA teacher saved David that year.

David had several of the same teachers for seventh grade as he had in sixth grade. Those teachers had formed their opinions of him during the previous year and had not changed them over the summer. School started in mid-August. By the end of the month, teachers had sent several negative notes home about David's behaviors.

In mid-September, Carol and Kevin went on a short trip out of state to celebrate their twenty-fifth wedding anniversary. On the second night they were out of town, Carol received a phone call from David. True to his natural tendency to rat himself out and never blame others for his problems, he told her he had received a detention for working ahead on one of his tests.

The day he received the detention, David and seven other students went with the special education teacher to her classroom to take an assessment and have it read aloud to them, in accordance with their IEP accommodations. She sat them around a table and read a question to them, reread as necessary, and waited until everyone answered before going on to the next question.

David answered the questions quickly and had to wait for the others to finish. While he waited, he was bored and started talking. The teacher asked him a few times to be quiet, so instead of talking, David moved on to working on the other test questions. When the teacher noticed he was doing that, she sent him to the hall to do the test on his own. A few minutes later, the principal saw him in the hall and told him to come to her office. According to David, Mrs. Smith didn't ask why he was out there; she had him follow her to her office, where she gave him a conduct detention because he was asking too many questions and being defiant.

The next evening, Mrs. Smith called Carol to tell her David had received a detention for being disrespectful to a substitute teacher and wanted to know what Carol was going to do about his getting two detentions in two days. Carol explained she was out of town, would be back the next day, and she would talk to David when she returned.

A little while later, David called and frantically told her about the second conduct detention. He was crying, panicking, and upset. He worried he wasn't going to be allowed to participate in any assemblies, field trips, or end-of-year activities, because if he got another conduct detention, he would lose those privileges. He told her he was scared to go back to school and didn't want to be there anymore. She was several hundred miles away listening to the pain in her child's voice. She couldn't hug him; she couldn't make things better for him; she just had to listen and tell him she would figure things out.

She finally calmed him down enough to tell her what happened. The substitute teacher he had in one of his classes was someone who worked daily at the school and knew all the students. They had been playing a game where they were given an answer and they had to come up with the question. The class had been broken into groups and David's group was tied for first with another group. When the teacher gave the answer, David knew the question. He excitedly raised his hand and jumped up and down. The sub looked at him and said, "I'm not calling on you because your answer will be stupid." David slammed himself down hard into his chair and pushed his desk away from himself, and things fell off his desk. The substitute sent him to the office where he was given his second conduct detention in twenty-four hours.

It was a while before Carol felt David was good enough for them to end their call. When she was off the phone with him, she called a few of his classmates' parents and asked them to check with their children about the events of the day. She didn't give them any details about why she was asking and asked the parents not to tell their child she was asking. As each parent returned her call, their children had all given them the same story David had given her.

As soon as Carol returned from her getaway with Kevin, she rushed to the school to talk with Mrs. Smith about the prior two days' events. When she shared her information, Mrs. Smith attributed their versions to the notion they were David's friends and were just trying to help him get out of trouble. To further prove her point, Mrs. Smith called David down to her office. She stood up behind her desk, raised her voice, accused him of lying to his mother and withholding information, and badgered him to tell his mom the whole true story.

Carol came unglued at that point. She said she told, probably yelled, at the administrator to stop badgering her son, that the school staff were wrong, and the substitute needed to apologize to David for calling him stupid. Mrs. Smith told Carol to calm down or she would call the police, and told David to go back to class. Carol wouldn't calm down and said David was not going back to class after Mrs. Smith berated him in such a way. Carol told her she wasn't leaving until the situation was resolved, and if the administrator felt threatened, she could have someone else join them.

Since Carol would not leave and would not allow David to leave, the principal left her office. David and Carol stayed in the office for about twenty minutes crying and calming down. Mrs. Smith did not call the police and did not call another person into the meeting. Although it was agreed upon that David wouldn't have to serve the detention, it remained on his record, and the substitute never had to apologize for his comment.

From that point forward, Mrs. Smith seemed to always be in David's business. If she heard from one of the teachers David had a missing assignment or had not been perfectly behaved during a class, she was talking to him, taking away his lunch recess, and giving him lunch detentions. The teacher in whose classroom the event happened and the substitute from that day also seemed to watch to catch him in some wrongdoing or did things to make him fail. He didn't get any more conduct detentions, so he was allowed to participate in end-of-year activities and field trips, but the scrutiny was relentless. David often came home and reported certain teachers and Mrs. Smith called him out of line or out of class and asked if he was behaving. Then they reminded him if he wasn't behaving, he would immediately be in the principal's office for the remainder of the day.

David's attitude worsened; after that incident, he did not want to go to school. Instead of just worrying that some adults seemed out to get him, he had proof. He had anxiety starting because he had to work with the substitute, after she put him down in front of the class. Since the principal could no longer try to blame David's behaviors on ADD/ADHD, she insisted David needed counseling. The school had a counselor who was in the building once a week, but her schedule never synched with David's so she could see him.

Carol paid a private counselor to work with David. Depending on how the principal and the staff worded their demands regarding assessment, medication, and counseling, they may have acted illegally again. The law stated school staff could suggest getting help, but because they were not usually trained in medicine or psychology, staff members could neither diagnose medical conditions nor demand the family seek care unless the school planned to pay for the service.

His social studies teacher in seventh grade used a brand-new curriculum. This new curriculum was much more driven by the students' ability to independently work and think through scenarios. Many nights, David, Carol, Kevin, and one of David's sisters tried to understand what the homework was asking. Kevin read and reread the chapter looking for answers; David's sister, who was doing online courses for college, tried to help find answers; and no one was successful.

Earlier in the year, Carol sent notes to the teacher asking for help on certain questions. When David turned in his work with those questions unanswered, the teacher told him it was incomplete and counted as a missing assignment or a zero. When Carol confronted the teacher about it, she said she never received or saw any notes asking for help.

Within the first few months of school, David had eight missing assignments and three homework detentions. When the school called to tell her about David's fourth homework detention, she responded, "That's fine, at least I know where he'll be after school."

Carol asked again for David to be moved away from a certain group of kids and put with higher-achieving students. They told her he couldn't be moved because he was getting an extra service by being with the lower-achieving group, and it was to his benefit to stay there.

As the year progressed and David continued to get low grades, missing assignments, and no extra help from the teachers, Carol told David to just write something in response to the questions they didn't understand. At least then it was just counted wrong and not as a missing assignment. Carol had reached the end of her rope trying to please the teachers. At one point during his seventh-grade year she told David, "They can't flunk you, just do what you want."

Carol called the special education district for her area and begged them to help her. She explained everything that had happened. She had several phone calls with the district office before an unofficial IEP meeting was called, a few weeks before Christmas break. The district psychologist, David's special education teacher, his homeroom teacher, and Carol met to discuss how to help David. The psychologist told the teachers that David needed to experience success and be positively reinforced for everything he was doing correctly. The team developed a plan, and Carol left the meeting feeling as if finally she had been heard, and David was going to get the help he needed.

A couple of weeks after Christmas break, Carol had not heard anything regarding how the plan was going, so she emailed the special education teacher. The teacher told her the plan had not been implemented, because the teachers really didn't believe it would work, nor did they have the time to implement it and keep the data. The teacher also hinted she was overwhelmed with students and trying to provide all they needed according to their IEPs. Since the meeting had not been official, the plan had not been written down in his IEP, and therefore the school could not be held accountable.

Carol was beside herself. She didn't know what else to do. No one was holding the teachers or the school accountable for their actions, yet David was always in trouble for his actions.

Every day from then to the end of the school year, both she and David went into survival mode. She tried to repair and rebuild his heart and mind on the way to school and cried all the way home. She felt like she was sending her son to the jungle every day and prayed while he was there that he survived. She worried all day about what was happening. How were things going? Was he having a hard time? Was he being given his accommodations and modifications? Was he being isolated again? She couldn't protect her son while he was in school. She couldn't explain to him that he was still loved, even though the teachers treated him poorly. She couldn't build him up with the belief he was a good person who sometimes had bad behaviors. She had to trust someone in the building had his back.

They found out in February Mrs. Smith, the principal who had given him such a difficult time for so many years, was retiring at the end of the school year. It was the hope he needed to make it to the end of the year. Carol marveled at David's ability to be kind to this person who had been so hard on him for so long. Every time he saw her, he greeted her with a smile and a wave. Sometimes he held the door open for her. He gave her the benefit of the doubt that she was going to treat him well. He seemed to forgive all her transgressions immediately upon learning she was retiring. It was just another example of David's good-hearted nature.

Carol described a time when the band teacher called to tell her how kind David had been to him. The teacher found out right before school started that one of his best friends had died. He told David's class he hoped they would give him a little grace because of his news. David went to him during a time the class was quietly working, put his hand on his teacher's shoulder, and said, "I'm sorry you lost your friend; that must really hurt."

David survived the remainder of his seventh-grade year, and at the time of his interview was doing well in eighth grade. He had a new principal and new teachers, and he knew it was his last year in the building. He decided he was going to finish on a positive note at this school.

Carol said the stress of David's struggles had a negative effect on her marriage. Many nights she had to work late and Kevin was left to help David with homework. The next morning she often helped David finish. Kevin had a more aggressive approach he wanted to try with the school over the years, while Carol tried to maintain a positive relationship with school personnel. They often fought over how to deal with all the situations.

Carol eventually accepted Kevin's more aggressive attitude toward the school, and she was no longer worried about maintaining a good relationship. When there was an issue with the staff's behavior and attitude toward David, she didn't back down. She was willing to call a meeting every month, if necessary, to protect her son and give him the education he deserved. She and David knew his high school years would be much better.

Carol advised other parents of kids with special needs to keep believing in their child, to keep building them up when the world tries to knock them down, and to try to maintain good relationships—but know when you need to stand your ground.

If she could go back in time and make it so he didn't have a specific learning disability, she absolutely would. She believed David would still be the same person, because her parenting style would have been the same. She understood all children have difficult times in their lives and felt David would have experienced other things that would have taught him compassion and how to see another person's perspective.

She said, "Every hard time is a learning experience; it's just awful it has to come at the expense of a child. Every child should respect themselves and return respect to others. Every child should have someone to look up to, something to look forward to, and something to chase as a dream. Who my child will become is not defined by the grades he earned in school. There are more important lessons to be learned, like patience, kindness, understanding, gratefulness, security, trust, belief, and many more that do not get graded."

Thank you, David and Carol, for sharing your story with me. You taught me how to think outside the box and demonstrated to me that behaviors are communication. Thank you for teaching me unconditional love, patience, the art of putting others first, and how to persevere through awful times and still maintain a good attitude through most of it. Thank you for showing forgiveness in action, giving people the benefit of the doubt, facing fears, and having faith in people to do the right thing. Thank you, Carol, for showing me how to stand in my child's corner and always have their back.

Section III

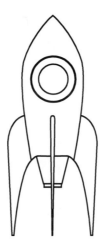

Rose

Dan and Maryanne were in the military and in their mid-thirties when they found each other—again. They had been stationed together before, but had not really known each other. When they each got on the transport plane to Korea, they had no idea the other was on the same flight nor did they expect the change that was about to happen in their lives.

They were mostly inseparable during their six months in Korea. When the ends of their assignments were drawing near, Maryanne said to Dan they should get married. They were married during a whirlwind trip to the United States so their children could be present at the ceremony. Maryanne already had one daughter, whom Dan adopted as soon as possible, and Dan already had two girls, but Maryanne and Dan knew right away they wanted to have a child together. A little over seven months after they married, they found out Maryanne was pregnant.

By that time, they had both been stationed stateside, but still not near family. Because Maryanne was thirty-six, the doctors considered her of advanced maternal age and at higher risk of having a baby with chromosomal problems. They wanted to test her baby for defects or abnormalities. When the doctor called Maryanne and Dan into the office to discuss the results of her amniocentesis and triple screen test, she immediately knew the results were not normal. The doctor told Maryanne and Dan when Maryanne was five months pregnant that their baby was a girl and would most likely be born with Down syndrome.

Down syndrome is the result of extra copies of some or all of chromosome 21. It causes cognitive delays, low muscle tone, distinguishing facial and physical characteristics, and an increased risk of medical conditions including gastroesophageal reflux, underactive thyroid, respiratory and hearing difficulties, and congenital heart defects.

The doctor told Maryanne and Dan that because they found out early, they could opt to end the pregnancy. They were very upset at the thought and immediately told the doctor abortion was not an option for them. Dan felt the doctor was pushing to end the pregnancy, because she kept bringing it up through Maryanne's second trimester, saying the law required her to tell them. Dan was still angry about those appointments and the doctor more than 19 years later.

Maryanne had knowledge of Down syndrome (DS) and understood the potential for heart defects, so they chose to go to a specialty hospital off base where they had ultrasounds done on the baby's heart. Her heart was perfectly healthy according to the tests. The remainder of the pregnancy went very well for Maryanne, physically. She had her moments of being sad and fearful of the unknown. She wondered if the baby would need constant care. Likewise, she pondered whether her daughter would ever walk and talk, or would she need to be carried or use a wheelchair. She felt God would not give her more than she could handle, so all would be fine.

Dan, on the other hand, did not know anyone with special needs and was very scared. He was scared he would not be a good dad, his child would have all kinds of medical issues, and he would not know how to treat her or what to do for her. Dan began researching online and in books, and asking doctors and anyone else he could think of who had knowledge of DS. Most of those sources talked of worst-case scenarios, so Dan's fears only became stronger. He wished he had found something, anything, that gave him hope or focused more on the positives of having a child with Down syndrome. He agreed to participate in interviews for this book partly because he wanted to provide hope and encouragement to other parents.

He told me about a time shortly after he and Maryanne found out about the diagnosis. They were sitting on the steps outside their house and he began to bawl. He was "freaking frightened" of the unknown and whether he would live up to being a good dad. Because Maryanne was so amazingly strong and confident that everything was going to be okay, his fears were alleviated a little. She believed the doctors when the test results showed no heart defects or problems. Dan held onto his doubts, but he also knew they would face whatever challenges lay before them as a team, and that was of some comfort to him.

They told the family members while Maryanne was still pregnant that the baby would be born with Down syndrome. Everyone was very supportive, but many people told them they were sorry. Maryanne's responses were cordial, but in her head, she was thinking, "It's not a death sentence or the end of the world—why are they saying they are sorry?"

Maryanne's dad became very quiet when she told him. He also had never had experience with someone with special needs and did not know what to expect, or whether it posed any potential health issues for his daughter or his granddaughter. While he was worried, he was very supportive and would provide her anything she needed. Maryanne said the minute her dad met Rose, he was "butta" (melted butter), and she never worried again.

Dan's two daughters, thirteen and fifteen years old, lived in another state with their mother when Maryanne was pregnant, but they were understanding and excited to have a new sister. Maryanne's daughter, Marie, was six and really did not understand what Down syndrome was, but was also excited to have a sister on the way.

Maryanne was scheduled for a cesarean section on October 22. Dan remembered there were two full teams of medical professionals waiting for them: one for Maryanne, and one for the baby. Maryanne recalled the delivery process as being unremarkable. Her labor and delivery nurse, Randy, was amazing, and the entire team knew the baby would be born with Down syndrome, so they were prepared. Randy was very informative throughout her cesarean section, letting her know what was happening (and how and why), and what she might feel or not feel.

Dan was awed by how strong and amazing Maryanne was throughout the C-section. She was awake, but numb in the area of the incision, and a curtain blocked her view. Dan sat up by her head and saw some of the procedure. He recalled how the doctors were moving her organs around to reach the baby, how they lifted Maryanne up a couple of different times to get her in the right position and to get to the baby, and how Maryanne just took it all in stride. Dan's memory was of being overwhelmed by all the doctors and Maryanne's strength. Once Rose was born, the second team of doctors took her for immediate examination. Maryanne was not able to touch or hold her until the next day.

Randy cared for Rose in the nursery and shared with Maryanne that Rose had markers of DS, confirming what they had been told in her pregnancy. Rose's neck was short, she had a crease across her palm, her tongue was large, and she had small ears. He told Dan to come with him. Dan was torn because he wanted to be with Maryanne, but also with his newborn. Maryanne, in her strength, pushed him to go with Rose; she would be fine, and Rose needed him more than she did at the moment.

After witnessing the complex delivery and seeing all the blood during the surgery, his nerves were overwhelmed. As he looked at his little girl, he almost fainted when he stood up. Randy was quick to help him. Dan said he felt like such a fool and did not want Randy to help him; he wanted Randy to make sure Rose was okay. Randy told him Rose was doing okay and Dan's reaction to everything was not unique. This helped Dan relax a little, and he followed Randy's orders. For the next seven hours, Randy did not leave Rose's or Dan's side.

Randy and the rest of Rose's medical team took Rose to the neonatal intensive care unit (NICU), where she remained for two days. Once they arrived in the NICU, Randy asked Dan if he wanted to touch Rose. He answered quickly with an emphatic "yes," and Randy allowed Dan to wrap his arms around Rose while she was in the incubator. It was only for a few seconds, but Dan said it was the most wonderful feeling. Randy had Dan sit next to the incubator, put Dan's hand on Rose's stomach, and told him to keep it there as a calming factor for both Dan and Rose. As Dan remembered seeing Rose in the NICU, he began to cry at the memory of all the tubes, IVs, face masks, and tests they performed on her that day. He said it was just dreadful.

Randy told Dan everything they were doing was standard for when a child was born with DS. Every test they performed came back with favorable results: bloodwork was good, her heart was complete and working as it should, and her Apgar score was good. Little by little, Dan began to relax. It was strenuous and frightening to see his newborn going through all the testing, but she did great. Dan did not realize at the time that Rose gave him a glimpse into the strength she possessed to handle things. She needed to be on oxygen for forty-eight hours because her blood oxygen saturation levels were low, but everything else was normal.

The nurses gave Maryanne updates throughout the day to afford Dan more time with Rose. Since Maryanne had not yet been allowed to see or hold Rose, as soon as Maryanne was awake the next day, she was determined to go see her daughter. Maryanne tried to walk to the NICU and made it about halfway there; a nearby nurse saw her before she passed out. Maryanne was given a wheelchair and taken to see Rose. By then, the only thing Rose had on her was the oxygen tubing.

Maryanne was only allowed to look at first. She was still recovering from a major surgery, and after her attempt to walk, they had to make sure she was stable enough before letting her hold Rose. Maryanne held her briefly several times that day. As the day progressed, Rose was weaned off the oxygen and moved to a regular room. They had one last issue they needed to address before they could go home. When Rose ate, she stopped breathing. It seemed she was just so hungry, she would forget to stop for breath. The medical team worked with her and Maryanne, figured out a solution, and they were released together when Rose was three days old.

When Maryanne and Dan took Rose for her well-baby checkup a week later, they were told Rose's pulse oxygen levels were extremely low, and they had to send her by ambulance to a children's hospital. Before the ambulance arrived, it was necessary to insert an intravenous (IV) line into Rose so they could begin to get oxygen into her system. Unfortunately, the medical staff were not able to insert the IV, and after several attempts elsewhere on Rose's body, they finally had to put it in her head. It was the worst experience of Maryanne's life watching the medical staff work to get the IV in on Rose while she was screaming.

Maryanne was permitted to ride in the ambulance with Rose and see things were okay. She wondered if this was what their lives would be like from now on. Dan drove himself behind the ambulance and wondered what was going on inside. While the drive was only about thirty minutes, to Dan it felt like hours. All the worries, fears, questions, negative thoughts, and more came flooding at him while he was driving. Every time he pushed one negative thought out of his head, another popped up. Being alone, for Dan, was the worst thing at that moment. He braced himself for the worst possible outcomes, because he was certain now that all the doctors and tests were wrong.

The doctors at the children's hospital immediately took her to the emergency room and began doing their own tests. The results were nowhere near what they had been at the previous doctor's office; in fact, they were within normal limits, which was very confusing to the medical team. They sent Rose to a room for observation and more testing later. They repeated the tests the next day, and the results were normal again. Eventually the doctor told Maryanne and Dan there was no way the levels were what the previous doctors said they had been. Her levels were normal at the children's hospital, and not enough time had elapsed from the doctor's office for it to have happened, even with the IV.

There was a lot going on in the emergency room and their subsequent stay in the hospital, but Maryanne was not scared. She looked at it as a learning experience. She learned how to stay calm when monitors were beeping, what to look for if Rose was really in distress, and what all the numbers, acronyms, and medical jargon meant. Maryanne realized in that episode that from then on, she and Dan needed to question things, ask for second opinions, and be Rose's advocates.

While Dan was immensely relieved Rose was okay, he still worried all the initial test results were wrong. Several years passed before he could really believe Rose was truly healthy. She had either acid reflux or a problem with gagging due to the size of her tongue for a while, but once her mouth caught up with the size of her tongue, food stayed down much better.

The only other major medical issues Rose has had in her lifetime were multiple sore throats and rounds of tonsillitis, and eventually, surgical removal of her tonsils and adenoids. Maryanne recalled sitting at the dinner table a few days before Rose's surgery, and big sister Marie was crying buckets because she was upset her baby sister was in so much pain. Rose could not even swallow mashed potatoes because it hurt so badly. Rose was a trooper throughout the meal, though. She sat slowly eating her mashed potatoes, grimacing in pain every time she had to swallow, and a little tear eventually trickled down her cheek.

Somehow, though, amidst all the pain, Rose managed to swallow a small magnetic metal ball the day before surgery. The ball had to be out of her system for the surgery to proceed; an X-ray performed before surgery showed all was clear. Rose did great with the surgery and recovery. Over the years, Rose has had only colds or a stuffy nose, and she was very good about telling Maryanne and Dan when she needs treatment for those.

Outside of those little things, Rose has led a very healthy life. Maryanne remarked how wonderful their experiences with the military doctors have been throughout the years. The doctors understood Maryanne and Dan were with Rose all the time and knew their daughter very well, so when they brought her in and said something was wrong, the doctors respected them, listened to them, and found them to be right. Rose had her first pediatrician for five years and the second one, whom she adored, for ten years. Besides her pediatrician, Rose saw an endocrinologist yearly for several years; an eye doctor once a year; and an ear, nose, and throat doctor when she had her tonsils removed.

Dan and Maryanne's lives were going through a lot of adjustments at the time Rose was born. First, they were still newlyweds. Second, Dan's daughter came to live with them. She was causing a lot of difficulty for her mother. Her mother realized Maryanne and Dan created a more stable environment and hoped Dan would be able to help their daughter make wiser decisions. They had a newborn with special needs, and there were no family around to offer support. Dan commended Maryanne and himself for getting through that time so beautifully. They really had to depend on each other for support and truly be a team. It was not always easy, but Dan felt they were stronger as a family because of it.

They contacted therapists right after Rose was born, and therapy started within weeks. These therapists came to Maryanne and Dan's home a few times a week. Rose received occupational therapy, speech therapy, and physical therapy. When she was about eighteen months old, the physical therapist told Maryanne that Rose would never walk on her own and they should consider getting her a walker. Maryanne refused to accept that information and asked the therapist to never come back. They found a new therapist, and two days before Rose's second birthday, she was a flower girl in her aunt's wedding. She very confidently walked down the aisle all by herself, even though the other, older, flower girls refused to walk.

When Rose was between nine and eighteen months old, she was easily frustrated because she could not communicate. The speech therapist taught her some sign language. Once Rose mastered the signs for more, help, and eat, and could communicate her wants so people around her understood, the frustration went way down. Rose continued these therapies for several years in her home. When she began public education, her therapies smoothly transitioned from the home therapists to the school. Rose received physical and occupational therapy until the fourth grade and continued in high school with speech therapy.

Marie and Rose were typical siblings, loving on each other one minute and fussing at each other the next. Dan and Maryanne had not treated Rose as a child with a disability; they treated her as a child. They did all the same things with her, with some adjustments, that they had done with Marie when she was little. They went on weekend camping trips; Dan took Marie on Thursday and set up the camp site, then Maryanne and Rose joined them on Friday. They brought a big round bathtub for Rose and her crib, but nothing else different than the other campers. Marie was a dancer and a cheerleader throughout elementary and middle school. Rose was her biggest fan and always the person Marie went to first to see if she had done a good job.

Marie was unaware Rose had a disability or was different from other children her age. Even though she had been told when Rose was born that her sister had a disability, Marie did not see it. Maryanne had explained there might be things Rose received or needed that Marie would not, but Marie was never hurt or felt she was missing out on anything. To Marie, Rose was normal and perfect.

The first time she realized Rose was not "normal" in other's eyes was when Rose attended elementary school and was not put in the general education class. Marie was ten or eleven years old and in fifth grade when Rose joined the special education preschool class at the same school. It did not change Marie's mind about her sister; she continued to treat her exactly the same. She began to notice others treated her not necessarily in a bad way, but differently. Maryanne recalled the time when Marie was seventeen and said something to someone about the way they treated her baby sister. It was nothing traumatizing for Rose, but hurtful for Marie to hear.

Maryanne and Dan coordinated their work schedules as much as possible so Rose did not have to be without both of them for long periods of the day. Maryanne worked earlier hours and Dan worked later in the day. Maryanne set out Rose's clothes the night before. Rose helped pick out her shoes and socks if she wanted to. Together, they put Rose to bed around eight to eight thirty in the evening.

Dan woke Rose up and helped her get ready for school. Dressing usually took about twenty to thirty minutes and bathroom activities took another twenty to thirty. Rose was capable of doing all the activities, with supervision, from about age four. She usually ate breakfast at the day care. While he enjoyed this time with Rose, he often found himself frustrated with the pace at which she got ready.

Many times, when she was finally ready, and Dan thought they were able to leave, Rose stopped in the hallway at a shelf with a ceramic bowl. Sometimes she just looked at the bowl and moved on, other times she had to move the bowl, and still other times she had to turn it. This often took several minutes, and Dan told Rose repeatedly they needed to go, or he nudged her in the direction of the car. Dan realized later his urging only delayed the process.

On the days Rose was left alone to do what she needed to do with the bowl, the mornings were much easier, and she was much happier and more cooperative. On the days when she did not get to do what she needed to, she was crabby for hours and uncooperative for Dan. Rose never explained why she needed those moments, but Dan eventually realized if he just let her do what she needed to do with the bowl, the morning routine finished more smoothly and quickly.

The wording here was significant: Rose needed time with the bowl. While none of us understood her need, she had a reason. Sometimes because we do not share a need, or it is not something that makes sense to us, we think it is wrong. That is not always the case. Some kids have to get their hair just right and spend time making it just so; Rose had to spend time with the bowl. Eventually, Rose grew out of the need, but even if she had not, it would have been okay.

Regardless of circumstance, human beings have this in common—we want to be heard and be validated. In the moment when Dan realized spending time with the ceramic bowl was an important need to Rose, he heard her and validated her. Dan regretted it took him so long to realize she needed the time. He wished there had been some literature or information on the Internet that cross-referenced other disability traits, and then maybe he would have realized sooner.

Rose's internal clock moved to a different beat than most people's. She had a very laid-back personality and performed tasks when she was developmentally ready according to her individual timing. Rose learned to do many things her parents and I were told she would never do. For example, even though Maryanne picked out Rose's clothing until she was in high school, she started dressing herself completely without supervision at the age of seven; though she didn't yet cut her own meat at the dinner table, she graduated from using a sippy cup when she was seven or eight. Maryanne worried about potty training and was sometimes disappointed it was taking so long. Rose's doctor told Maryanne that Rose would do it when she was ready.

Dan and Maryanne both told the funny story of "The Poop Slide," a universally recognizable story of parenthood. When Rose was about eighteen months old, Dan and his daughter Sara were with Rose at home when she had the kind of very runny, poopy diaper that was so full it was coming out the sides before anyone realized how bad it was. Dan was standing near their kitchen counter when he figured out what was happening. He scooped her up and told Sara to get paper towels because there were no baby wipes nearby. After she gave him the paper towels, he instructed her to go get the baby wipes from Rose's room. He laid her down on the counter, pulled the tape off of the diaper, and there was poop everywhere. He wanted to get her out of the mess, so he gently picked her up and managed to avoid getting anything on himself. He was just starting to wipe her off with the paper towels when he lost his grip on her back. Down his arm she slid, making a poop slide from his wrist to his elbow. Sara returned with the baby wipes just in time to see Rose sliding down her father's arm.

She had been my student for several years, and one of the many things we did to help the process was encourage her with a "Good job, Rose," every time she urinated on the potty. One day, when Rose was around eight, my sixty-year-old paraprofessional took her to the bathroom. Rose was on the toilet for an extended period of time, and the paraprofessional needed to use the restroom too. She thought it was okay if she quickly used the stall next to Rose.

When Rose heard liquids splash, she said, "Good job, Miss Joan." The paraprofessional was gracious and thanked Rose for her kind words, and we got a good chuckle out of the story. Maryanne said Rose often did the same thing with her or Sara. I wonder, how many adults did Rose congratulate on their potty skills? This was the only area Maryanne wished she had known more about before it all began, so she could have been more diligent helping Rose develop this skill. Rose was fully potty-trained at age ten.

Maryanne and Dan could not have been happier with Rose's elementary school experience. Many times over the years, Maryanne heard people with children with special needs complain about their children's school setting. She always told them about her great experience and how supportive Rose's school was to their special-needs population.

Rose was part of a group of kids who were known throughout the school for good reasons. She was included in general education classes when appropriate and included in all sorts of school activities with her general education peers. I taught her academic classes when it was no longer appropriate for her to be taught by the general education teachers.

Every teacher and almost every student in the building knew her name through the years. Staff, faculty, administration, and students loved her. Rose developed a very outgoing, happy personality by the time she was in her late primary grades. She still had her moments, and sometimes days, of being crabby, but even then, she was personable and cooperative most of the time.

When she was in eighth grade, there was an instance when she did not communicate verbally (though her body language expressed a lot), she refused to get up off the floor and to work, and kept turning away every time someone tried to talk to her. None of the usual things we did were working.

I went to our only male teacher in our hallway, who was also dean of students for the school, and asked him if he could talk with her. I explained I needed him to treat her as he would any other student who had exhibited those behaviors, and he said he would try. When I told her he wanted to talk to her in the hallway, she listened and went to him.

He had a stern voice with her, told her she needed to listen to her teachers, and had her promise him she would go back in the room and cooperate. She did, and the remainder of our day was good. Later, the teacher told me it was one of the most difficult discipline situations he ever had to undertake. He was a high school baseball coach and could discipline those big guys with no problem, but disciplining her almost broke his heart.

Rose worked, moved, and processed at her own pace. When she was upset, she withdrew, did not talk, and tried not to interact with anyone around her. Usually, when she was having a rough day, we could convince her to talk about what she was feeling. From those conversations we could figure out what was causing her rough day.

Sometimes, something had happened at home (think ceramic bowl) or at day care before she came to school. If she talked to us and finished processing whatever it was, she was fine and did her work. Sometimes, she had not slept well the night before, or she was not feeling well. In those cases, if it was severe enough, we would let her lay down for fifteen or twenty minutes.

I realized early on with Rose that I could either take a small amount of time with her and help her through whatever it was, or I could take a large amount of time trying to force her to do what I wanted her to do. Since I figured this out in my first one or two years with her, the remainder of my years with her were pretty smooth.

Rose moved at her own pace even in pressing situations. Dan shared a story from Rose's adulthood about her lack of urgency. They were at an amusement park when a thunderstorm hit, so the park had to close. Dan and Rose were at the farthest point away from the entrance when the rain started. Dan tried to hurry Rose along, but Rose continued to move at her slow pace. By the time they reached the front gate, they were soaked, and Rose did not care at all. Through the years, her parents and teachers tried to find keys to unlock a faster pace consistently, to no avail. We all just got used to Rose's pace as we would have with someone who was always on the go.

Some readers might think I did not discipline Rose or I was too soft on her, based on my actions. That would be very far from the truth. Think about yourself when you had a bad night's sleep, you argued with someone before you arrive at work, or you were not feeling well. What do you do? You talk about it, you take steps to feel better, and you work out the issue in your head.

Rose was considered nonverbal and had a much below-average intelligence quotient (IQ). She did not know what was bothering her, or could not express her feelings through typical language, so she behaved inappropriately. In our conversations, she did not just come out and say, "I'm tired." We figured it out through a series of questions and addressed the root cause. She was then held accountable for whatever work she had missed or disruption she had caused. We taught her that her feelings were valid, and her actions had consequences, positive or negative. Maryanne, Dan, and I were in complete agreement about this system and they implemented it at home as well.

Dan and I had many talks over the years. He had such a soft heart toward Rose. It was difficult for him to tell her no or see her unhappy, so he often let her get away with things. Sometimes he asked my advice, and sometimes I offered it unsolicited, but he was always willing to heed my advice. Then we began implementing my Time for Time system at school and though it was tough for him, he agreed to implement it with her at home. He saw the benefit quickly and continued to hold her accountable to a higher standard of behavior. He said their relationship actually improved, and he truly felt like he was finally able to claim "good dad" status.

Dan, Maryanne, and I had a wonderful relationship from the very beginning. They described how invaluable it was that we communicated via email, a mode that worked well for them and helped involve them when needed. They knew they could trust me to keep them updated and did not worry about Rose while she was under my care because of our communication system. Dan felt the relationship we had made us all better, and in turn made things better for Rose and her success.

Near the end of my second year with Rose, I asked Dan and Maryanne if my family and I could take Rose to a local Buddy Walk. My daughter and Rose were just a few weeks apart in age, so I thought it would be perfect for them to get to know each other.

The Buddy Walk was a fundraising event sponsored by the National Down Syndrome Society to raise awareness of and appreciation for Down syndrome. Participating local agencies received some funding from the event, and the rest of the proceeds went to the national organization. This event was only in its second year and was happening in a place I was very familiar with.

Dan and Maryanne agreed she could come with us, but when the day arrived and we picked Rose up, they were acting a little differently. I went over the details of where we would be and how long I thought we would be gone, and I gave them a number to call me if necessary. They still seemed a little nervous. As Dan buckled Rose into our vehicle, Dan said to me, "You know, you are the first person we have ever trusted to take Rose away from us."

I replied, "You mean the first person outside of family?"

He said, "No. Ever."

Rose was eight. Several times in my daughter's eight years, she went to friends' houses and had sleepovers with friends and family members, and different babysitters had cared for her. The tone of his voice, the look on his face, and his words left me speechless and

I suddenly felt a great weight on my shoulders. I had never thought about this event from their perspective.

Suddenly, my carefree attitude was gone. The enormity of the day from Dan and Maryanne's perspective became painfully real. I realized the thoughts they must have had in deciding to let us take her. The amount of trust and faith they had to have in me to protect their child, treat her in an honest fashion, drive cautiously, and bring her back safely, was almost too much. I felt as though I had just been given charge of every rare and precious jewel in the world, and in their minds, I had been. While all parents have to believe in the adults with whom they entrust their child, this level of trust was so far beyond that in my mind, it is difficult to describe. Thinking of how monumental that moment was for all of us increased my tension and made my blood run cold and my palms sweat.

Maryanne said, "You want to trust that people have your child's best interest at heart, but the reality is there are bad people in the world. Rose cannot tell me if something is wrong." Rose's parents had to push aside their fears of car accidents during our half-hour drive to the event. They had to push aside fears of not seeing their daughter again. They had to fight off the fear of someone hurting their nonverbal daughter physically, sexually, or emotionally; people with DS were statistically three times as likely to be abused. They did not really know my husband, so they had to trust my judgement that he was a good guy and a safe driver. Every negative thing in the world that could happen to a child ran through their heads, and they still had an enormous amount of faith and trust in me to let her go with my family that day. It still gives me chills.

When Dan and Maryanne walked back into their house after we left, they did not know what to do with themselves. Outside of the birth, it was the scariest thing they had done when it came to Rose. For more than eight years, they had not been alone with just each other and had not been in their house without Rose. Maryanne walked around inside the house, and Dan walked around the outside, each a bit numb at first, trying to figure out what to do. Maryanne felt empty and weird. They went through the motions of their day, but could not really tell me what they did until Rose returned home. She was the center of their world and suddenly the center was gone.

Throughout the day, they looked repeatedly at the time and wondered what she was doing, how things were going, and if it was almost time for her to be back. When we pulled into the driveway, Dan was sitting on the tailgate of his truck. The biggest smile came across his face, and I think I breathed for the first time since we picked her up. Dan had been anxiously waiting there for at least thirty minutes. Maryanne was out the door in a heartbeat when she heard the vehicle in the driveway. Two other times, my family took Rose somewhere. Each time was a little less stressful than the time before, but it was never easy for any of us.

We all have to trust strangers to some extent, but there was one main issue of trust Maryanne and Dan had to worry about more when it came to Rose. Rose started her menstrual cycle when she was twelve. She quickly became very regular, which was good for planning the necessary supplies at school and helping her be prepared.

Several years after starting her cycle and being extremely regular with her start days, she was late by two weeks. Maryanne tried not to panic and tried to think the best of every male in Rose's circle, but the thoughts still came. Rose was acting no differently, and when Maryanne questioned her if anything out of the ordinary had happened, Rose did not tell her anything unusual. She wondered if Rose would even know to tell her if something had happened—or what if someone had told her not to tell? Maryanne was so relieved when Rose's cycle started that month.

In blessed addition to the stressors of keeping Rose safe, Dan and Maryanne had many fond memories of Rose's elementary years; Maryanne refers to the years spanning fourth through eighth grades as her fondest. In fourth and fifth grades, Rose joined a dance team outside of school and performed beautifully in two recitals. She was a cheerleader for the boys' school basketball team in seventh and eighth grades.

In seventh grade, Rose learned to do something very few people thought she would. She learned to read. I had spent nine years with Rose—one of the great things about my position. During year eight, I found a reading curriculum that clicked for her.

An administrator told me I should be focusing my efforts on teaching life skills to Rose and others in my care, not on teaching reading. But through the years, my students worked on letter and sound recognition and blending sounds, and when we found the magic key in a curriculum that made sense to Rose, she amazed us all.

She quickly recognized and read sight words, found those words among other words, and sounded out words. She learned community signs, safety signs, and her family's names, and suddenly a new world was available to her. It was such a joyous day when Rose read her first complete sentence totally on her own. She often picked up books during down time and read them to herself or her classmates.

I was so proud of her and her skills, I took her all around the school and had her read to teachers and students. I also made sure to take her to all the administrators, especially the one who commented she would never read, and let her show off her skills. The administrator did not believe Rose was actually reading; she thought Rose had just memorized the book. She pointed to words and asked Rose to read them.

Rose thought for a second on some of the words, but figured them out. I cannot express how proud and justified I felt in that moment. Rose progressed to reading multisyllabic words and labels on food.

In her eighth-grade year, the school celebrated National Down Syndrome Day by having Rose and her parents on the morning announcements. They wore T-shirts that said "Rockin' that extra chromosome," and explained Down syndrome and the effect it had on their lives.

At the school's end-of-year party, Rose and two of her friends sang several karaoke songs for the entire school and all the volunteers. The final fond memory of elementary school was her graduation, when she crossed the stage in her cap and gown and accepted her diploma, and her classmates asked to be in pictures with her.

When it was time to transition from elementary school to high school, they participated in an IEP meeting with the local high school. Dan recalled the meeting was very positive and a great collaboration. The local high school superintendent admitted they did not have an appropriate program for Rose. Dan and Maryanne were already aware of this and had requested a representative from a different high school to attend the meeting. The entire team worked beautifully together to give permission for Rose to attend the other school.

The other high school was in a different town, so the school car (Rose called it "her car") picked her up and dropped her off every day at her door. Dan noted it was a huge help in transitioning from elementary to high school. The driver came to the house a week before school started, met Rose and her family, allowed her to get in and out of the vehicle, and just spent some time with her. It helped Dan and Maryanne feel a little less nervous about this person who was alone with their child for a thirty-minute one-way drive every day.

High school was not the same as elementary school; her exposure to the general education population changed, communication and her relationship with the teacher was different, and she was not able to be a cheerleader. Even so, Rose learned new things and had many positive experiences in high school. Her reading improved, she learned how to spell many words, and she usually earned a perfect score on her weekly spelling sheet. Her math skills progressed to a higher level. She learned life skills, including reading recipes, getting around in her community, and helping in the kitchen.

She went to Workshop several days a week, where she had several different jobs she could do. Her pay was determined by which job she did and how efficiently she did it. She complained about going, but was always happy when she received her paycheck.

The biggest highlight of Rose's life so far happened in high school: she attended her senior prom in spring 2019. She looked beautiful and had an amazing time.

When Rose turned eighteen, she became a legal adult in the United States. Maryanne and Dan had to file for legal guardianship of her, which was an arduous and expensive ordeal. They all appeared in court before or on Rose's eighteenth birthday, sent letters to her siblings to ensure no one else should become or wanted to become her guardian, and involved lawyers in the proceedings.

Rose lost many of her independent rights that were hers as a legal adult. Maryanne and Dan became her guardians as a way to protect her from other people's abuse. By becoming her legal guardians, Maryanne and Dan helped with her finances, made wise decisions regarding health care, living options, and employment, and generally protected her from any outside person trying to take advantage of her.

Outside of school, Rose had many positive experiences. She asked her dad to teach her to play chess. Both of her parents worked on laundry, cooking, and cleaning skills with her. She took up bowling in the last several years and was good enough most days to beat her dad.

While Rose did not have a driver's license, Maryanne said she was a backseat driver. If Maryanne did not move as soon as the light turned green, Rose was telling her to go. Every bump in the road, Rose complained to Maryanne as if Maryanne did it on purpose. Recently, Maryanne went over a pothole in the road and Rose said, "Oh my fucking gawd, Mom." Maryanne laughed on the inside, but scolded Rose for using the curse word.

Since Maryanne and Dan were both veterans, they and Rose have participated in several Veterans Day parades in their area. No matter what town they were in, people recognized and shouted Rose's name. When she was on the back of her mom's motorcycle, she waved at everyone.

In 2014, the family went to a zip line park. The instructor rode with Rose on the first two, and on the third one she told everyone she could do it by herself. She rode the other seven zip lines that day by herself, used her brake correctly, and even did some tricks.

Maryanne and Dan decided early in Rose's life that they would do special things for and with her at times when other people her age celebrated some sort of milestone Rose would probably not reach at the same time. For example, for her twelfth birthday, she attended a Justin Bieber concert. Whereas Rose's sister received help to buy a car when she turned sixteen, Maryanne and Dan celebrated Rose's sixteenth birthday with a VIP package to a Taylor Swift concert. Her seat was right on the aisle; Taylor walked down the catwalk, took off her sunglasses, and handed them to Rose. This special concert experience and other celebrations made Rose so happy, and she did not mourn for milestones missed.

Rose loved to be silly and sing, had a great sense of humor, and enjoyed life most of the time. At a swimming pool, another swimmer lost a padded insert from her bikini top. The insert floated near Rose, so she picked it up and walked over to the woman. As she handed it to the stranger, she said, "It's okay, it happens." Of course, the woman was embarrassed, but Maryanne thought it was hilarious.

Rose also loved to do cannonballs into the water to make the biggest splash she could and walked on her hands across the pool whenever possible. At a water amusement park, Rose told Dan repeatedly, "Dad, you are amazing." Dan planned to take her back to that park every summer because of how much she enjoyed herself.

She loved silly, fun food challenges and playing games. For one challenge, she took the biggest bite she could take and attempted to say "chubby bunny" without spitting food everywhere. Another food challenge she tried was to eat mashed potatoes with her hands behind her back. She, Maryanne, and Marie often played charades on their girls' nights.

Recently, Dan pointed to a truck and commented to Rose about how nice it was. Rose shrugged her shoulders a little, and he told her it was his favorite color. She looked at him and said, "Brown?"

He replied with, "No, it's red."

"Dad, you're color-blind, that is brown," she said sarcastically. Dan actually was color-blind, and he had to laugh at Rose's honesty as well as her sarcasm.

One of Rose's favorite activities to do was sing. She wore headphones, listened to her music, and sang right along with the artist. One day, Dan recorded her and showed her the video. She became very upset and said it was not her singing in the video. Dan assured her it was her voice, and she sounded beautiful. Rose insisted it was not and stomped off to her room. After Rose became upset, Dan and Maryanne realized Rose's perspective of her singing voice was quite different from their view. They thought she knew how she sounded, but her reaction to the video indicated she did not. They concluded that when Rose sang with the headphones on, she probably did not hear her own voice and thought she sounded just like the artist.

Dan and Maryanne had some scary and negative experiences with Rose too. The negative moments often came at the hands of others, in the form of stares and whispers. As Rose grew older, she noticed when people, especially kids, stared at her. She has told Maryanne several times in the last year that people stared at her, and she wanted to know why. Maryanne did not know how to tell Rose she was different than most people, and people were curious about differences when they were not educated. Maryanne said, "Rose's totally normal to herself."

Maryanne recounted an instance at a concert where a child was staring rudely at Rose for a very long time. Finally, Maryanne said to the adult who was with the little girl, "You might want to teach your child about kids with special needs so they do not stare at them." Dan and Maryanne preferred people ask them questions about Rose rather than treat Rose rudely.

The scariest experiences were most often the times when Rose exercised her escape artist skills. When she was little, she managed to leave the house without being noticed a few times. More than one of those times, she ended up by the neighbor's pool. She never went into the pool, but it was enough to scare them into installing locks high up on the doors. Rose also thought it was fun to hide in the clothing racks when she and Maryanne shopped. Maryanne did not find the humor in those episodes.

When Rose was six, the family took a cruise to St. Maarten. Maryanne and Marie went ashore to shop while Dan stayed in the cabin with Rose. He went to the bathroom and Rose was lying on the bed. When he came out of the bathroom, Rose was gone. He saw the door was open and ran to the hallway. She was nowhere.

He quickly found a staff member and explained what happened. The staff member called his supervisor, put Dan on the phone, and they started a search. He gave a description of Rose and frantically looked up and down the hallway, hoping to catch a glimpse of her. He feared the worst. He imagined her falling overboard, getting hurt, wandering off the ship, or someone taking her. His mind raced, his heart pounded, and he was paralyzed with fear.

He had to stay in the room in case she came back. He tried to think positively as the seconds ticked by. He tried to figure out what to say to Maryanne when she returned. He would never forgive himself if anything happened to his little girl. Finally, after several minutes, they found her. She was safe, sitting on the floor in the next section of the ship.

Something similar happened when Rose was eighteen and at an amusement park with Maryanne. They had gone to the park with a friend of Maryanne's. They were walking to the next ride and talking when Maryanne turned around to speak to Rose and she was gone. A quick look around in all directions confirmed Rose was nowhere in sight. Maryanne quickly found an employee, explained the situation, described Rose's attire, and the search began.

Maryanne had the same thoughts as Dan had earlier. Where had Rose gone? Had someone taken her? Was she hurt? What would

Maryanne tell Dan? She was frantic, looked in all directions, and repeatedly called her name. After the longest four or five minutes of Maryanne's life, Rose was found safe, sitting on a bench. She was tired from all the walking, saw the bench, and decided to rest.

In general terms, Maryanne and Dan worried about Rose's health and well-being, her level of physical activity, and her maintenance of a healthy weight. They were concerned about knowing when they can no longer physically take care of her. Along with those worries, Dan hoped the transition from high school to adult life would be smooth and graceful for all.

Dan was worried about the significant schedule shifts he and Maryanne needed to make after Rose finished high school. He wanted to be involved as much as he could for as long as possible, but he was not yet eligible to retire from his employment. His fear was that the lion's share of Rose's care would fall to Maryanne. In her view, though, Maryanne was ready for when Rose finished high school. She thought she and Rose would travel around the country in a recreational vehicle, visit family, and see the sights.

Neither Dan nor Maryanne worried about Rose taking care of herself in everyday life. She set up and followed her own daily routines.

At Maryanne's, she laid out the clothes she chose for the next day, and went to bed around eight thirty every night. On school mornings, she arose between six and six fifteen, and her car arrived about 7:40 a.m. She used every minute of that time to get ready. She dressed herself, took care of her personal hygiene with no help, ate the breakfast Maryanne prepared, and made her bed every morning. After she accomplished all of those things, she sat in the living room with her iPad and had her jam session until her car arrived.

When she returned from school, she gave Maryanne whatever was in her backpack and became upset if Maryanne looked in her backpack to check for papers. Then she made herself a snack and a drink, and watched her iPad in her room until dinner. Sometimes she helped with dinner. She always helped with the dishes, and after they were finished, she took her shower and got ready for bed. Whatever time was left before her bedtime was her time to do whatever she wanted.

When she arrived at Dan's, she took her overnight bag to her room, put her toiletries where they belonged, hung her dirty laundry bag on the closet door, and then she was ready for whatever Dan had planned for them.

She was very much like a typical person her age, with two major differences. First, Rose did not have a concept of time. Not only did she operate at a different pace than everyone else, she truly did not understand questions related to time, unless they were worded in a very specific way. Dan and Maryanne figured out the specific wording so they could converse with her.

The other significant difference was that Rose had many invisible friends with whom she started seriously interacting around the age of twelve. She often talked to one of them at school and sometimes would get mad at her. I acknowledged she had a friend, and told her that her friend was not registered to be in my class. The friend had to wait for her at home. It took my telling her a few times and a reminder every once in a while, but eventually, Rose left her friend at home.

Years later, these invisible friends were still present. Rose talked with them constantly and has had arguments with them to the point of slamming her door and stomping down the hallway. The distinction here between imaginary and invisible was deliberate. Everyone who knew Rose truly believed she thought her invisible friends were as real as the ones the rest of us could see.

Dan's biggest worry was how to prepare Rose for the inevitable day when he and Maryanne pass away. Will Rose understand what it means when they die, and will she be able to cope?

A moment that was etched in Maryanne's mind and gave her some solace was Rose's reaction to a death in the family. Rose was about ten years old. Maryanne explained to Rose her great-grandmother died, but she felt Rose did not really understand what that meant. When Rose saw her great-grandmother in the casket, Maryanne could see on Rose's face that she understood.

Maryanne told Rose her great-grandmother had gone to heaven, and Rose could see her in the first star that came out every night. Since that time, Rose has experienced the death of her grandpa and several beloved family pets. When she was told of each death, she said "Aw," and moved on. However, when the stars came out at night, she said hello to Papa, her beloved pets, and her great-grandmother.

Maryanne and Dan wanted Rose to be her happy, healthy, goofy self for the rest of her life. They hoped she would always be well cared for after they were gone, and took steps to make sure Rose's future would be secure. Maryanne and Dan agreed, and so did Rose's sisters, that Rose will live with one of them. Moreover, Maryanne and Dan prepared financially for Rose to be taken care of—though, of course, they worry whether it will be enough.

Dan's advice to other parents who discovered they were going to have a child with special needs, or just found out their child had special needs, was to read stories like this one, that speak of the positive sides of having a child with special needs. He also said to read the information over and over again and not to second-guess themselves. He suggested, if at all possible, talking to other parents who had a child with special needs.

He learned from Rose and believed he became a better person, dad, and manager because of her. While he was freaking frightened at her initial diagnosis and throughout her early years of life, he was extremely grateful for the blessing of having her in his life.

He hoped for parents that good resources were easier to find than they were when Rose was younger. When he and Maryanne were raising Rose, friends told them help and agencies were out there, but no one knew exactly where to go or who to ask. They appreciated the advice, but they did not have the time or the energy to search for the help and therefore never found it. They always put their main focus on raising Rose the best way they could figure out together.

Maryanne hoped Rose will get to do the things she wants and that she will keep swimming, both literally and figuratively. Maryanne's advice to parents was that even when it feels like the end of the world, it is not. She said parents should not let their child's diagnosis define who the parents are or who their child is or will be. She suggested parents of children with special needs go with the flow as much as possible and to always advocate for their child with doctors, schools, and other people.

Thank you, Rose, Maryanne, and Dan, for sharing your lives and your time with me for all these years. Thank you for allowing me to see behind the scenes of your lives and for sharing your story.

Rose, you have taught me a whole different approach to life and happiness. You have taught me patience, gentleness, compassion, unconditional love and acceptance. You have taught me that there are causes behind behaviors, that behaviors are communication, and that there are more ways to communicate than just through words. You have shown me perseverance even when the task is difficult. Thank you for being a wonderful student of mine and teacher to me.

Dan and Maryanne, thank you for the trust, faith, and belief you had in me all those years ago. Thank you for being partners with me and allowing me to share in the joy of teaching your daughter.

Kathleen

Kyle and Carrie were pleasantly surprised in autumn 2000 when they found out they were expecting child number four. The pregnancy went along with no complications, just like the other three. Looking back, the only odd thing was that at twenty weeks the ultrasound "could not visualize the baby's stomach." Carrie explained that as a baby swallowed amniotic fluid, the stomach should become visible on an ultrasound. At the twenty-four-week visit, the doctor wanted another ultrasound. This time, everything was normal, and they found out they were having a girl. Carrie remembered being terribly disappointed they were going to have all girls. Kyle looked at her and said, "How do you think my mom felt when Dean was born and he had so many problems? We want a healthy child."

Doctors induced labor when each of Carrie's previous three pregnancies lasted at least five days past its due date, so she was expecting this one to be the same. Baby Kathleen had other plans for her mom. Ten days before her due date, Carrie started having pains. She was unsure whether they were Braxton-Hicks contractions or true labor pains, so she called the doctor's office when the pains were about five minutes apart. She and the staff member agreed she could wait until her regularly scheduled checkup in a couple of days unless things became worse. The doctor monitoring this pregnancy was not the same doctor Carrie saw for her first three pregnancies. Her regular physician was scheduled to have a baby of her own around the same time Carrie was due.

228 | Those Who "Can't..." Teach

Carrie found this out early enough to switch doctors; however, she did not know this doctor as well, and that proved to be a downfall.

At her appointment, Carrie found out she was six centimeters dilated. She was so excited. She lived close to the hospital and asked if she could go home and get her things. Since her water had not broken, they allowed her to do so. She called Kyle, asked him to pick up Hardees for her, and had him tell the older three the baby was on the way. Carrie emailed the news to her family and Kyle's. She returned to the hospital, and her parents, Kyle's parents, Carrie's grandmother, and the girls all arrived shortly after.

Three hours later nothing was happening, so the family decided to get a bite to eat. Dr. Burns, the delivery room physician, told Carrie approximately twenty minutes after they left that she could start pushing, but Carrie wanted to wait until the family returned. Dr. Burns said she could wait a few minutes because of the epidural. The family arrived back at the hospital about twenty minutes later, and Carrie started pushing. Everything was fine with the delivery; Carrie and the baby were healthy throughout the contractions and pushing. The doctor told Carrie just one more push, and the baby would be out.

The moment the baby came out was the biggest, most memorable negative reaction to her child Carrie had ever seen. Carrie remembered thinking something must be horrifically wrong, as the delivery room nurse's expression was one of anguish, shock, and horror all rolled into one. Instead of elation, excitement, and happiness, this nurse's reaction to seeing Kathleen for the first time was spine-chilling. Carrie immediately became frightened and confused. None of the medical professionals in the room said a word.

Carrie's grandmother, who was sitting across the room, could see Kathleen and said, "Oh, she's got a cleft lip." Neither Kyle nor Carrie had even a glimpse of Kathleen. Dr. Burns quickly and silently took the baby from the room. Carrie did not remember how long it was before the first time she saw and held Kathleen. The next few minutes felt like hours. Without speaking, the nurses stitched Carrie up, cleaned her up, and made her as comfortable as possible. Her mother, grandmother, and Kyle left the delivery room to tell the other family members. Carrie was alone and confused. Her mother told her later that when Kyle's mom heard about Kathleen, she went screaming in despair down the hall.

Eventually, the nurses brought Kathleen in and gave her to Carrie. Kyle was by her side again, and they saw their little girl for the first time. The nurses had given her some sort of pacifier, and therefore Carrie did not really get a look at the cleft lip. Carrie was numb. The obstetrician finally came back into the room, touched Carrie's hand, said congratulations, and snuck out of the room again.

Cleft lip and cleft palate are very common birth defects in the United States. In utero, the tissues in a baby's mouth and nose do not fuse properly or at all; results include a split in the upper lip (cleft lip) and a hole in the roof of the mouth (cleft palate). A person can have either condition, or both.

Cleft lip and cleft palate can cause problems with breathing, eating, hearing, speaking, and tooth development. Bullying over appearance can also present sizeable social and emotional challenges.

Doctors do not know for certain why it happens, but evidence suggests a combination of genetic, health and environmental triggers could be the cause. Either parent can pass on the genes for the condition. Cleft palate and cleft lip are treated with surgeries.

Due to the severity of the cleft lip, the hospital where Kathleen was born was unable to address her needs appropriately. Within an hour or so, she was rushed to a bigger hospital about an hour away. The local hospital put Carrie in a private room and then Carrie said the staff "basically left me all alone. Nobody came in, and nobody talked to me all night." Carrie was numb, in shock, and sad all at the same time with no one to help her understand what was happening or help her process her feelings.

The next day, the doctor stuck her head in the room, avoided eye contact, and told Carrie bluntly, "You can go." The impact of the reaction from the local hospital staff and doctors at Kathleen's birth never left Carrie and created a fervent desire that no one else will ever have to feel so alone, confused, abandoned, and frightened as she felt.

Kyle had to take care of the family business as well as their first three daughters, so Carrie called her mom to come pick her up. Together they went to the children's hospital an hour away. Kathleen was in the neonatal intensive care unit (NICU). A nurse was at each of the six or seven incubators, which were spaced out to accommodate all the equipment needed for each child. Carrie had to walk through double doors, scrub up, and put on a sterile gown, booties, and mask. Staff told her Kathleen was in this area, but she was not.

She asked again, and they told her Kathleen was in the next room. Carrie walked through another set of doors into a dimly lit room the size of a closet, and there was Kathleen—all by herself. She had oxygen and was swaddled and asleep. She had not been assigned a one-to-one nurse like the other babies. Carrie said to her mom, "Well obviously she isn't doing too bad. I mean, she's in here all by herself sleeping, with no one hovering over her."

Eventually, Carrie was told Kathleen had a bilateral cleft lip and a cleft palate, but Carrie had seen her for only a few minutes at the local hospital and was unaware of the extent and severity of both. Kathleen's appearance, pulse, grimace, activity, and respiration (Apgar) and her weight and height were all within normal limits. The doctors and nurses at the children's hospital kept mentioning something about Kathleen's toes, but Carrie did not understand. Kathleen was wrapped up when Carrie saw her at the local hospital for those few minutes.

Thus began Carrie and Kyle's "journey to Africa," as Carrie put it. While they expected to be going to a familiar place, they ended up arriving somewhere completely different. This place was unfamiliar, and the language, sounds, expectations, and how to get around were all very different.

Carrie eventually found out what the fuss was about. Kathleen had syndactyly; two toes were webbed together. She was also born with low, small set ears and hypertelorism, which is an abnormally large distance between the eyes, possibly due to her cleft palate. This cluster of items was leading the doctors toward a genetic diagnosis or syndrome, but they were not sure what it would be.

The doctors barraged Carrie and Kyle with questions. Their answers revealed Kyle's brother, Dean, had also been born with a cleft lip and palate. The genetics team was called in to test Kyle and his family. Since there had been no such developments on Carrie's side of the family, she and her family were not tested. They expected the results would be back in a week or so.

During the week, Kathleen remained in the NICU and Carrie stayed with her. Because her lips and palate were not formed completely, Kathleen was unable to make her lips and mouth form the sucking position required to nurse or drink from a bottle. Carrie had to learn a new way to feed Kathleen. One tool many families of cleft lip and cleft palate babies found useful was a squeeze bottle. Carrie pumped her breast milk, transferred it to a squeeze bottle, and squirted a few drops into Kathleen's mouth at a time. Thankfully, her swallowing had not been affected. During this week, everything else seemed to be normal with Kathleen; she ate, had typical bodily functions, and slept. After seven days in the NICU, they were ready to take Kathleen home.

Just as Carrie was ready to walk out with Kathleen, she had her second worst experience with medical professionals. She was called back into the nearest empty room, close to the exit, to meet with a geneticist, three nurses, and a counselor. There was no gentle lead-up or softness to their voices as they informed her of the test results and Kathleen's diagnosis. In a cold delivery of hard facts, the geneticist said Kathleen's problems were genetic—an "unbalanced translocation of chromosomes, blah, blah, blah,"—and the rest sounded like the same syllables over and over again, like the teacher in the Charlie Brown shows.

Once the doctor told her Kathleen definitely had a syndrome or disorder, time froze, and she could only process that bit of information. She realized to them it was just a medical diagnosis, but to her and her family, it was an every-minute-of-every-day-for-the-rest-of-her-daughter's-life diagnosis. It was gut-wrenching.

Kathleen had an unbalanced translocation of chromosomes seven and eight. Approximately one in five hundred people has a balanced translocation of chromosomes. The unbalanced translocation can happen when this person has a child. Each person is completely unique in how it will affect them. It depends on the exact chromosomes affected, as well as the other parent's chromosomal makeup. Kathleen is the only person in the world with her exact makeup and effects.

When Kathleen was born and Kyle's mother, Vivian, received news of her granddaughter's cleft lip and palate, she went screaming down the hall. It reminded her so strongly of when her own child was born, she was overcome with emotion. When the doctor shared the genetic testing results with the family, both Kyle and Vivian felt some guilt for passing on the chromosomal translocation. After Carrie, Vivian had the hardest time dealing with Kathleen's diagnosis. There were so many similarities to her own child: cleft lip and palate, same chromosomes affected, the large space between the eyes, the hole in the heart, and probably the cognitive delays as well.

When Kyle's brother, Dean, was born, about fifty-five years prior to Kathleen's birth, the outlook on children with disabilities and birth defects was very different. One of Dean's doctors basically said to let him die. Vivian's husband told Carrie that when it was time to leave the hospital, he and a nun had to convince Vivian to take Dean home.

At that time, people with disabilities were institutionalized, and no one Vivian knew had ever raised a child who looked like Dean. Kyle's mother was in such a state of shock and so heartbroken, her newborn's doctor seemed unwilling to help, and she did not know what to do. She was frightened and felt all alone. After some months had passed, another doctor was willing to help, but by then Dean had developed pneumonia and had lost weight. Even with this doctor's help, by one year of age, Dean only weighed nine pounds.

Dean lived until his mid-forties, but he never walked; he only said a word or two his entire life; he was missing his gallbladder and a kidney since birth (which was not known until he was in his thirties); and he was never able to attend school due to his low cognitive ability. Eventually his parents made the very tough decision to put him in a home for people with severe disabilities. Carrie said once he was in the home, he did learn how to do some things on his own, and he received very good care until he passed away.

Carrie knew Kathleen had physical defects and suspected she had Down syndrome, but to sit there in the test results meeting and be told her child had more than that, and it was probably exactly what her husband's brother had, was overwhelming and devastating. She remembered the doctor asked her if she was disappointed it was not Down syndrome. Her response was, "I'm just sad you are having to talk to me at all."

Carrie was trying to process all of this when she noticed the group of people standing up. She regained her focus and realized they were telling her goodbye. They had just given her the most devastating and heart-wrenching news of her life, and now she was expected to leave. They offered no help, guidance, or support.

Carrie's mom picked up Carrie and Kathleen from the hospital that day. In a dazed state, Carrie buckled Kathleen into her car seat. As soon as Carrie was situated in the passenger seat, she began to sob. She sobbed the entire hour car ride home, the rest of the day, and several more days. She was sitting in a chair sobbing one day when Kyle hugged her, and she told him, "I think I could cry a million tears, and it wouldn't be enough."

"The level of devastation was just ridiculous," Carrie said.

Carrie began to cry as she recalled the memories of that time. Kathleen, her beautiful now-seventeen-year-old daughter, sat right next to her. The pain on Carrie's face and the tears coming down her cheeks prompted Kathleen to reach over and offer her mom her grilled cheese sandwich.

I had the privilege of teaching Kathleen for ten years and never met a more empathetic and sympathetic person. Local school bands came to play for the students at our school and several times during sad parts of the music, Kathleen cried or felt sad at appropriate times. Many times, she was the only student out of a group of several hundred who understood what the music was portraying.

She always understood and recognized sadness and pain and reached out to comfort those who were going through it. Kathleen was nonverbal, so it was always with her actions and facial expressions that she offered comfort. Sometimes it was a hug or a hand on the other person's shoulder or hand. Sometimes it was a head on a shoulder or it was through tears. Sometimes it was the offer of food as it was on this day.

When she got this devastating news, Carrie went through a teetering phase. She wanted to know everything possible about her daughter's diagnosis, yet did not want to know. She wanted things to be "normal," yet she loved Kathleen exactly as she was. She wanted to take a break from reality, but wanted to push forward to find answers or help. She wanted to live in denial for just a minute, but knew she could not.

She was frightened and confused, had a million questions, and did not want to be in this nightmare. She wondered, "Why am I here, and how did I get here?" There were no answers and no turning back or changing the situation. Carrie felt powerless and hopeless. It was such a mixed bag of emotions. She felt grief for what could have been, but joy for who Kathleen was.

Carrie said the period of time shortly after Kathleen was born was like going through the stages of death. She was bitter, intensely mournful, and overwhelmed. She was surrounded by her family and friends who all tried to understand, but without a frame of reference, they really could not understand. Carrie felt broken in a million pieces and all alone.

Outside of the family, Carrie knew of only one other child in the world who was similar but not exactly the same as Kathleen. There was no support group specifically for people dealing with this extremely rare condition, nor was there much definitive information on what could and could not be done or accomplished. Carrie met with countless doctors, residents, and specialists over the past seventeen years, and many of them had never heard of what Kathleen had. Many of them tried to find more information or even a cure, but none were successful.

Carrie remembered the worst and best thing Kyle said to her during this time. He told her she needed to basically accept the situation as it was and take care of their beautiful little girl. This was the worst thing because he left every day to take care of the family business, and therefore 99 percent of the care fell on Carrie's shoulders. He did not face the situation as often as Carrie. He did not have the exhaustion from being up multiple times throughout the night for feedings. He had been through this with his brother and had some idea of what was going to happen, but Carrie had no experience at all with someone with special needs and was overwhelmed with fear and sadness.

It was also the best thing he said, because he was right. Sitting in her chair crying all the time was not helping Kathleen. Though Kyle did not make this comment flippantly or maliciously, it was not what she needed to hear at the time. She had to grieve in her own time and way, as well as take care of Kathleen. While she never physically lost a child, she felt she lost the child she thought she was going to have. Carrie said through tears, "At the time Kathleen was born, my heart was torn into millions of pieces I thought would never be put back together. But God is faithful, and He took all those pieces, and He did put them back together."

According to Carrie it was "quite a period of time" for God to put all those pieces together, but He did. Most days she sat on the floor in the shower and prayed for strength to get through the day. Sometimes, she had to pray to get through a minute or an hour. It was a very stressful and straining time on her, their marriage, and their family.

Carrie described how the rest of the family reacted to Kathleen in the beginning. She said, "She was their sister and they loved her." Carrie did not remember any questions, shame, or fear. She did remember many times when the sisters held Kathleen and treated her just like any other baby. One time, Kathleen was still small enough to be in a bassinet. Kelly was around age three, Courtney was about four and a half, and Chloe was about six. The big sisters all stood around the bassinet, just looking at Kathleen with love, and Kelly reached her hand out to Kathleen. It was one of Carrie's fondest memories.

It took Carrie some time to stop comparing Kathleen to other children or even to her sisters. She said if she had not stopped thinking "Oh, she should be babbling, walking, driving, graduating, doing whatever..." she would have never gotten out of that chair. "I had to accept what I had been given and accept her for who she was, and love her as the individual she is. I tell you the truth, if I had that other child, I wouldn't be here. She wouldn't be the same person she is today, and I love this person—exactly as she is."

Once Kathleen was released from the children's hospital, Carrie needed to establish her with a general practitioner for a well-baby checkup. Carrie told the receptionist on the phone the genetics team was supposed to send a letter regarding the results. The receptionist confirmed they had received the letter and replied "everybody thought it was really weird." Carrie quickly concluded the letter—with very personal, very private information about her husband and daughter—had been shared with everyone in the office, whether they had a need to know or not. Carrie felt violated that so-called professionals shared such information around the office. Since this was one incident and it was during the time when Carrie was still processing everything, she didn't pursue the situation any further.

One of Carrie's biggest and most time-consuming jobs, as with any infant, was feeding Kathleen. The cleft palate and lip did not allow Kathleen to suck, but she was able to swallow. Carrie used the squeeze bottle to drip a few drops of breast milk at a time into Kathleen's mouth. When fused properly, the palate protects the mouth from the nose. In Kathleen, that protection was completely missing. Oftentimes while swallowing, Kathleen's tongue pushed the milk onto the roof of her mouth, but there was no roof, and the milk went in her nose and caused her to gag. When her gag reflex was triggered, Kathleen often vomited the milk she had consumed. Kathleen was also burdened with gastric reflux, which meant if she managed to get the milk down, she may have thrown it up anyway. Her reflux was so bad in those first few months, she had to be hospitalized.

An average one-month-old infant eats eight to twelve times a day. From one to two months, the feedings decrease to seven to nine times, and decreases again to five to seven times a day until they are about a year old. Every day for the first eight months of Kathleen's life, Carrie went through this feeding process five to twelve times a day. The typical amount of time it takes to feed an infant varies between twenty and forty minutes; however, this situation was not typical.

First, Carrie pumped the milk in about thirty minutes. Then, she squeezed tiny amounts of milk at a time into Kathleen's mouth. Almost every feeding resulted in milk coming back up at least once and required a cleanup, the scope of which depended on how much she had consumed to that point; this stage added another thirty to forty minutes or longer. Finally, if Kathleen hadn't spit up, Carrie had to try to burp her, which added ten more minutes. The total time for one feeding was anywhere from seventy to eighty minutes or longer. When Kathleen was a newborn, this process was even longer.

Most people think eating is a natural behavior; in truth, it is a learned behavior most infants pick up rather quickly. A newborn with either a cleft lip or palate, or both, will be delayed in learning how to eat and suck. Carrie had to put the drops at the back of Kathleen's mouth and let gravity help the milk go down before Kathleen pushed it up into her nasal area. Kathleen's severe reflux complicated her already difficult feeding problems.

When Kathleen was a little over three months of age, her first surgery was to repair the bilateral cleft lip. A few days later, Carrie took Kathleen to her general practitioner for her well-baby checkup. The infant scale was located in a small hallway between the inner offices. The nurse weighed Kathleen, and Carrie spoke with the assistant about what medical items would be checked during the appointment. While they talked, Carrie noticed someone walk by, but didn't think much of it. Then she noticed, one after the other, multiple medical professionals walking by Kathleen and staring at her to "check out the weird kid." Carrie felt like her child was an attraction at a freak show.

This was the second instance of unprofessional behavior with this doctor's office, and Carrie had enough. Throughout Kathleen's life, people have stared at her, but Carrie never felt as horrible as that day. Her recommendation—no, demand—was that medical professionals think about their actions and words. She understood curiosity, but she felt others should have understood privacy and should have been mindful of the person they were talking to and of their feelings. When a patient came in with something "never before seen," she insisted the medical staff should remember the patient was a person, and unless they had been given express consent to examine the person, they were being rude and disrespectful. She found a different doctor, forty-five minutes away.

Kathleen never lost any weight during those first eight months because of Carrie's extreme diligence with her feedings. Carrie kept detailed records of how much Kathleen was taking in and how much she was spitting up. She figured out the caloric intake and added calorie supplements to the milk to keep Kathleen from losing weight. Carrie's mom referred to her as the "food nazi" because of how obsessed she seemed to be regarding what Kathleen was eating. At eight months, Kathleen was diagnosed with "failure to thrive." It was true she had not lost any weight since birth, but she really had not gained any either. The doctors talked to Kyle and Carrie about a gastrostomy tube.

A gastrostomy tube (also called a G-tube) is a tube inserted through the abdomen that delivers nutrition directly to the stomach. Carrie knew this day would probably come, but she really hoped her meticulous attention to feeding Kathleen would prevent it. No parent wants to hear what they are doing is not good enough, and no parent wants their very young child to go through any surgery, let alone two within six months.

In hindsight, the G-tube proved to be a lifesaver, but at the time, it was a very difficult decision to make. The tubes needed to be replaced every three to six months, or more often if an infection occurred. When Kathleen first had it, a doctor needed to change the tube. Over time, Carrie learned how to change the G-tube on her own. The part of the tube that stuck out of the skin was called a Mic-Key button or "button." Many children need a button in the early stages of life, but most of them are able to grow out of the need. In Kathleen's case, she still had hers at seventeen years of age.

For a time after the button was implanted, Carrie was still able to feed with breast milk. By around fifteen months it was time to switch to a nutrient-rich type of formula. At first, Carrie was able to order this through the state Medicaid office and have it shipped directly to her house. Around Kathleen's second birthday, Carrie was told she had to go through the Women, Infants and Children (WIC) office in a town thirty minutes away. This added more stress to an already stressful life.

Carrie went to the WIC office, filled out papers, picked up the vouchers, went to a local grocery store that ordered the formula, and finally returned to the store days later when the formula came in. This process occurred every four to six weeks. The first time Carrie went into the office, she had filled out a form at the request of the WIC office. The form asked for all sorts of personal information, including how often Kathleen ate, the amount she ate, and how many wet diapers she had. The WIC lady said she had never seen anyone fill it out so completely, including the caloric intake. Carrie just chuckled and thought, "The food nazi strikes again."

In Kathleen's first year, she had sixteen specialist appointments and regular checkups with the pediatrician, as well as appointments for vaccines and when she was sick. One day Carrie went through the cafeteria line at the children's hospital, and the cashier tried to give her an employee discount because she had seen Carrie so often, she thought she worked there.

"Thankfully," Carrie said, "God has always taken care of Kathleen." The financial cost of everything was not quite the burden it could have been. When Carrie became pregnant with Kathleen, she and the family were on private insurance because they ran a family business, and Carrie did not work outside the home at the time. A representative at the private insurance company told Carrie she could and should apply for Medicaid. She did all the paperwork, not thinking she would be approved, but she was. Within the first year of Kathleen's life she needed multiple surgeries and other trips to the children's hospital, totaling well over one hundred thousand dollars. Thanks to their private insurance and Medicaid, they only had to pay a small portion out of pocket.

Carrie worked as a lab technician, but felt with all her experience with Kathleen's health issues, she earned a medical degree the hard way. The degree wasn't from a university, but from years of interacting with all the doctors, specialists, and interns; understanding the issues during appointments, hospitalizations, and surgeries; and learning general knowledge of Kathleen's diagnosis. She often felt she knew more than many college-educated doctors, especially when it came to her daughter.

It was always up to Carrie to inform doctors of what all the other doctors were doing and thinking they might do. It was up to Carrie to share all the information at each individual doctor's appointment about feedings, symptoms, upcoming surgeries, test results from other professionals, upcoming tests, weight gain and loss, milestones achieved or not, and Kathleen's medical history, every time there was a new doctor or intern, or even a doctor she hadn't seen in a while. Any time Kathleen saw a new doctor, it was imperative they knew all of Kathleen's history to treat her correctly.

Carrie was Kathleen's biggest advocate. She chose not to be intimidated by therapists, doctors, medical professionals, teachers, and administrators to get the absolute best she could for Kathleen. She was not always liked by these professionals because she questioned, discussed, sought other opinions, did her own research, and stood up for what she felt was best for Kathleen. She has been scoffed at, scolded, questioned, talked to like a child, given dirty looks, and reminded many times she was not an expert in a certain field. Her response was, "I may not be an expert in your field and while I appreciate and respect all the degrees hanging on your wall, I am an expert in my child."

She found a doctor she learned to love. The doctor was very knowledgeable, and she and her staff were always professional. In fact, this new doctor was so helpful and knowledgeable, she likely saved Kathleen's life. Several times in her first eighteen months, Kathleen had respiratory syncytial virus (RSV), a respiratory virus that can cause pneumonia. One case of RSV was so severe, Kathleen had to be hospitalized. This new doctor gave approval for Kathleen to get a vaccine. While this did not seem like a big deal, special permission had to be granted because of Kathleen's current and future potential health, and typically the vaccine was only given to premature babies and infants younger than twelve months.

During a routine visit when Kathleen was about eighteen months old, a different doctor in the practice examined Kathleen. As soon as the doctor walked in, she smiled brightly and said, "Oh, I remember Kathleen." Carrie had never seen this doctor and was confused as to how this woman knew her daughter. The new doctor explained she had been doing her residency when Kathleen was at the children's hospital. She remembered the doctors and nurses being very concerned for Kathleen, wondering if she would survive, and not knowing exactly what was wrong with her.

While the doctor said all this, Carrie recalled arriving at the hospital and seeing Kathleen all alone, wrapped up, and on oxygen; she found irony in the different perspective. Carrie thought this was kind of funny, but the next thing the doctor did was even funnier in Carrie's mind. She became very serious, looked Carrie right in the eye, and with complete sincerity said, "You do know Kathleen has a really rare chromosomal abnormality, don't you?" Carrie almost burst out laughing, thinking to herself, no, in all this time I never knew that.

Along with the cleft lip and palate, Kathleen was born with an atrial septal defect (ASD). An ASD, put very simply, is a hole in the heart that does not close on its own and causes potentially serious health issues. Before a baby is born, the heart typically has several holes in the wall between the upper chambers, to redirect the blood flow as organs develop. Shortly after birth, the holes normally close or become so small they do not cause problems. With ASD, the hole stays big enough that too much blood is allowed to flow into the lungs, which overtaxes the lungs, arteries, and heart, and damages them over time. The hole may require surgery to close. The cause of ASD is unclear, but doctors think genetic and environmental factors contribute.

When Kathleen was about eighteen months old, doctors determined she had pulmonary stenosis, a condition related to her ASD. One of her heart valves was not closing properly as a result of the blood flowing incorrectly. By the time Kathleen was about thirty-three months old, the ASD had grown into a hole with a diameter of over one inch, about the size of a half-dollar, and her heart had become slightly enlarged from doing all the extra work. She needed a cardiac catheterization to repair it.

For Carrie, it was another procedure for her young child, another time of worry, another time of weighing pros and cons, and another time of recovery. The surgery used a "hubcap," or ASD adaptor, to fix the opening. The cath was successful, her heart decreased to its normal size, and the hole was repaired. Subsequent X-rays revealed something that looked like a hubcap or spider web right in the middle of her chest. Occasionally doctors said they heard leaking when they listened to Kathleen's heart, but it was not a concern anymore.

Kathleen had a major five-and-a-half-hour surgery to repair her cleft palate when she was not quite two years old. After the surgery,

Kathleen was all bandaged up, swollen, and black-and-blue from the procedure with tubes sticking out of her. Her little arms were wrapped in such a way as to keep them away from touching her face and out of her mouth.

Carrie was sitting there alone with Kathleen, when in walks a priest Carrie recognized from Vivian's church. Carrie thought what a nice thing for this priest to drive the over hour-long drive and check on her and Kathleen. The priest sat down next to her, looked at her, and said "You know, Vivian is having a really hard time with this." When Carrie thought back on the conversation, she did not recollect the priest asking her how she was doing or attempting to give her or Kathleen any sympathy. It was all about Vivian.

By the time Kathleen was two years old, she had had more surgeries than I have had in my entire life, and she was not finished with them yet. At three months, she had her bilateral cleft lip repaired; at eight months she had the G-tube implanted; around eighteen months she had the cardiac catheterization; at thirty-three months, she had her cleft palate repaired. She had to have plastic surgery on her nose two more times to make it a proper size and shape after cleft palate surgery; she has had plastic surgery on her lip because of growth; and she had heel cord surgery when she was about ten. There was the possibility of another surgery to Kathleen's lip, as she seemed to have lost some of her ability to make certain sounds. Carrie felt it was because Kathleen continued to grow and thrive, but the repaired area was not keeping up with her growth.

People have said to Carrie it must have been an easy decision for her to approve a surgical procedure, since Kathleen has had so many surgeries. Carrie wanted readers to know that was the exact opposite of the truth. Every surgery, from the first procedure to the possibility of another one, was agonizing to consider. She had to weigh the pros and cons of the effects of having the surgery. She had to consider if the benefits could outweigh any potential negatives. She knew Kathleen experienced pain if she opted for surgery, but would Kathleen have pain—emotional or physical—if Carrie opted not to? She had to consider her child was under anesthesia, as well as the side effects that anesthesia alone could cause. The length of a time a person was under anesthesia and the overall health of the person before surgery also affected how the brain reacted. No parent easily decided to allow their child to have surgery, no matter how many they have had.

Carrie brought Kathleen home from the hospital. As they settled into a routine (if one could say chaos is a routine), and as Carrie regained her footing, she reached out for therapies. The state in which Carrie lived was set up so agencies such as Head Start, Department of Human Services, and Department of Specialized Care for Children provided services for children from birth to three years old. When a child turned three, those agencies released the child to the public education system.

During the first three years of Kathleen's life, agencies were very kind and helpful, and seemed to genuinely want to do all they could to help Kathleen thrive. The system was designed to help each child develop as many building blocks as possible. Carrie had therapists at her house several times a week for occupational therapy (OT), physical therapy (PT), and speech language pathology services (SLP), and she had to do follow-up checks with the heads of the departments several times a year. Carrie referred to the experience as "all love and fluff."

That was not her experience when Kathleen was three and no longer eligible for services outside of the school system. Whereas the birth-to-three services were very broad in what they covered, there was no concern about how the services related to education. Once Kathleen arrived in the public school system, any services she received had to be tied as an important factor in her education.

According to the United States Department of Education, in 1975, the Education for All Handicapped Children Act was passed in the United States. This act was amended and renamed the Individuals with Disabilities Education Act (IDEA) and it ensured a free appropriate public education (FAPE) was provided to all students, regardless of ability. This was directed by a document called an individualized education plan (IEP).

These acts were supposed to be supported financially by the federal and state governments at more than 50 percent of the cost. However, promised money was often not delivered. School districts and special education cooperatives were often left juggling the cost of extracurricular activities like band, art, and sports, and the promised services for students with special needs.

Many schools in the state where Carrie and Kathleen lived had operated in the red for several years, even after their administrations made hard decisions and cut back as much as possible. The state had mismanaged education funds of all kinds for so long, they were not able to provide their share of education funding for transportation, general and special education, and safety concerns on time or at all. The public schools provided services to children with special needs, but the services were as basic as possible. It was legal in many cases because of the word "appropriate" in IDEA. The school did not have to provide the best, but what was appropriate for each individual student.

Every year, the school held a review meeting to update the parent on what the child with an IEP accomplished and what, if anything, the child still needed to strengthen. Every three years, the child was reevaluated to make certain they still needed an IEP. There were people who were legally required to attend these meetings: the parent, a general education grade-level teacher, a special education teacher, a representative of the local education agency, a school psychologist, and any therapists or related service personnel who worked with the child.

At Kathleen's first IEP meeting with the nearest public school in 2003, Carrie was shocked. Sitting around the table were the superintendent of the local school, the preschool teacher, the early childhood teacher, an occupational therapist, a physical therapist, a speech language pathologist, and a school psychologist, none of whom Carrie knew. Seven experts sat around the table and Carrie sat at the end by herself, facing all these people. All the love and fluff she felt with the earlier agencies was now replaced with roadblocks because certain things did not tie into the education of her child.

Carrie very quickly realized she needed to be able to explain to a panel of experts how those services related to her daughter's education, if she wanted Kathleen to continue to receive comprehensive services. She also quickly realized public school therapies were tied to money, something most of the schools in Carrie's area were lacking in abundance. She chose right then not to be intimidated by all these experts. She chose to stand strong and advocate for her daughter. It was never easy, but it became easier.

The law was updated in 2004 to require a free and appropriate education for all students with disabilities. Its focus was on individualized plans to provide each student the knowledge, tools, and services that equipped them to continue their education, secure jobs, and live on their own. This addition to the law did not begin to trickle to the local school districts for compliance for several more years.

Carrie said the school became a type of enemy, because every time she dealt with them it felt like a battle. She had to fight to get what she felt were basic therapies and services for Kathleen: getting around the school building safely, keeping her balance, writing, feeding and toileting skills, and feeding her through her tube several times a day. Carrie said there were some therapists as Kathleen got older who just seemed to "want her off their caseload." One of her biggest pet peeves was when she attended an IEP meeting at her daughter's school and everyone at the meeting said they were an expert, but treated her as if she knew nothing.

If it was not for Carrie and her devotion to and love for her daughter, Kathleen would not have been as advanced as she was. Carrie knew she did not raise Kathleen all on her own. She knew, appreciated, and understood it took a whole village of people to get Kathleen to where she was. Carrie was always at the center of the team; she maintained all the information—educational and medical—from year to year and deserved respect for her knowledge. The special education law stated Carrie was an equal member of the IEP team; however, Carrie was rarely treated as such.

Carrie unfortunately did not always have the best experience with the school districts and the IDEA 2004. When Kathleen was ready to move from the elementary school where I was her teacher to a high school setting, Carrie was met with much opposition and did not feel the law was on her side. She felt the law needed to change again. It was too vague and very difficult for parents of children with special needs to get an appropriate education for their child. The wheels of education moved very slowly when it came to change, and unfortunately the special-needs population was being harmed the most.

In the first several years of Kathleen's life, not only was Carrie dealing with all of Kathleen's medical and cognitive needs, but her second daughter, Courtney, was having difficulty in school. Carrie asked the school about testing her daughter to see if she had a specific learning disability, but the school did not think it was necessary, as Courtney was doing okay in all of her classes. She was not at the top of the class, but she was doing all the school thought she was capable of.

Carrie did not let the school change her mind. She had Courtney privately tested, and the results showed Courtney did have a specific learning disability. The testing was so precise, Courtney was told she had dyslexia, which means difficulty with reading. Carrie took the results to the school and convinced them to evaluate Courtney. However, at the meeting where the results were discussed, she was told Courtney did not qualify. By this time, Courtney was in fourth grade and her teacher told Carrie she was labeling Courtney as a C student, and she was only ever going to be a C student. Carrie chose to take care of the matter on her own.

She found a private school that offered summer classes specifically for students with learning disabilities. This school was approximately ninety minutes away. Carrie and Courtney drove there every day for weeks during two summers. When Courtney was in high school, she thanked Carrie for taking her to those classes. She said she never would have been as successful without the tools and skills she learned there.

Courtney graduated from a college preparatory high school with honors and from one of the nation's top fifty colleges with a chemistry degree. When Courtney started at her college, she took the documentation from the private school and presented it to the Student Disability Resource Center. The director of the department looked over her paperwork and was astounded she had never had an IEP or help of any kind by her elementary and high schools.

In college, she qualified for some accommodations and modifications, such as extra time to complete assignments and take tests, ability to take her test in a separate location so she can read it aloud to herself, and someone to verify she is reading the numbers correctly for measurements. She not only showed the fallacy in her fourth-grade teacher's thinking, but blew it out of the water.

I joined the school district where Kathleen attended when she was a part-time kindergarten student in 2005. When I first met Kathleen, she was so tiny, even as an almost five-year-old. I thought she looked fragile, but her eyes were the most sincere and happy of any child I had ever seen. She greeted me with her best smile and welcomed me into her life wholeheartedly. She completely trusted me even though she had no idea of me—we had just met. I had not taught anyone with needs as severe as Kathleen's, but I decided the very first time I met her that I would do my best to give her the best education I could. I had the privilege of teaching her for ten years. Her smile and her love for me and anyone around her still can bring me to tears.

I had the great opportunity to teach Kathleen to move around the school independently without having to hold anyone's hand and eventually go from one place to another in the building without anyone walking beside her. She could walk up and down steps and bleachers, even though she was terribly afraid of big open spaces and heights. She learned to write her first and last name, identified many numbers, memorized all the letters by name and many by sound, and learned to look at books properly. She could read some sight words and stories about her family and the school.

Kathleen knew how to open her own locker and put her things away when arriving to school and how to get them out again at the end of the day. She became potty trained during the last couple of years I was her teacher. She was able to feed herself using different utensils, including cutting her food, and she learned how to trace lines, and how to cut paper with scissors. Kathleen was able to suck through a straw and blow bubbles through the same straw, learned how to cook some basic foods, and could dress herself.

Farther afield, she memorized street signs and practiced how to safely cross the street. She also learned about recycling and helped do the recycling around the school. Kathleen was able to use an iPad to answer questions, tell jokes, recognize shapes, put one-dimensional puzzles together, work with money, and tell her address and her parents' and siblings' names. She served others by wrapping silverware and setting up cafeteria tables with condiments, napkins, and silverware. She learned how to work with others and wait her turn, how to be respectful and polite, and so much more.

She showed love and compassion to all those around her. She taught "normal" kids she liked many of the same things they did and definitely liked to have fun in many of the same ways they did. She became a celebrity in our school and her town, because she was friendly to everyone and everyone knew her name. She flirted with boys and had crushes on a few, as well as on a male teacher or two over the years. She got into trouble and had to be sent to the principal's office once. She went through the teenage hormonal mood swings like all teens. She wanted to be accepted and have friends like her classmates.

I may have been biased, but I felt she had a better attitude toward school and learning than many kids her age. She came in almost every day I had her and was willing to put forth a ton of effort, even though she did not progress as much as "normal" kids. She rarely complained and even more rarely was disrespectful to herself, her classmates, teachers, or the administration. She brought joy to everyone she encountered who paid attention to her on an almost daily basis.

When Kathleen was in seventh grade, she displayed some new behaviors. She held her stomach and complained she was tired, her heart raced sometimes, and occasionally she had some staring. Since Kathleen was nonverbal, it was often difficult for us to know if anything was happening or hurting, and what it was. Carrie took her to several different doctors, did her own research, and used that knowledge to determine Kathleen was having seizures. We who had worked with Kathleen for several years knew her nonverbal cues. However, her doctors at the time did not have that benefit.

I recalled one day when Carrie came back from a doctor appointment and told me the doctor put his hands on her shoulders, moved really close to her face, and almost in a whisper said, "You know your child has serious cognitive delays, right?" Again, Carrie thought how ridiculous it was that a professional said that to her. At the time, she told me she wanted to answer with, "What? No, I had no idea. I'm so shocked and upset with myself, I didn't recognize it and shame on all the other doctors over the years who never told me." I asked Carrie if she still remembered that instance. She said after a while of seeing so many different doctors and hearing so many similar things, those types of stories just became the norm, unfortunately.

When Kathleen started high school, the staff there required a lot more of Carrie than we did in the elementary school. In the first year, Carrie felt she was there several times a week and received phone calls multiple times a day when she was not there. Kathleen's school had never had anyone with her complex needs (of course, neither did we when she first joined us), and by the way they treated Carrie and Kathleen, it appeared to Carrie they did not want her there. For example, the school did not understand Kathleen needed, not wanted, to be fed through her G-tube twice a day at school. They thought she should just learn to eat more. Kathleen had a diagnosis of Graves' disease, an autoimmune disorder that caused hyperthyroidism, or overactive thyroid. One major side effect of this was weight loss or not being able to gain weight.

At seventeen, Kathleen barely weighed ninety pounds and was about five feet tall. She needed to be fed nutrients through her G-tube three times a day to keep what small amount of weight she had, and she ate three meals a day, plus snacks. One day at the beginning of her high school career, the person who was trained to feed her via the G-tube had gone home sick before it was time to give Kathleen her nutrients for the afternoon. The school sent a note home that afternoon telling mom no one gave Kathleen her afternoon nutrients, and they hoped it was okay.

In another instance, the teacher and aide who were trained were both going to be out on the same day. The school nurse told mom Kathleen just had to learn to eat more, because it was too difficult to train enough people for when situations like that happened. The one person who should have known or been the most willing to learn was not the one trained and did not think she should be trained. She also thought it was too much work to have more than two people trained to give life-sustaining nutrients.

I did not know how to give Kathleen nutrients when she first came to me, but I learned. It only took a few minutes to do and was quite simple. We had a smaller staff at the elementary school and had six people trained, and none of those people was a person with a nursing degree. The high school had a certified nursing assistant program as part of their curriculum choices. The students enrolled in this program could have been trained (with mom's permission of course) and supervised to give these nutrients, as it would have been good for them to know for their future careers. However, this never crossed the school nurse's mind.

While her title was school nurse and she held a nursing degree, she was a teaching nurse, not one who had ever worked in the medical field. Carrie worked in a hospital as a lab technician and because of her job there, and as the mother of a child with such severe needs, she had more experience in the medical field than the person at the school with the title. Carrie had to go in and train the nurse on how to feed through a G-tube. (She trained us at the elementary school also, but we were educators, not medical professionals, and therefore Carrie understood the need and did not mind.) She also had to train her on what to do if it ever came out, how to properly clean the area, and what to do if any gastric juices were present.

Even after training, Carrie had to go several times to the school to answer questions regarding the tube and drop off supplies and the cans of nutrients. To Carrie, it felt like the school nurse was trying to aggravate her enough that Carrie would stop the tube feedings at school. The school nurse insisted Carrie have a prescription from the doctor stating exactly how much liquid was needed to flush the tubing, how many ounces of nutrients to give, how many ounces of fluid to flush the tubing again, and how many times a day this had to be done. Carrie understood this was a way for the school to be released from any legal responsibilities if something were to go wrong; however, it was just "one more thing" on her list to take care of.

It was interesting to note the school superintendent had the option of sending Kathleen to another district that had a program already in place that would benefit her, but he refused to send her there. He was adamant the school was developing a program where she would be served appropriately. It seemed that while he may have thought that, his staff had a different and probably correct opinion. After her first year, the school implemented a program that was appropriate for her.

Kathleen may not have been as advanced in academic intelligence as her peers, but she was still able to convince people she could not do certain things, even though she was able. When she was in the upper elementary school, she often pretended she had an upset stomach or headache to attempt to get out of doing work. We learned very quickly when she was faking and how to address the situation, but the high school did not want to believe she faked feeling bad.

Kathleen learned very quickly certain behaviors got her sent to the nurse, who then called her mom to come get Kathleen. When the nurse described the symptoms as holding her stomach or her head and not working, Carrie told her to send her back to class if she had no fever. This was the protocol for the rest of the students in the building, and Carrie knew Kathleen was either faking, or it was nothing that warranted leaving school.

The school insisted several times that Carrie come and get Kathleen because they were worried it could be something more, and they did not want to be responsible. As soon as Carrie arrived, Kathleen was usually all smiles, acting normally. Carrie tried to get the school to allow Kathleen to stay, but they still insisted she be taken out of school.

After a few times, Carrie explained to Kathleen if she continued faking being sick, she would be in trouble at home. Kathleen either did not understand or did not believe her mom, so she tried one more time to get out of school. When they arrived home, she had to sit and do nothing for the rest of the day—no iPad, no TV, no music, nothing. Kathleen rarely tried to fake sickness to get out of school after that.

Every day Carrie had a list of things she needed to do for Kathleen. She was always running the list through her mind, prioritizing and re-prioritizing. Things on the list included a wide range of tasks: making and keeping doctor appointments; being aware of Kathleen's weight and what her caloric intake was for the day; paying attention to when Kathleen last had a bowel movement; keeping her healthy and showered; making sure she had clean clothes; checking on her feeding tube and Mic-Key button; making sure insurance paperwork was up-to-date; preparing for IEP meetings; planning for who will be home when Kathleen was home, as she cannot be home alone; providing proof that a nurse or nurse's aide needed to be at the house twenty or more hours a week; making sure the iPad was charged; ordering medical supplies and medicine on time; obtaining prescriptions for occupational and physical therapy for the school systems; bringing Kathleen for fittings and adjustments for orthopedics; getting adjustments for orthodontia; procuring prescriptions for G-tube feedings for the school; sending clean clothes to the school after Kathleen had an accident; bringing supplies to the school for feedings; signing permission slips; and checking homework. And that was for just one child.

As a school teacher, I knew Carrie had a lot of things on her mind because not only did she have Kathleen, but she had her own job, the family business, three other children, her husband, the dogs, the household, and eventually scheduled nursing. Oftentimes I sent reminders home and texted or called her to ask for things. I noticed a few times when Carrie almost seemed frustrated about the reminders. I never thought she was a bad mom, but I knew she had a lot on her plate, and I thought I was being helpful. It turned out those helpful reminders were more frustrating than helpful. She always had a list running through her head of what needed to be done for Kathleen, organized by most to least important. What I considered important really was not in the grand scheme of Kathleen's and Carrie's lives.

There was a time when Kathleen had a hard plastic brace on her foot that went to her mid-calf. It always seemed to rub on her ankle bone and the back of her ankle, which caused redness and swelling. This brace had to fit snugly, almost as tight as skin, to do what it was supposed to do. If she complained that it hurt, or we had to change her clothes because of a toileting accident, we checked it. If the cushion, usually a thick Band-Aid, had come off, we replaced it with a Band-Aid Carrie supplied or one from our office supply.

Once a week, our physical therapist assistant came in, took the brace off, took off Kathleen's sock and checked the ankle area. Frequently, the physical therapist assistant called Carrie to let her know the cushion was missing. She would have been remiss if she had not done that; however, Carrie saw these phone calls as a nuisance after a while. She stopped answering the calls and did not respond to texts for a day or two sometimes.

I understand now why that was the case, but at the time we had no idea we were just piling on to her long list of things. There were several times over the years when Kathleen came to school at the beginning of the year with her change of clothes in case of an accident, diapers, wipes, all her school supplies, a month supply of her nutrients, the tubing for feedings, a toothbrush and toothpaste, and a hair brush. In the early years of my working with Kathleen, Carrie was usually very quick to respond to messages or a text saying we needed more of something. However, as the years progressed, we went through a period of time where her answers and the response for getting replacement clothing took longer. Those, I found out later, were the times Carrie placed our list of needed items on the bottom of her priority list, or the times when

Kathleen packed her suitcase with all the clothes she could find and they all needed to be washed. It was frustrating to me at the time because I did not understand.

During the beginning of Kathleen's second year of high school, the school insisted she get updated prescriptions for occupational and physical therapy, as well as one for her feedings. Those had to be three separate prescriptions. Carrie called each doctor, explained exactly what needed to be written on the prescription, and then drove to each of the doctor's offices to pick them up. This was a Friday, and Carrie immediately put them in Kathleen's folder to take to school on Monday.

Unfortunately, over the weekend Kathleen decided to play school. She took the prescriptions out of the folder and colored on them to the extent that two of them were unreadable. Carrie made this discovery on Monday morning as she was helping Kathleen get ready for school. She had to call the school to let them know what had happened, drive back to those doctors' offices, pick up new prescriptions, and take them to the school. Thankfully, these doctors' offices were within thirty minutes of her home and the school. Again, the list was shuffled to address the priority level of each item.

These were issues the family of a neurotypical developing fourteen-year-old probably did not have. Carrie said "when you have a child with special needs, you are fighting constantly—medical conditions, issues, problems, needing prescriptions—and you have to be willing to do it all, every day, for the rest of your life or your child's life." Any given day can bring new challenges, new obstacles, new frustrations, and of course, new joys.

Carrie recalled a time when her cousin was visiting. This cousin had a child about the same age as Kathleen, around three years old. The cousin had forgotten a sippy cup and asked Carrie if she could borrow one. The cousin found a cup where Carrie told her, but could not find the stopper that keeps liquid from freely flowing out of the sippy cup. When she asked Carrie where the stopper was, Carrie realized she had not thought about her cousin's child needing it. Since Kathleen could not suck, Carrie had thrown all the stoppers away. This was just one more example of how different Carrie and Kathleen's lives were from others.

Carrie felt the education system needed to realize kids like Kathleen benefited from being around others like her, as well as those not like her. Kathleen had a great education because it looked different than anyone else's. She was with kids like her for most of her day, for the majority of her education career in elementary school. She grew and learned more than anyone expected. Carrie believed if Kathleen had been fully included in a general education classroom like some people believed was best, she would not have achieved as much as she had, academically or socially. She said the laws needed to change, districts and legal teams needed to remember the first word of the law's name was "Individual," and each person and situation should be considered in that light.

A pet peeve of Carrie's was when people said to her, "Oh you must be so special because God would not give you more than you can handle. You must be a very strong person . . . yada, yada, yada." To Carrie, this sounded like this person thought God gave Carrie and Kyle a choice. She knew it sounded horrible, but if God had come to her and asked her to give her seal of approval for what He had planned, she would have said, "NO. No. I want her to be everything my other daughters are." She felt when people made those statements, they thought she chose this for her daughter, and given the option, she would choose this for her daughter or another child if she had one.

Carrie believed God gave her Kathleen, and knowing who Kathleen is, she would not change a thing about her, because that would change who she was. She said this did not make her a strong person or a saint, or make raising Kathleen easy. She believed sometimes God gave people things that were going to purify them as described in Zechariah 13:9 when God said He "will refine them as silver is refined, and will try them as gold is tried."

"Gold is put through many phases in order to get the beautiful element we know as gold. It goes through many trials and fires to get all the unnecessary and junky stuff out. Our lives need to have these trials and some sadness because if we do not know anything but happy and good, how can we truly appreciate happy and good?" pondered Carrie. As a Christian, Carrie believed in Jesus and His resurrection and that one day, because Jesus died on the cross for each one of us, we will have perfected bodies in heaven. She had hope through Jesus Christ that one day in heaven, Kathleen and all of us will have perfected bodies that will allow us all to do whatever we need to do perfectly.

Over the years, people have stared at Kathleen, made comments regarding her being worthless and a waste of space, and asked why we have to educate her or medically care for her. Carrie truly believed Kathleen was here for those around her to be challenged to be better. She again referred to biblical scripture citing Jesus's words in Matthew 25:45, "Then he will answer them, 'Truly I tell you, just as you did not do it to one of the least of these, you did not do it to me.'"

Carrie asked the questions, "Will you smile? Will you lend a hand? Will you keep any negative thoughts to yourself? Will you educate yourself?" Carrie wished that instead of people saying to her "You must be special" or "God doesn't give a person more than they can handle," that people said with sincerity, "I know this has got to be a hard road, but you sure seem to be doing a good job, that's a beautiful child." She also said that everyone was only one breath, one accident, or one severe illness away from being just like Kathleen, and how did they want to be treated then? If people thought about that when they saw people with special needs, maybe they would be more considerate and welcoming.

As Kathleen became older, many of the problems from her childhood were distant memories, but new problems were developing. Kathleen was losing strength and stamina with her walking and often preferred to be in a wheelchair. She also developed some sensory problems and was oftentimes overstimulated. Carrie thought when Kathleen used the wheelchair, it gave her a bit of a break from sensory overstimulation. The chair provided a gentle squeezing pressure on her body, which had a calming effect, and when Kathleen did not have to focus on walking and all that entails, she could process everything else around her.

Carrie said being a long-term caregiver was a very difficult job, especially when the one receiving the care was a loved one. Most people who became caregivers with no choice in the matter were the children or spouse of someone who needed care. Those types of caregiver positions typically ended in less than ten years. However, when a child was born with special needs, especially as severe and complex as Kathleen's, the caregiver's role could last anywhere from twenty to fifty years. The way this caregiver's role ended was usually with healing or death of either the caregiver or care receiver.

Carrie talked with a woman who had been a caregiver to her own child for about a year until the child was healed. The other mother was telling Carrie how their situations were so similar and she understood Carrie's life. While Carrie was very happy that the other child healed, she did not feel their situations were similar at all, and it made her a little angry that this mother thought she knew what Carrie's life was like. That mother's child was well and able to do all sorts of things that Kathleen was not, and never will be, able to do. That mother's struggle was over, and she could go about her days very differently compared to what Carrie needed to do for the rest of her life. That mother may have had an idea of what a small, brief portion of Carrie's life was like, but to say she understood it perfectly felt like a slap in the face to Carrie. Indeed, there were times taking care of Kathleen was a whole-family responsibility.

Kathleen's sisters have always been fiercely protective of her. They never wanted Kathleen to feel any sadness or think she was different. They have always told her she is beautiful or cute. Even when Kathleen got on their nerves, as siblings will do sometimes, they did not stay mad or aggravated with her. In fact, they gave her a different name for when she misbehaved or was having a bad day. They called her Veruca. When she tore up their homework, scribbled on prescriptions for therapies, scribbled all over her own homework, changed the settings on the iPad, or was just sassy to them, they referred to her as Veruca, her evil twin. Kathleen did not seem to mind being called Veruca and appeared to understand why they called her that at times. She gave the impression that she enjoyed the good humor behind the name.

Kathleen was closest to her sister Kelly, not only in age, but in relationship. Kelly was always the sister who gave her the most care. Chloe was in junior high and in another part of the school by the time Kathleen started school; Courtney was in the same hall, but at the end of it; and Kelly was just a few doors down, in fourth grade. Every day, one of the girls held Kathleen's hand and walked her into her classroom, then came to the classroom after school, took her by the hand, and walked her back to the bus. Kelly, of course, did this the longest. Kelly also sat with Kathleen on the bus to give her comfort, and provided an extra layer of protection from other kids, or situations that might occur on the bus.

Kathleen was always small for her age and easily thrown off balance. Her sisters were worried she would get knocked down and possibly injure herself or damage the plastic surgeries that had repaired her lip and palate. In fact, at first, the girls were upset with me when I allowed Kathleen to walk down the school halls without holding someone's hand. We always protected her on all sides, but were teaching her independence and responsibility to be as aware as possible of her surroundings. Even when Kathleen was in fifth grade and very capable of walking unassisted, Kelly still held her hand everywhere they went.

When the girls arrived home after school, oftentimes Carrie was at work, and the girls watched Kathleen for a few hours. The girls did not have jobs outside the home; they were needed to help Carrie with Kathleen while Kyle took care of the family business. Many times, as Carrie's shifts changed to evenings, the girls were responsible for helping Kathleen with her homework, feeding her dinner, helping her bathe, and preparing her for bed, as well as doing all those things for themselves.

At the age of seventeen, Kathleen's mental and physical abilities fell in the late preschool to kindergarten level. Due to eye-hand coordination difficulties, there may be some things, like shoe tying, that Kathleen will never be able to do completely on her own. When she was in the early elementary years, the sisters took turns with her so none of them felt overwhelmed and could get their own studies, showers, and dinner completed.

However, as Chloe and Courtney progressed to high school and college, more of Kathleen's care fell upon Kelly's shoulders. She was closest in age to Kathleen and had the least amount of school activities and homework. Kelly spent countless hours playing with Kathleen, bathing her, feeding her, and getting her ready for and tucking her into bed. Because of all this time spent with each other, the two of them became best buddies. Kelly, after Carrie, was Kathleen's biggest protector, cheerleader, and fan.

As the girls became older, Kathleen was not content to just play with dolls and toys; she wanted to be like her big sisters and have an iPad, watch television, and listen to music. One could think this might make caring for her easier, as she would be able to be alone for periods of time. Some evenings, Kathleen sat and listened to music or watched YouTube videos, but most evenings she needed to be watched carefully so she would not get into trouble. When she was bored, Kathleen would try to change the channel or switch to a different application on the iPad, and not remember how to get back to what she had been doing. Then she either became frustrated or decided to find something else to do.

When she decided to do something else, as long as she was quiet, she may not be noticed for a little while. Around the age of twelve, she was infatuated for a time with country singer Luke Bryan, and she was going to see him. Kathleen found a suitcase and took every piece of clothing she could reach—out of the drawers, closet, and hamper—and put it into the suitcase. She also packed books, toys, and whatever she thought she would need. Several times Carrie came home from work to find Kathleen packed and ready to go live with Luke Bryan.

Thankfully, she was never strong enough to pick up her full suitcase and leave the house. However, since she packed every piece of clothing she had, Carrie had to wash it all; she was not sure what was clean and what was dirty before it went into the suitcase. When Kathleen was bored, she also went through stacks of papers, some of which were the other girls' homework, and draw on them. She never did anything dangerous. She just did things that required a little technical knowledge or cleaning up.

Carrie did not want to talk about the negatives, because she would rather have people think her life is perfect and struggle-free than have someone think Kathleen should not be here, was a waste of space, or was not worth living. Carrie tended not to talk about the struggles, because when she talked about the burden, the stress, how it changed her life, how she was not footloose and fancy-free, and how she could not do whatever she wanted when she wanted, people thought badly of Kathleen and others like her. Carrie's reality was that she always had Kathleen to think about and it was very limiting on her life.

"Most people don't understand and I tend not to focus on those things, because I do not want people to get the impression I have less love for Kathleen, or I see her as something less than what she should be, or that all the terrible assumptions people have about my child are true," says Carrie. But the fact of the matter was, she was limited. She could not have a bad day, be sick, go on a girls' weekend, or do any of the things "normal" moms could do every once in a while. Finding a sitter was still necessary for Kathleen even at the age of seventeen, and if Kyle or one of Kathleen's siblings was not available, then Carrie was just out of luck. Extended family and friends were not available or physically unable to take care of Kathleen for many reasons.

The amount of trust Carrie had to have in a person to leave them to care for her seventeen-year-old, nonverbal, very affectionate, medically complex, intellectually challenged daughter was astronomical and impossible to muster. This was Carrie's life every day for either the remainder of her life, or the remainder of Kathleen's life.

That brought tears to Carrie's eyes as she pondered what will happen to Kathleen when Carrie passes away. While I do not want my child to be sad when I pass away, and therefore try to make as many happy memories now as possible, I do not worry about how my child will be taken care of when I'm gone. This was a huge reality for Carrie—something she had to plan and prepare for Kathleen's future. This was a heavy weight on Carrie's mind that she thought of almost daily. She had to consider where Kathleen will live, how she will be taken care of financially, medically, and emotionally, and who will help her with those decisions.

One step Carrie had to take when Kathleen turned eighteen was filing for legal guardianship. Parents of typically developing children did not have to do this, but many parents of children with special needs had to, for the safety of their child. This was important to do so others cannot take advantage of their child's finances, living decisions, medical decisions, and more. This was just another item Carrie had to add to her list of daily care items for Kathleen. She had to start the process months in advance, involve a lawyer, and go with the family to court so a decision can be made.

Having a child with special needs for Carrie was one giant emotional roller coaster ride. There were, of course, the highs of seeing Kathleen reach a milestone or witnessing the joy she had inside her and shared with everyone, and those fleeting moments when Carrie forgot for just a second her daughter had exceptionalities. Then there were those moments when life crashed around her with the reality of her situation and Kathleen's. Some days she was mentally, physically, and emotionally exhausted and was not sure she could continue to do this daily. She felt guilty for having these feelings. However, those feelings did not last very long. They were soon replaced with the joy Kathleen's smile brought as she rode her horse at a therapy center (her favorite activity), or danced to her favorite songs, or hugged Carrie and expressed her love for her.

During the ten years I had with Kathleen, I think I learned just as much, if not more, than she did. I learned that even when something was difficult or seemed impossible, a good attitude was still possible. I learned hard work could look very different from one person to the next. I learned compassion in a much deeper sense. I learned patience beyond what I thought possible—not with me for her, but her for me. I learned humans could express themselves without using words and sometimes more beautifully. I learned love was actions more than words.

Kathleen taught me to appreciate all I had and could do and to celebrate all victories. She taught me strength, persistence, unconditional trust, unconditional love from a non-family member, the practice of finding true joy in the simple things of life, courage to face fears on a daily basis, and kindness all the time, anywhere, to anyone. She taught me not to underestimate her abilities or knowledge or to put limits on what she could do or learn. She taught me to be a better person.

Thank you, Kathleen and Carrie, for sharing your story and lives.

Wyatt

Wyatt was Kim and Roger's first child and first pregnancy; they were both 30 years old. Kim had a condition known as polycystic ovary syndrome (PCOS) which had many side effects, one of which was infertility. The doctor warned Kim that becoming pregnant for the first time would be difficult and could take a long time. She dieted and began taking metformin, a common drug choice for women with PCOS who were trying to get pregnant.

The doctor's warning was unnecessary, and they were quickly expecting. The pregnancy was an easy one. Kim experienced very little morning sickness, her weight gain was good, she ate right, and her pregnancy seemed to meet all milestones. She talked with her mom and her sister about their pregnancy and birth experiences. She took classes, read books, and did everything she could think of to prepare herself.

Even while doing all this preparation, Kim realized things may not go by the book, or like her family's experiences, or even like her birth plan. Her plan was to have a natural birth—no medications during the delivery. She also wanted to make sure she followed the doctors' directions. She had a family member who did not listen to the doctor, and things went wrong.

About a week before she was due, Kim noticed the baby did not seem to be moving much. The doctor's office staff told her it was normal, and unless the baby's movements were fewer than three times an

269

hour, she need not worry. The baby was moving three times an hour, but barely.

The next day, at her regularly scheduled doctor's appointment, a week before her due date, the doctor noticed something was wrong with the baby. The baby's heartbeat had decreased quite substantially from the week before. The doctor told her, with no urgency or tension in his voice, that they may have to induce her. He left the room to go check on something. Though she was still concerned for her baby, Kim felt a sense of relief, because they had identified a problem and were taking action on it, and she realized the day had finally come to meet her baby.

The doctor returned almost immediately; something had changed his mind. Much later, they told Kim the baby's heart rate was low and had dropped dramatically during the exam. With urgency and concern in his voice, the doctor told Kim she needed to go to a prep room immediately. She needed to have her baby by emergency cesarean section (C-section).

Kim and her husband worked about an hour away from the doctor's office, the hospital, and their home. Roger was at work because they did not think this appointment would be anything other than routine. Kim was scared, confused, worried, feeling very alone, and hoping her parents or Roger could make it to the hospital at least on time for the baby's birth—if the baby was born alive. Kim began thinking the baby may not make it or maybe had already died. She had a million more negative thoughts running through her head and no one there to talk to or comfort her. Minutes felt like hours.

Every second she wondered what was happening: What was wrong? Was there a problem with the baby? Was there a problem with her? Why had the doctor's attitude changed so quickly? She knew something would go wrong; should she have called the doctor sooner? How long had the baby's heartbeat been low? How long had the movements been right at three per hour or less? Would Roger or anyone make it to the hospital on time? Was this some sort of punishment for the times she missed a prenatal vitamin or ate some junk food during her pregnancy? Was this some kind of trade-off for having become pregnant so easily or for having such an easy pregnancy? Was the baby's life in danger? Was her life in danger? Had she wanted this too much? Had she done something during the pregnancy to cause this? Was this the other shoe dropping?

While she was worried, Kim was also a pragmatist and thought if there was a problem with the baby, at least the baby would be taken care of right away and not have the trauma of going through the birth canal too. She was in such a state of shock, she did not really remember being taken to the operating room or getting prepped for surgery. She appeared on the outside like she was calm and in control, but inside was chaos. The medical staff brought in the big needle to administer the numbing medicine so they could perform the C-section, and she did not react. She just followed the directions she was given and showed no emotion, almost like a robot or being on autopilot. Kim hoped for the positive in all situations and simultaneously prepared in the back of her mind for the negative. In retrospect, Kim believed she was able to endure what was happening to her physically and remain calm and quiet during this time, because she mentally prepared herself for the negative.

Kim watched the medical team take care of her newborn and wondered what was happening to her son. She did not get to hold him or see him. She realized she would lose out on those precious first moments with her child she wanted so badly. She realized she had taken for granted those moments so many of her friends and family talked about. She would not experience the doctor placing her newborn baby in her arms. She felt selfish for having the thought, but she shared it with me because it was part of her journey.

The medical team took her baby to another part of the hospital, and she began to cry silently as she realized her baby's life was in more peril than she had allowed herself to think. Shortly after the team left with their baby, Roger arrived with Kim's parents. They had missed the entire C-section. They did not realize all Kim had seen, heard, and gone through. When they arrived at the room, the looks on their faces told a very serious story, and Kim knew her baby's life was in danger.

Both Kim's dad and Roger had commented to a nurse about how beautiful the baby's skin was, and how he looked like a porcelain doll. The nurse soberly responded that babies were not supposed to look like that when they were born; they were supposed to be red, purple, or a flushed color. The baby was born extremely pale; his Apgar score was well below normal.

Kim tried to stay calm and to remember to breathe right after she gave birth. She was relieved her baby had been born alive, but she still worried about how long he would live. She felt numb. In a way, she was protecting herself from what could happen. The doctor was very serious and gave her only the facts. There was no warmth to his voice. He was not softening the blows as he told her something was wrong. Kim's inner chaos was growing, but she had to hold herself together so she could hear what the doctor was saying. It was difficult to focus as her thoughts kept returning to her fears. Would she ever get to hold her son? Would he die?

The decision was made that the baby's condition was too critical for him to remain at the small hospital. He was airlifted to a hospital with a neonatal intensive care unit (NICU). Kim was shocked and scared. She went through the same mental turmoil she had experienced earlier in the day when she was being prepped for the C-section. How could this happen when her entire pregnancy had gone smoothly, and there had been no indication anything could or would be wrong with her child?

Kim was finally able to see her baby but was only allowed to kiss his forehead as the medical team rushed to the helicopter. When she kissed him, he felt so real and soft, and it was hard for her to fathom he may die at any minute. The memory of this moment was etched into her mind in excruciating detail, causing her to cry years later. She did not know exactly what would happen to her baby. She thought the kiss could be her last moment with her son.

Roger and her parents left for the NICU when the helicopter did. Kim was alone and panicked because she could not get answers from anyone. One doctor told her to be prepared for the possibility Wyatt may not make it. She returned to the thought that her pregnancy had been too good to be true. She had wanted so badly to be a mom for so long, and the pregnancy had gone so well. It seemed almost natural that something bad would happen.

Kim had no choice but to stay at the local hospital for a couple more days, recovering from the C-section. The hospital did not seem to know what to do with her. Other babies were being born, the hospital was running out of room, and Kim did not have a baby with her. The hospital moved her out of the birthing suite and into a small corner exam room situated away from other new moms and babies. Nurses in the birthing unit were focused on taking care of babies. Kim did not have a baby in her room, so nurses were not checking in very often. She again found herself dealing with an unexpected and scary situation by herself. While she understood their reasoning for leaving her alone, her feelings of not being a mom took firmer root in her isolation.

Though he was able to stay strong when he was alone at the NICU, Roger was an emotional mess when he was with Kim and did not really know how to help her. She resented him for a while, because she felt she had to endure this unexpected situation by herself. She did not want to be the strong one. She wanted someone to take care of her, to comfort her, and tell her everything would be okay. In retrospect, she was proud that Roger was strong for Wyatt and was proud of herself for holding it together and being strong, too, even when she did not want to be.

While at the hospital, she pumped her breast milk and sent it to the NICU. Every new experience was a reminder of how things had gone wrong. She was going through the motions and doing things new mothers do, but she did not feel like a mom and spent a lot of time wondering what she had done wrong. The medical staff told her it would help her healing if she walked; she was very glad they told her that. Walking helped her feel less isolated and gave her an opportunity to think about what had happened, and what might still happen.

Before Wyatt was born, Kim had not given a lot of thought to the moment when a mother and child meet for the first time. When other mothers told stories about the instant connection they shared with their baby, Kim secretly thought it was an exaggeration. Until she had Wyatt and could not hold him, she had not realized the beauty that moment can hold. The three days Kim could not see Wyatt were torturous. She agonized over when she would see him and what it would be like.

When the time came and she was finally able to hold Wyatt, she did not instantly feel he was hers. She knew he was hers, but she did not have instantaneous connection and joy. It felt like she was holding someone else's baby. The feeling began to change when, at the urging of the hospital staff, she held Wyatt using skin-on-skin contact. She had not realized how much she had both craved and mourned the loss of those precious first moments after Wyatt was born. She felt she had lost a piece of connection with Wyatt, and was skeptical about whether the skin-on-skin connection would help. She felt guilty she had not been there when Wyatt needed her, and she had let him down.

That small skin-on-skin connection worked. She finally had the feeling she had been missing and was able to start working through her anxiety and guilt. Looking back, Kim remembered building the bond as being different than her experience with her other three children, but not less or worse. The bond just took a little longer to happen and, over time, became something as special and extraordinary as Wyatt himself.

When Wyatt arrived at the NICU, doctors determined he was anemic and needed a blood transfusion. After the transfusion he perked up, and within a few hours became the color he was supposed to be. While Wyatt's health no longer seemed to be in jeopardy, he remained in the NICU for one week for observation.

During the week, Kim still struggled to deal with all the emotions she was feeling and often cried. When she walked around the NICU, she began to feel guilty for a different reason. Most of the babies in the NICU were premature or were visually struggling. After the transfusion, Wyatt looked like a beautiful, healthy, full sized baby. The visual difference between Wyatt and the other babies was striking, and many of the other parents smiled at him and commented on how good he looked. Kim felt ashamed, because the other babies' lives were still in peril and their families were in real distress, while she was crying over a beautiful, healthy baby. She felt as though her emotional turmoil and tears had been over dramatic and unwarranted.

Some tests done on Wyatt and Kim a few weeks after he was released from the NICU revealed that instead of her placenta giving red blood cells to her baby, it began taking them from him. Doctors explained Wyatt may have side effects from the lack of oxygenated blood during the final days of the pregnancy. When Kim knew it was something her body caused, her guilt increased tremendously. She still battles with the guilt, though not as much as when Wyatt was first born.

Kim and Roger stayed at the Ronald McDonald House the week Wyatt was in the NICU. Kim and her family were so grateful to the Ronald McDonald House and the wonderful services they provided. Except for clothing, every item a parent needed to stay close to their child during a medical crisis was provided at no cost to the families. The apartment-style residence featured a playroom, kitchen with meals and snacks, bedrooms, and bathroom with fully stocked toiletries. Kim found out how much it had meant to her mother after her mother passed away, and her funeral plans included directions for people to donate to Ronald McDonald House in lieu of flowers or other memorials. Kim recommended Ronald McDonald House, both for its services to families and as an organization worthy of donations.

When Kim and Roger brought Wyatt home, they were so thankful he was alive that they held him and watched him for hours at a time. It took some time for the realization he was going to live to completely set in. They marveled at every little thing he did. He hit his milestones of rolling over, crawling, walking, and talking like any other baby.

At around the age of two, he became very defiant. His speech regressed, and refusals became his primary form of communication. He refused to do anything he was asked or told to do. Kim did not worry too much, because she thought it was the terrible twos phase. He often thought about what he was being asked or told to do, and after he said no, eventually gave in and did what was requested.

While he had plenty of meltdowns or temper tantrums in his young life, his parents and doctor agreed his behavior was not uncommon for his age. However, some friends and family had noticed the behavior and thought there was reason for concern. They began asking Kim if she had ever thought about having him evaluated.

One woman asked Kim if she had ever had Wyatt evaluated for autism. Autism is a developmental disorder that impairs the ability to interact and communicate. Kim thought this was rather bold of the woman and pushed it aside, because the woman had no expertise or experience with autism. She felt this woman was just saying this because Wyatt was not behaving, and maybe the woman was annoyed. Kim felt bad later for having those feelings and was disappointed in herself for being so unaware of her child's developmental delays.

She thought Wyatt did not show the same types of signs or behaviors people in movies or on television showed. She thought all people with autism were very obviously different, nonverbal or oddly verbal, idiosyncratic in their tendencies, and did not want to be touched. At the time, Wyatt was not bothered by sensory stimuli, he talked, he did not have any obvious idiosyncratic tendencies, and he was affectionate. Years later, he was still very affectionate and did not have many of the behaviors that quickly identified a person as being on the autism spectrum. Even on their doctor's diagnostic questionnaire for autism, he did not fit the criteria for most of the questions.

Kim and Roger's home state offered a preschool program based on academic needs for children when they turned three. At the screening, Kim and Roger had expected Wyatt's scores to be low, since they were expecting his noncompliance from home to carry over. They did not expect his scores to be as low as they were. For Kim, it was like being hit over the head.

Up to this point, he had always met his milestones, and the pediatrician voiced no concerns. Kim began to think back to the earlier mentions of autism she had brushed aside. The results of Wyatt's evaluation showed he would benefit from an early childhood learning program, and he was allowed to join at no cost to Kim and Roger. The scores prompted Kim and Roger to seek a diagnosis for Wyatt.

Wyatt began the pre-kindergarten program, and Kim signed him up for an evaluation from a highly recommended group of specialists from a local university. The next available time for an evaluation was nearly a year later. Kim recommended that parents who want to have their child evaluated should call as soon as possible; expert evaluation is in high demand.

While they waited for Wyatt's evaluation, Kim began working with the pre-kindergarten program to support their work with Wyatt. The faculty and staff at the school cared a lot about Wyatt and worked well with the family. When Wyatt had behaviors in his preschool program, the staff called Kim and discussed a plan for how they wanted to help Wyatt learn appropriate behaviors.

In the meantime, she began to process all the feelings from when he was born. She finally allowed herself to think of all the things that had gone wrong. She started to realize how many unintentional expectations she had for what Wyatt's life would be like. She began to mourn all the things she thought Wyatt would participate in and experience, and all the things he would be, if he were "normal." She wondered if he would be able to land a job, live independently, go to college, or have a wife. Then she remembered she almost did not have a son at all. She was overwhelmed both with shame for her thoughts and with gratitude for Wyatt's life.

The uncertainty of what path Wyatt would take and what would happen to him when she and Roger pass away were the thoughts that kept her up at night. When she was a child, there was a young man in her town who was disabled and lived with his mother. Though he was nonverbal, he was a member of the choir at the church she attended. He made sounds at the notes rather than sing the words. Kim did not interact with him much, as he was older, and she only saw him at church.

He was an adult, but unable to care for himself when his mother passed away. All at once, he had to deal with the loss of his mother, and he was moved to a group home. She wondered how much this man understood about his situation, whether he had anticipated his mother's death, or was it even something he could comprehend, and what sort of trauma did all this change cause him. She began to worry about whether Wyatt would have similar experiences.

Wyatt finally met with the evaluation team right before he began kindergarten. They confirmed what Kim had grown to expect; Wyatt was on the autism spectrum. Hearing the diagnosis opened the door to a very different reality than what she had unintentionally expected. She began the same cycle of fear, resentment, and shame she had experienced periodically since Wyatt was born.

Thoughts of the young man from her childhood came racing back. If something happened to her, who would take care of Wyatt? Where would he live? Who would put his needs above their own or think about how things would affect him? After the fear came resentment when more unintentional expectations raced to her mind. She had wanted to be a grandmother, and now it did not seem possible; she wanted to enjoy "normal" things with her child, and now it did not seem possible; she wanted to be like any other mother, and now it did not seem possible; why was this happening to her? She was the most ashamed of these thoughts.

Kim felt this struggle was Wyatt's, and while she walked along-side him, it was not about her. She sometimes became upset with her-self for thinking about her broken expectations, because she felt they were the ultimate in selfishness. However, she also felt it was a normal thought process, and according to my experience with other parents, she was correct.

She came to believe that no matter what she did or did not do, Wyatt would be who he was, because that was who he was supposed to be. If somehow Wyatt could magically have the autism taken away, she would not want it to happen, even for all the money in the world, because then he would not be the Wyatt she knew and loved.

Moments of mourning were brief because she always remembered something about Wyatt's uniqueness that made her smile. All parents have hopes and expectations for their child, whether their child has ex-ceptionalities or not. When reality does not measure up to their hopes, parents begin to question and wonder.

Even before she was pregnant, Kim tried to temper her expecta-tions for her children. She had heard so many other parents comment about how their children were not living up to their expectations. Kim did not want to have those feelings, or pass those feelings along to her children. Like most parents, she presumed her children might struggle with making right choices, standing up to peer pressure, and being a good friend. Never did she imagine her child would be on the autism spectrum or that she would have to face and reevaluate the expecta-tions she had tried to avoid.

As Kim, Roger, and Wyatt began to learn and adjust to the diagnosis, they decided to add to the family. Right before Wyatt turned four, they welcomed his brother Oscar into the family. More changes were in store a year later, when Roger changed employment and the family moved to another state. Moving to a different state meant a seismic shift in services available to special-needs children, both in and out of school.

In a short period of time, Wyatt had to deal with changes to his family, home, school, teachers, and all of the everyday things that were familiar to him. Kim reached out to a few contacts who had experience with school services in their new location. She became aware that moving to the new location meant a new individualized education plan (IEP), fewer services, and more reliance on out-of-school support.

One of the recommended services outside of school was the March of Dimes. They provided a helpful service that assigned a trained social worker to come into their home, observe, and train her and Roger on autism strategies and interventions to help Wyatt. It was introductory rather than ongoing support, and it required insurance. They were fortunate to be covered, and recognized others may not be. She hoped someday there will be a service that comes to families' homes regularly and trains parents and caregivers how to help their children with special needs grow their abilities as much as possible.

It soon became apparent Wyatt had a pattern of good behavior followed by regression. In the first few weeks of school, he started with good behavior, then began to withhold participation, then acted out and tested boundaries. He eventually turned the behavior around, returned to better behavior, and made academic progress. After a few weeks the cycle began again. This cycle continued throughout most of his elementary school years.

He made good progress, but it did not always fit the teacher's definition of acceptable. His first-grade teacher halted his progress when he would not perform academic tasks as she wanted him to, even though it was directly caused by his autism, not willful behavior. For example, he often used incorrect pronouns, such as confusing gender, during his reading assignments. She stopped him and did not allow him to proceed until he read the passages perfectly. The result was that he did not progress at all.

This occurred over the course of a year before Kim and Roger became aware of it. His second-grade teacher was great. She recognized Wyatt was capable, but delayed due to his behaviors and his lack of progress the year before. She eventually recommended an additional year in her class so she could help him get back on track. Kim and Roger agreed repeating second grade worked out for the best.

While Wyatt was struggling in his new situation, Kim was looking for a prekindergarten program for Wyatt's brother, Oscar. Unfortunately for Oscar, their new state did not offer the kind of free prekindergarten services that had been so helpful to Wyatt and his parents. Kim found a tuition-based program run by their new school district. It seemed like it might provide similar service. It turned out to be a very different experience with rigid expectations and very few interventions or accommodations for atypical children. According to Kim, they wanted Oscar to be perfectly behaved at all times. When he was not, they sent him home and told Kim she needed to fix his behavior before they allowed her to bring him back.

In one incident she recalled, Oscar was three years old and they called her to pick him up. When she arrived, they told her he had run out of line and then had a temper tantrum. Kim asked if Oscar could hold hands with someone in line, or if one of the adults could hold his hand, and she was told the school was not allowed to restrain kids in that manner.

Kim and Roger eventually decided to find a different school after another concerning experience. One day Oscar went to the bathroom and inexplicably stripped completely naked. His teacher, a state award-winning teacher, left him in the bathroom for over an hour. She said she could not go in and get him because it was against school policy. The safety issue of a teacher alone with a student would have been solved if she asked another employee to go into the bathroom with her. The only reason Oscar came out of the bathroom was because the school staff called Kim to pick him up.

The staff at Oscar's school did not know how, or refused, to implement a behavior program for him and oftentimes made his behaviors worse by their actions or inactions. He was not permitted to move around, express his feelings, fidget, or talk out of turn without getting into trouble. It was a tall order for any three-year-old.

After a couple of years, the family moved back to their home state. The family experienced the same whirlwind of changes as the last time they had moved. Kim gave birth to twin girls, Emily and Valerie, and the family had a new home, in a new neighborhood, with new school, new teachers and new surroundings. This time, the educational challenges were fewer and the new schools had more services and interventions. In retrospect, Kim felt this was the best decision for their children. Oscar and Wyatt thrived in their home state school systems and received the help they needed and deserved.

Wyatt was finally moving past his persistent refusals and began to show real progress, often surprising Kim. However, she began to notice other areas where Wyatt was not progressing in a typical way. Sometimes she realized Wyatt was at an age when his peers were doing a certain thing, and he was not; she caught herself going through the same cycle of shattered expectations, fear, resentment, and shame.

Kim often felt under qualified to work with Wyatt. She did not know where to go or whom to ask for help, and if she found the right person, she did not know what to ask. She wished there had been support groups or that she had friends who were going through similar issues so she would not feel so alone. Advice from someone who had already been down her path would have been exceptionally helpful. "You don't know what you don't know until someone enlightens you," she said.

Like Wyatt, she was making progress. The more she noticed her feelings, the more she began to accept them and forgive herself. She found when she stopped defining what her children were, or what she wanted for them, she did not mourn the images she had in her mind of what Wyatt, Oscar, Valerie, or Emily would be like.

The feeling Kim struggled with the most was anger at how the world looked at Wyatt, and how the opportunities he had because of his uniqueness were different than what others had. She told the story of going to the zoo in a big city when he was in elementary school. He was not interacting with kids his own age in a typically expected fashion. Kim believed this was partly due to his autism, and partly because she and Roger did not have many social interactions outside of their family. They were each other's best friends and enjoyed spending their time with each other and their children the most. She felt maybe they did not set the best example for their children on social skills.

At the zoo, Wyatt approached a boy and girl sitting on a bench and attempted to engage them in a conversation. Kim beamed with pride because Wyatt was putting himself out there and trying to interact with kids close to his age. The kids scooted away from him, gave him the "oh, you're a weird kid" look, and said something along the lines of "What's wrong with you?" Kim immediately grabbed Wyatt's arm and hurried him away from the children.

She quickly went from proud mama bear to angry mama bear saying uncharitable things about those kids and their parents in front of Wyatt. Later, she looked back at her reaction and knew she handled it badly. She wondered if she should have used the moment as a teachable one for the other children and for Wyatt. Could the situation have turned around if she had taken the time to speak to those kids and remained calm? Even as she shared the memory with me, she became angry again. For people with an invisible disability, being mistreated happens often, and it was a challenge for Kim to overcome her emotional response and to consistently educate herself and others.

I had the privilege of teaching Wyatt for one year, when he was in fourth grade. He was a very bright student who was close to grade level. Wyatt had been improving academically, behaviorally, and socially for the past few years. Kim described Wyatt's behavioral pattern from his earlier school years. She shared how he started the school year fine, but within a few weeks his behavior regressed, so I was prepared.

He had a rough day or part of a day within the first few weeks of school, but those behaviors did not last long. He was processing a lot of new information, as he was in a new school building, and had all new teachers, routines, foods, smells, sounds, rules, and classmates (two schools merged at fourth grade). At home he was adjusting, too, most notably to life with two toddlers.

If I gave Wyatt time to process whatever was causing some inappropriate behaviors and then talked to him about it, he was usually fine within a very short amount of time. When my students had time to process what happened, talked about why they had those behaviors, and decided what options were acceptable for the next time, they always did much better. Wyatt thrived in this type of setting. I kept a daily behavior log for him on his desk, and rarely did he score less than 85 percent for the day.

Some people might think I should have been happy only with 95 percent or better. For some students, that might have been the acceptable percentage and a standard they could achieve, but if we looked at ourselves and most other students, no one was really on task, following directions, sitting quietly, respecting everyone at all times, staying in their seat for hours at a time, interacting and getting along with everyone whether they liked them or not, and doing things whether they enjoyed them or not, without complaining, 95-100 percent of the time. We demand children comply with a lot of things we do not expect adults to do and get frustrated when the child does not comply.

A child with autism has difficulty meeting many basic expectations. For example, some kids with autism are very factual and literal. They are not trying to be disobedient, rude, or sarcastic in a conversation; they're stating facts. This was Wyatt in many instances, although through language training, he understood and used increasing amounts of figurative language.

Expectations, however, are a two-way street. The world is full of oddities that challenge the expectations of a child like Wyatt. They do not easily understand figures of speech, idioms, or abstract concepts. While Wyatt was in my class, we discussed his experiences, and I helped him understand not everyone's experiences were exactly the same. Some words were even pronounced differently based on the person's family or location. This helped him understand his textbook materials, and his interactions with other people improved too.

Wyatt's sweet personality shined through some of these moments. There was an idiomatic phrase Wyatt had a really difficult time grasping for a good part of the year before he understood. While I was proud of him in his moment of clarity, the random moments that followed made me smile. He tried to convince me he still did not understand the phrase, but his cute smile turned into a giggle very quickly when we talked about it. He often used it incorrectly on purpose, just to see if I would catch him.

I very much enjoyed these interactions, because he was proud of himself. He wanted me to see he really did understand. Kim and I observed that while sometimes it took Wyatt a little longer to comprehend something, he was capable of grasping almost all concepts. As soon as Wyatt agreed with me that something was important, or he understood the why behind something, he mastered it more quickly.

Unfortunately for Wyatt and many children who learn differently, finding their way through the educational system was challenging, even with the services and interventions available in the best of school districts. And sometimes even educators can be as misguided and misinformed as those children who mistreated Wyatt at the zoo.

The teacher Wyatt had for fifth grade had gotten to know him and his ability level, because our classrooms were right next to each other. By the end of the year with her, he was on grade level in math. In sixth grade, his new special education teacher, who did not know him, lumped him in with her other special education students and their curriculum. At the end of his previous year, he was doing multiplication and division and working with fractions. His sixth-grade teacher had him adding and subtracting single digits. Kim sent a note early in the year asking about this work and received very little response. The work continued to be well below his ability level.

At parent and teacher conferences at the end of October, she questioned the teacher again. This time the teacher said it was the whole class curriculum, and when she gave him the test at the beginning of the year to determine his baseline, that was where he scored—three years below grade level. The teacher seemed defensive. She gave the excuse that it was just her and an aide with ten kids and implied it was too difficult to individualize the curriculum.

Kim felt like this was the first-grade teacher all over again. She explained what math skills Wyatt had mastered the year before and stated she believed he could do higher-level math skills. She showed in his IEP from the previous year he was doing those math skills with success and expressed her concern he would fall behind his peers if this was all that was expected of him. The teacher agreed there were a few students who might be able to do higher-level skills, and she would attempt it with him and those other students.

After a couple of weeks, Kim received a note from the teacher saying Wyatt was able to do the work, although it was difficult for him, but he was putting in great effort. When Kim asked Wyatt about it, he replied the work was not any more difficult than what he had been doing before. He was taking it all in stride. Kim knew from his behaviors at home he was not struggling with the math. If the new work had been too difficult for him, she would have seen his stress increase on the first day of higher-level math.

Kim felt teachers did what was easiest for them until someone spoke up. She felt helpless. She worried things would not change, and all the progress he made in the previous two years would have been for nothing. His grades were A's, but to Kim it did not mean anything, because he was working on material that was too easy for him. She preferred he be challenged, even if it meant a lower grade on his report card. Kim continued to be proactive when it came to Wyatt's math curriculum. At the end of the school year, Wyatt finished at grade level again for his math skills.

For this reason and many others, Kim pondered the effect of having a different special education teacher every year. When she asked Wyatt's school district staff the same question, they were very defensive. She said, "It is as if the school is just waiting to be offended or blamed." Kim wanted to be an equal member of the IEP team as the law provided and felt without all the information, she truly was not equal. She was not looking to lay blame; she just wanted to know more information or get educators' opinions on things.

Through it all, Wyatt had a great outlook and was always cheery. Kim worried someday he would lose his great disposition and give up, or worse, get angry. Kim believed some members of her family and of Roger's had negative outlooks on life, even though their lives were "normal." Her big fear was of Wyatt picking up the negativity as kids and adults mistreated him.

Despite her fear, she had a great hope that if Wyatt maintained his good attitude and continued to put in effort, he would be okay. Her hope grew as she saw Wyatt improve and progress. In one of the first parent-teacher conferences I had with Kim, she was concerned about Wyatt going to college and getting a degree. She was worried he would not be able to handle the social, behavioral, and independent parts of college. I spoke to her of options for college degrees and assured her if he continued to progress every year as he had done in my classroom, he would be able to achieve those things.

At the most recent annual review of Wyatt's IEP, she raised the concern again. She was given great insight into programs already available to people with disabilities who wanted to attend college, with the hope of even more options by the time Wyatt graduates high school in six years. Kim's fears were less and less each year. She felt very thankful autism was becoming more socially accepted, and disabilities in general were becoming more widely accommodated.

As Wyatt matured, Kim's and Roger's families noticed the positive changes, and seemed to worry less about his future. In one of many signs of his growing maturity, Wyatt developed a morning routine. He got up at a certain time, dressed, prepared and ate his breakfast of Froot Loops cereal and milk, and brushed his teeth. On a recent morning, they were out of Froot Loops, and he calmly asked Kim if they could go to the store. When they arrived at the sparsely populated local grocery store, Kim asked Wyatt if he wanted to go in and buy the cereal on his own. He did.

Into the store he went, cash in hand. He came out with Froot Loops, milk, and a few other items which Kim questioned him about. He told her that he wanted the other items and had calculated the amount of cash he had, compared it with the cost of the items, knew he had enough, and thought it was okay. He also told her when he went to get the milk, he deliberately checked the expiration dates and chose the container with the longest shelf life. While this may not have seemed like a big step to some, this was huge for Wyatt.

There were a lot of skills involved in this transaction from start to finish: he remained calm when his routine was thrown off; knew he could ask to get more; asked his mom if they could go to the store; engaged successfully in social interaction in the store; kept a running total of the cost of the items; knew how much money he had; navigated around the store; planned the checkout process; knew he should get change at the register; and calmly explained to his mom about the extra items. After this great experience, Kim looked for more opportunities for Wyatt to do things independently. She hoped to find an overnight camp in her area for Wyatt to attend and have the experience of spending the night and taking care of himself outside of mom and dad's protection.

For every step forward, though, he seemed to take an unexpected step backward. Wyatt had speech and language therapy when he was younger, and when his speech patterns were at grade level, he was released from this therapy. However, recently, Wyatt developed an irregular speech pattern, pausing at the syllables in every word. Kim thought Wyatt had some control over this, because when he was told to stop, he usually did. At the times when he did not stop, Kim noticed he appeared to be smirking.

Kim's parents noticed his peculiar speech pattern too and, out of concern, had mentioned it many times to her in front of Wyatt. At the time, she wished they would not do that. She did not want to feed into a behavior by giving it attention, and if it was not a behavior, she did not want to feed his fears. Over time, her opinion shifted. She said sometimes hearing from someone other than parents could be a powerful tool, and she felt it could be helpful to include the child in a discussion about their concerns.

As the oldest child in the family, Wyatt started to realize his siblings looked up to him. He helped out more around the house, took on more responsibility helping his siblings, and worked diligently on being a good example to them. Kim was very happy this was happening, with one caveat: she was concerned Wyatt inherited her tendency to be a people pleaser. She wanted him to know he did not have to do things just because it appeared it would make someone happy. She was uncertain whether he would stand up for himself if it was dangerous or something he did not want to do. As he approached puberty, this became an even greater concern for her.

People's expectations create a major difficulty for people with an invisible disability like autism. People forget, do not know, or do not believe the person has a disability and often treat the person inconsiderately or downright cruelly. She saw the people-pleasing trait in Wyatt and worried he could be taken advantage of, or easily convinced to do things that were not in his best interest. So far, Wyatt had not had any cruel interactions, but it did not stop Kim from thinking it will happen in the future.

When Valerie and Emily were three, they participated in the same needs-based prekindergarten program Wyatt had benefited from, and which Kim wished Oscar had been able to attend. The program was in their home school district and offered to bus all their preschool students. This was extremely helpful for Kim, because it alleviated the complex logistics required to load all her children into the car every morning.

During the school year, the girls were in two different classes. At first, Kim was concerned how Valerie and Emily would do being separated, but they made some discoveries for which she was very thankful. Some areas of need came to light for each of them that may have continued unnoticed if they had stayed together; they each compensated for the other's weaker areas. Additionally, this separation allowed the girls to develop their own distinct personalities, which Kim described as delightful.

Eventually, Kim and Roger discovered all of their children had either behavioral or developmental delays. Kim looked back at her journey with Wyatt with gratitude and felt better prepared to handle the challenges that come with special-needs children. Kim shared a little about a typical day in her household, which illustrated the accommodations required to guide her children, especially when they did not focus on accomplishing the task at hand. Wyatt was thirteen, Oscar was nine, and Valerie and Emily were four. Kim was a lawyer working for an online university. A few days a week she had someone come in to spend time with the children so she could complete her work. Roger worked outside the home.

On the day of my interviews with Kim, the twins were at a summer preschool program that met a few days a week for a few hours each day. Wyatt was spending the week with his grandparents. Oscar was home, working on an online summer curriculum Kim purchased through a local university.

Within a minute of beginning the interview, Kim heard Oscar doing other things and reminded him to work on his homework. He told her he had to go to the bathroom. As he walked toward the bathroom, he began to undress. When she reminded him they had company and to wait until he was in the bathroom, he giggled. While he was in the bathroom, he hummed the entire time. Kim pointed out he never missed an opportunity to entertain.

After several minutes, he came out of the bathroom, wandered over to us, and tried to climb into Kim's lap. She reminded him he had not done any work the day before and had promised to do all of his work today. He went back to the computer, returned within a minute or so, and crawled around his mother's chair. She spoke to him about his behavior and gave him two options: get back to his work or go to his room for a timeout break. He told her he did not like either of those options and complained he could not find the backpack with his homework.

At this point we took a small break, and Kim helped him get situated. We were ten minutes into the interview. We began again, and Oscar did a great job of working independently for about five minutes. He then snuck over quietly, placed his notebook behind Kim's back in her chair, and snuck away again. I did not say anything, and the interview continued. After a couple of minutes, Oscar came back, took the notebook, and pushed it into Kim's eyesight. She read it and became upset.

She walked Oscar back to his study area and told him he needed to finish his homework. They exchanged some words which I did not hear, and finally I heard Kim say, "When you complete one set, you can have thirty minutes of play time on your gaming system. As soon as those thirty minutes are up, you must come back to work or you will not get play time again until you are finished." Oscar responded to her that she could set the parental controls to thirty minutes and then he would not be able to go over the thirty-minute time limit. I chuckled at his knowledge of parental controls and his innocence in telling her about them. His voice was not defiant or whining; he was just being factual. He reminded me of Wyatt.

Wyatt began exploring activities outside of home and school. One activity that greatly benefited Wyatt and his family was Special Olympics basketball. In his second year, Wyatt's team did so well they competed in the state Special Olympics tournament and won. Kim and Roger were thrilled with the outcome, yet the overall experience came with mixed emotions.

"Recently, we bought him basketball shoes for the Special Olympics basketball team on which he plays. As I saw him standing there with his shoes and uniform on, I thought how wonderful he looked. He is tall, thin, broad shouldered, very handsome, and he looks like an athlete. I look at him, and I think 'he's never going to have that' (experience of being a 'normal' athlete)," Kim said.

She began crying again and said, "I don't know why that bothers me so much; I should just be happy he is alive. A part of me mourns the fact he won't have those 'normal' experiences. You know, he's standing there looking all handsome and athletic in his new basketball shoes, and then he does his little gallop and handshake thing typical of kids with autism, and I am reminded he's never going to have that experience. That's okay though, I wouldn't want him any other way. I love him as he is. It isn't an affliction; it is just the way he is." She emphasized Wyatt did not feel like he was missing out on anything. He did not look at other kids playing a sport and wish he could join; he enjoyed other things instead, and that made him happy.

Participating in Special Olympics was an eye-opening experience for Kim. She was not around families like hers every day, so she was excited to be in a stadium full of special-needs families. What she did not expect was having her heart broken. She did not see in many other parents' eyes the same hope she holds for Wyatt. From her perspective, many of the parents seemed burned out or were in a coping mode, and some parents seemed to have even given up on their child.

Athletes came from all over the state, most of them with family support. Some groups did not have the same encouragement; maybe some of the adult athletes did not have any family members who could come to cheer them on. Kim's heart hurt for the competitors who were alone. Other athletes without family present came with coaches, teachers, and group home facilitators, and Kim was in awe of the love and support the non-family members gave those groups. She was thankful for the experience, because it helped her look at her family differently and with more appreciation.

Kim still thought a lot about what parents of special-needs children go through and what she went through, especially when Wyatt was born. The responsibility of being a child's entire world for nine months could be daunting, yet mothers took on the responsibility over and over with joy. Some, like Kim, went to great lengths for the privilege. She still found herself returning to thoughts of unmet expectations and blame.

Kim often blamed herself for Wyatt's uniqueness. She wondered if she should have done something different during her pregnancy. Did she eat the right foods? Drink the right drinks? Take all the vitamins she should have? Get all the rest she should have? Exercise enough or too much? Did she expose herself to something that could have caused this? Why didn't her body perform like it was supposed to?

"I believe God gives you what you can handle, and He also gives you what will help you become a better person," she said through tears. "There is nothing wrong with different. Different adds spice to life. I look at my son today and I see a handsome, beautiful, healthy boy."

When asked what advice she might give other parents, she returned to the concept of expectations. She suggested as parents picture what the future might hold for their children, parents should keep in mind a broader idea of what happiness, success, or independence looks like, rather than significantly narrow down the picture.

When we define our expectations for our children too specifically, we potentially set ourselves up to be disappointed. Children seem to sense when parents are disappointed, and even when the disappointment is unintentional, it can be damaging. Kim was thankful Wyatt was her oldest, and she had learned that lesson already, because it benefited her as she raised her other three children who all possess unique capabilities.

Kim advised other parents to research their options, not just go with what was convenient or already being done. When she was pregnant with Wyatt, she chose a hospital close to home. It was a very nice, newer hospital, close to her doctor's office, with state-of-the-art rooms.

However, it did not have a NICU, nor were any doctors on staff prepared for most emergencies.

When Kim and Roger moved to another state, they immediately began searching for specialists and top-rated doctors and hospitals in the area, even if it meant driving an hour or more from their home. Kim recommended women find a doctor who specialized in high-risk pregnancies as soon as possible, if they were concerned at all that their pregnancy might develop problems.

Kim had no problems during her second pregnancy and delivery. By her third pregnancy, she was considered high risk because of her age. That she was pregnant with twins bumped her risk even higher. They joined a support group of other women with high-risk pregnancies. Kim commented how much of a positive difference it was to have the support and to be at a hospital with doctors who were experienced in emergency situations.

Finding the right pediatrician and dentist took some research too. When Wyatt was little, he did not have any sensory differences, though as he grew older, he did not like to have his scalp or his teeth touched. The scalp issue was difficult during showers and brushing his hair, and they found ways to help him cope. The teeth-touching issue required them to find a dentist who was experienced in treating someone with sensory differences and autism. They had to try out a couple of different dentists before they found the right one for Wyatt and his siblings.

Other advice Kim gave parents was to admit they do not know everything, learn what they can about the disability, and be compassionate with themselves when they make mistakes—because they will make mistakes. Parents also need to study their child. Much communication happens nonverbally, and learning what their child is communicating even without speaking a word can become very important.

She advised parents to think about the behaviors their child currently displays (like screaming to get their way, nose picking, or hugging everyone they see) and contemplate what the behavior could look like down the road as the child ages. Often parents think a child will just outgrow certain behaviors. While that may be true for typically developing children, it is often not the case with children who have special needs. If it would not be an appropriate behavior in three, five, or ten years, Kim recommended parents work to prevent the behavior from becoming a habit that will be even harder to manage later.

She advised parents not to take it personally that their child may have a disability. If parents deny their child has a disability and refuse to get support, they hurt their child. When Kim was in college, she worked at a day care with a little girl who was having some difficulty with a project in a full classroom. Kim took the student to another room with fewer distractions, thinking this would be helpful. When the student was still unable to grasp the concept and work on the project, Kim made a comment to her director that maybe the child would benefit from extra help. She did not realize the child heard her.

The next day, the child's angry father came in and yelled at Kim for thinking and saying his daughter could possibly need extra help. He told her what a good parent he was, how he had worked with his daughter, and his daughter was just fine. All the emphasis was on him, not his daughter. Kim understood the father's initial reaction but said at some point parents must step back and ask themselves if the comment making them upset or uncomfortable could be true. She was grateful for this experience and learned from it. She believed parents must put what was best for their child ahead of any insecurity or hurt feelings. She and Roger did their best to turn this philosophy into action with Wyatt.

Thank you, Williams family, for allowing me to tell part of your story. Your family has taught me acceptance, unconditional love, and perseverance. You've shown me how to overcome adversity and have a great attitude through it all. I look forward to watching your family grow and seeing all the wonderful things the children will accomplish.

Notes

Chapter 2:

    Raymond Interview with a parent, [June, 2019]

Chapter 3:

    Allen Interview with a parent, [August, 2018]

Chapter 4:

    Mike Interview with a parent, [June -July, 2018]

Chapter 5:

    Linus Interview with a parent, [June, 2018]

Chapter 6:

    James Interview with a parent, [July, 2019]

Chapter 7:

    David Interview with a parent, [September, 2019]

Chapter 8:

    Rose Interview with a parent, [June, 2019]

Chapter 9:

    Kathleen Interview with a parent, [June-July, 2018]

Chapter 10:

    Wyatt Interview with a parent, [October, 2018]

Selected Bibliography

American Heart Association. Accessed September 4, 2020. https://www.heart.org/.

Bow Foundation. Accessed September 4, 2020. https://gnao1.org.

Cerebral Palsy Group. Accessed September 4, 2020. https://www.cerebralpalsygroup.com

Cleft Lip & Palate Foundation of Smiles. Accessed September 4, 2020. http://www.cleftsmile.org.

Crisis Prevention Institute. Accessed September 4, 2020. https://www.crisisprevention.com.

Individuals with Disabilities Education Act (IDEA). Accessed September 4, 2020. https://sites.ed.gov/idea/about-idea/.

March of Dimes. Accessed September 4, 2020. https://www.marchofdimes.org.

National Down Syndrome Society. Accessed September 4, 2020. https://www.ndss.org.

Ronald McDonald House. Accessed September 4, 2020. https://www.rmhc.org.

Social Security Administration. Accessed September 4, 2020. https://www.ssa.gov.

Special Olympics. Accessed September 4, 2020. https://www.specialolympics.org.

About the Author

Shelley is a wife, mother, dog lover, special education teacher, speaker, and education consultant. She believes that while we each know who we are today, we don't know who we will be tomorrow. The example she uses to shed light on this is the caterpillar turning into the butterfly. Shelley believes in promoting acceptance, inclusion, and having no limits when it comes to people with special needs and their potential. Shelley was a special educator for over two decades and helped her students accomplish more than doctors, teachers, peers, and family members thought those students ever would. She believes in making the world better for all, one IEP at a time.